THE
BELEAGUERED
CITY

THE
BELEAGUERED
CITY

THE VICKSBURG CAMPAIGN
DECEMBER 1862–JULY 1863

SHELBY FOOTE

THE MODERN LIBRARY
NEW YORK

1995 Modern Library Edition

Biographical note copyright © 1994 by Random House, Inc.
Copyright © 1963 by Shelby Foote
Copyright renewed 1991 by Shelby Foote and Random House, Inc.

Originally published in 1963 by Random House, Inc., New York, as a
section of Volume II of *The Civil War, A Narrative: Fredericksburg to
Meridian* by Shelby Foote.

Jacket photograph © 1995 by Huger Foote

LIBRARY OF CONGRESS CATALOGING-IN-PUBLICATION DATA
Foote, Shelby.
The beleaguered city: the Vicksburg Campaign, Dec. 1862–July 1863/
Shelby Foote.—Modern Library ed.
p. cm.
Originally published as part of v. 2 of The Civil War, a narrative.
ISBN 0-679-60170-8 (acid-free paper)
1. Vicksburg (Miss.)—History—Siege, 1863. I. Foote, Shelby.
Civil War, a narrative, v. 2.
E475.27.F66   1995
973.7´33—dc20   95-6789

Modern Library website address:www.modern library.com

Printed in the United States of America on acid-free paper

12 14 16 18 19 17 15 13 11

SHELBY FOOTE

Shelby Foote comes from a long line of Mississippians. He was born in 1916 in Greenville, Mississippi, and has had a consuming interest in the history of the Civil War since boyhood. From an early age he devoured books on the subject much as others read detective stories. Foote attended high school in Greenville, and later the University of North Carolina, with novelist and essayist Walker Percy, who later joked that his literary example launched Foote on a writing career. Yet Percy's guardian, William Alexander Percy—the free-spirited planter-poet-lawyer whose autobiographical *Lanterns on the Levee* (1941) paid eloquent tribute to the bygone agrarian traditions of the Mississippi Delta while gloomily assessing the spiritual health of Western civilization—greatly influenced both young men, introducing them to the world of books, music and art. A literary figure and something of a spokesman for the South, the elder Percy was a bachelor who oversaw a great rambling house that became a standard stopover for all manner of visitors, including William Faulkner (who came to play tennis, but whose racket never made contact with the ball) and Carl Sandburg (who broke out his guitar and sang). Meanwhile, Foote and Walker Percy set up shop in another section of the house building model airplanes.

Shelby Foote's own career as a writer began and advanced rapidly in the years following World War II (during which he had served in the European theater as a captain of field artillery). After working briefly as a reporter for the Associated Press and selling the first postgraduate short story he ever wrote to *The Saturday Evening Post*, he published his first novel, *Tournament*, in 1949. The story of a delta landowner who revives a plantation that has been blighted by the Reconstruction years, the book was hailed by *The Christian Science Monitor* as "a tragic tale of frustrated energy, ambition and pride." Foote's next novel, *Follow Me Down* (1950), a mesmerizing account of faith, passion, and murder set in modern-day Mississippi, was praised by *The New Yorker*: "Mr. Foote's writing is marvelously exact and positive. His attitude toward his people is respectful and human, as though he had thought about them a great deal and knew too much about them ever to take them for granted." *Love in a Dry Season* (1951), the story of a small cotton town that is turned into a sexual battleground as two wealthy Mississippi families are manipulated by a fortune hunter from the North, further consolidated Foote's reputation. "Shelby Foote ably fashions a drama as modern as today's newspaper, as old as Mosaic law," said *The New York Times*.

But it was *Shiloh*, a genuine tour de force that appeared in 1952, which proved to be Foote's breakthrough composition. A fictional recreation of the battle of Shiloh—a work that conveys not only the bloody choreography of Union and Confederate troops through the woods near Pittsburg Landing, Tennessee, in April 1862, but the inner movements of the lower-ranking combatants' hearts and minds—it was acclaimed by *The New York Times* as "imaginative, powerful, filled with precise visual details . . . a brilliant book." "*Shiloh* is the best novel of the Civil War I have ever read," wrote Van Allen Bradley in the *Chicago Daily*

News. Foote's next novel, *Jordan County* (1954), was a fictional chronicle—"a landscape in narrative"—of seven haunted generations in a Mississippi county, a place where the traumas of slavery, war, and Reconstruction are as tangible as rock formations. An ambitious, troubling work of fiction that builds on the traditions of William Faulkner and Stark Young, *Jordan County* was praised by *The Saturday Review* for its "extraordinary inventiveness of narrative and descriptive detail . . . and a supple prose style which supplies a whip-lash effect to the unexpected turns of events with which its stories bristle."

While completing *Jordan County*, Foote received a letter from publisher Bennett Cerf asking him if he'd like to do a short history of the Civil War. "They wanted only about two hundred thousand words," Foote recalled, "and it seemed like a good way to spend a year or two." Before finishing one hundred pages, he realized that he would have "to go spread-eagle, whole hog on the thing." The result, of course, became the epic three-volume narrative, *The Civil War*, that took twenty years (during which time Foote was awarded three Guggenheim fellowships) to complete. The first part, *Fort Sumter to Perryville*, came out in 1958 and was immediately deemed a classic of its kind. "Here, for a certainty, is one of the great historical narratives of our century, a unique and brilliant achievement, one that must be firmly placed in the ranks of the masters," said the *Chicago Daily News*. When the second installment, *Fredericksburg to Meridian*, appeared in 1963, the *Washington Post Book World* called it "one of the historical and literary achievements of our time." By the time the last volume, *Red River to Appomattox*, was published in 1974, *Newsweek* wrote: "To read this chronicle is an awesome and moving experience. History and literature are rarely so thoroughly combined as here; one finishes this volume convinced that no one need undertake this particular enterprise again."

In between researching and writing *The Civil War*, Foote took time out to serve as novelist-lecturer at the University of Virginia and playwright-in-residence at the Arena Stage in Washington, D.C. After completing the twenty-year project, he returned to fiction with *September September* (1977), a tense and haunting novel of the South set on the eve of integration in Little Rock and Memphis. He served as consultant and presiding spirit on the celebrated nine-part PBS television series *The Civil War* that aired in 1990. At the time he remarked: "Any understanding of this nation has to be based, and I mean really based, on an understanding of the Civil War. I believe that firmly. It defined us. The Revolution did what it did. Our involvement in European wars, beginning with the First World War, did what it did. But the Civil War defined us as what we are and it opened us to being what we became, good and bad things. And it is very necessary, if you're going to understand the American character in the twentieth century, to learn about this enormous catastrophe of the mid–nineteenth century. It was the crossroads of our being, and it was a hell of a crossroads."

Shelby Foote died at the age of eighty-eight in June 2005.

THE
BELEAGUERED
CITY

★ 1 ★

Haste made waste and Ulysses S. Grant knew it, but in this case the haste was unavoidable—unavoidable, that is, unless he was willing to take the risk of having another general win the prize he was after—because he was fighting two wars simultaneously: one against the Confederacy, or at any rate so much of its army as stood between him and Vicksburg, the blufftop river town that was his goal, and the other against a man who, like himself, wore blue. That was where the need for haste came in, for the rival general's name was John McClernand. A former Springfield lawyer and Illinois congressman, McClernand was known to have political aspirations designed to carry him not one inch below the top position occupied at present by his friend, another former Springfield lawyer and Illinois congressman, Abraham Lincoln. Moreover, having decided that the road to the White House led through Vicksburg, he had taken pains to see that he traveled it well equipped, and this he had done by engaging the preliminary support, the active military backing, not only of his friend the President, but also of the Secretary of War, the crusty and often difficult Edwin M. Stanton. With the odds thus lengthened against him, Grant—when he belatedly found out what his rival had been up to—could see that this private war against McClernand might well turn out to be as tough, in several ways, as the public one he had been fighting for eighteen months against the rebels.

In the first place, he had not even known that he had this private war on his hands until it was so well under way that his rival had already won the opening skirmish. McClernand had gone to Washington on leave in late September 1862, complaining privately that he was "tired of furnishing brains" for Grant's army. Arriving in the capital he appealed to Lincoln to "let one volunteer officer try his abilities." His plan was to return to his old political stamping ground and there, by reaching also into Indiana and Iowa, raise an army with which he would descend the Mississippi, capture Vicksburg, "and open navigation to New Orleans." Lincoln liked the sound of that and took him to see Stanton, who liked it too. McClernand left Washington in late October, armed with a confidential order signed by Stanton and indorsed by Lincoln, giving official sanction to his plan.

By early November, at his Grand Junction headquarter fifty miles east of Memphis, Grant was hearing rumors from upriver in Illinois: rumors which were presently reinforced by a dispatch from General-in-Chief Henry W. Halleck, whom the three former lawyers had not taken into their confidence. Memphis, which was in Grant's department, was to "be made the depot of a joint military and naval expedition on Vicksburg." Alarmed at hearing the rumors confirmed, Grant wired back: "Am I to understand that I lie still here while an expedition is fitted out from Memphis, or do you want me to push south as far as possible?" Halleck was something of a lawyer, too, though he now found himself at cross-purposes with the men who had not let him in on the secret. "You have command of all troops sent to your department," he replied, "and have permission to fight the enemy where you please."

Grant considered himself unleashed. Organizing his mobile force of about 40,000 effectives into right and left wings, respectively under William Tecumseh Sherman and Charles S. Hamilton, with the center under James B. McPherson, he began to move at once, southward along the Mississippi Central Railroad from Grand Junction. Ordinarily he would have preferred to wait for reinforcements, but not now. "I feared that delay might bring McClernand," he later explained.

Vicksburg was 250 miles away, and as he saw it the town belonged to the man who got there first. By mid-November he was in Holly Springs, where he set up a depot of supplies and munitions, then continued on across the Tallahatchie, leapfrogging his headquarters to Oxford while the lead division was fording the Yocknapatalfa, eight miles north of Water Valley, which was occupied during the first week of December.

The movement had been rapid and well coordinated; so far, it had encountered only token resistance from the rebels, who were fading back before the advance of the bluecoats. Presently Grant discovered why. John C. Pemberton, the Confederate department commander —whose strength he considerably overestimated as equal to his own—was avoiding serious contact while seeking a tactical advantage, and at last he found it. He called a halt near Grenada, another twenty-five miles beyond Water Valley, and put his gray-clad troops to work improving with intrenchments a position of great natural strength along the Yalobusha River. Approaching Coffeeville on December 5, midway between Water Valley and Grenada, the Federal cavalry was struck a blow that signified the end of easy progress. Still 150-odd miles from Vicksburg, Grant could see that the going was apt to be a good deal rougher and slower from here on.

Something else he could see as well, something that disturbed him even more. While he was being delayed in the piny highlands of north-central Mississippi, facing the rebels intrenched along the high-banked Yalobusha, McClernand might come down to Memphis, where advance contingents of his expedition were awaiting him already, and ride the broad smooth highway of the Mississippi River down to Vicksburg unopposed: in which case Grant would not only have lost his private war, he would even have helped his opponent win it by holding Pemberton and the greater part of the Vicksburg garrison in position, 150 miles away, while McClernand captured the weakly defended town with little more exertion than had been required in the course of the long boat ride south from Cairo. That was what rankled worst, the thought that he would have helped to pluck the laurels that would grace his rival's brow.

But as he thought distastefully of this, it began to occur to him that he saw here the possibility of a campaign of his own along these lines. "You have command of all troops sent to your department," Halleck had told him, and presumably this included the recruits awaiting McClernand's arrival at Memphis. So Grant, still at his Oxford headquarters on December 8, sent a note to Sherman, whose command was at College Hill, ten miles away: "I wish you would come over this evening and stay tonight, or come in the morning. I would like to talk with you."

Sherman did not wait for morning. Impatient as always, he rode straight over, a tall red-haired man with a fidgety manner, concave temples, glittering hazel eyes, and a scraggly, close-cropped beard. "I never saw him but I thought of Lazarus," one observer was to write. A chain smoker who, according to another witness, got through each cigar "as if it was a duty to be finished in the shortest possible time," he was forty-two, two years older than the comparatively stolid Grant and once his military senior, too, until Donelson brought the younger brigadier fame and a promotion, both of which had been delayed for Sherman until Shiloh, where he fought under—some said, saved—his former junior. He felt no resentment at that. In fact, he saw Grant as "the coming man in this war." But he had never had better reason for this belief than now at Oxford, when he was closeted with him and heard his plan for the sudden capture of Vicksburg with the help of a kidnapped army.

As usual in military matters, geography played a primary part in determining what was to be done, and how. Various geographic factors made Vicksburg an extremely difficult nut to crack. First there was the bluff itself, the 200-foot red-clay escarpment dominating a hairpin bend of the river at its base, unscalable for infantry and affording the guns emplaced on its crest a deadly plunging fire—as Admiral David Farragut, for one, could testify—against whatever naval forces moved against or past it. As for land forces, since they could not scale the bluff itself, even if they had been able to approach it from the front, their only alternative was to come upon it from the rear; that is, either to march overland down the Mississippi Central to Grenada, as Grant was now attempting to do, and thence along the high ground lying between the Yazoo and the Big Black rivers, or else debark from their transports somewhere short of the town and make a wide swing east, in order to approach it from that direction.

However, the latter was nearly impossible, too, because of another geographic factor, the so-called Yazoo-Mississippi alluvial delta. This incredibly fertile, magnolia-leaf-shaped region, 200 miles in length and 50 miles in average width, bounded east and west by the two rivers that gave it its compound name, and north and south by the hills that rose below and above Memphis and Vicksburg, was nearly roadless throughout its

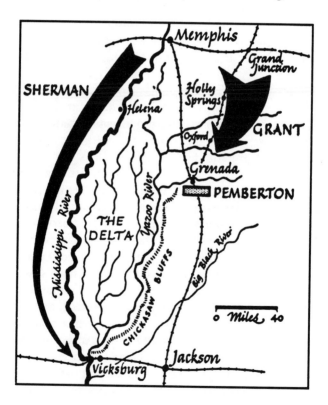

flat and swampy expanse, was subject to floods in all but the driest seasons, and—except for the presence of a scattering of pioneers who risked its malarial and intestinal disorders for the sake of the richness of its forty-foot topsoil, which in time, after the felling of its big trees and the draining of its bayous, would make it the best cotton farmland in the world—was the exclusive domain of moccasins, bears, alligators, and panthers. It was, in short, impenetrable to all but the smallest of military parties, engaged in the briefest of forays. An army attempting to march across or through it would come out at the other end considerably reduced in numbers and fit for nothing more strenuous than a six-month rest, with quinine as the principal item on its diet.

Anyhow, Grant did not intend to try it that way. He had his eye fixed on the mouth of the Yazoo, twelve miles above Vicksburg, and it seemed to him that an amphibious force could ascend that river for a landing on the southeast bank, which would afford the troops a straight shot at the town on the bluff. True, there were hills here, too—the Walnut Hills, they were called, the beginning of the long ridge known as the Chickasaw Bluffs, which lay along the left bank of the Yazoo, overlooking the flat morass of the Delta—but they were by no means as forbidding as the heights overlooking the Mississippi, a dozen miles below. It was Grant's belief that determined men, supported by the guns of the fleet, could swarm over these comparatively low-lying hills, brushing aside whatever portion of the weakened garrison tried to stop them, and be inside the town before nightfall of the day they came ashore.

That was why he had sent for Sherman, who seemed to him the right man for the job. Sherman happily agreed to undertake it, and Grant gave him his written orders that same evening. He was to return at once to Memphis with one of his three divisions, which he would combine with McClernand's volunteers, already waiting there. This would give him 21,000 troops, and to these would be added another 12,000 to be picked up at Helena on the way downriver, bringing his total strength to four divisions of 33,000 men, supported by Porter's fleet. Grant explained that he himself would continue to bristle aggressively along the line of the Yalobusha "so as to keep up the impression of a continuous move," and if Pemberton fell back prematurely he would "follow him even to the gates of Vicksburg," in which event he and Sherman would meet on the Yazoo and combine for the final dash into the town.

Delighted with the prospect, Sherman was off next day for Memphis, altogether mindful of the need for haste if he was to forestall both McClernand and Pemberton. "Time now is the great object," he wired David Dixon Porter, commander of the river squadron above Vicksburg. "We must not give time for new combinations."

He did not make it precisely clear whether these feared "combinations" were being designed in Richmond or in Washington—whether, that is, they threatened the successful prosecution of Grant's public or his private war. By mid-December, however, Grant's worries in regard to the latter were mostly over. Sherman was in Memphis, poised for the jump-off, and McClernand's men had become organic parts of the army the redhead was about to take downriver. There was still one danger. McClernand outranked him; which meant that if he arrived before Sherman left, he would assume command by virtue of seniority. But Grant considered this unlikely. Sherman was thoroughly aware of the risk and would be sure to avoid the consequences. Besides, with Halleck's telegram in his files as license for the kidnap operation, Grant felt secure from possible thunder from on high. "I doubted McClernand's fitness," he later wrote, "and I had good reason to believe that in forestalling him I was by no means giving offense to those whose authority to command was above both him and me."

The arrival of a telegram from Washington on December 18, instructing him to divide his command (now and henceforward to be called the Army of the Tennessee) into four corps, with McClernand in charge of one of those assigned to operations down the Mississippi—which meant of course that, once he joined it, he would be in charge of the whole column by virtue of his rank, unless Grant himself came over and took command along the river route—did not disturb the plans Grant had described in a letter home, three days ago, as "all complete for weeks to come," adding: "I hope to have them all work out just as planned." Sherman was ready to leave, he knew, and in fact would be gone tomorrow, before McClernand could possibly arrive from Illinois. Blandly he wired his new subordinate word of the Washington order, which dispelled McClernand's illusion that his command was to be an independent one. Instructing him to come on down to Memphis, Grant even managed to keep a straight face while remarking: "I hope you will find all the preliminary preparations completed on your arrival and the expedition ready to move."

★ ★ ★

McClernand found no such thing, of course. All he found when at last he reached Memphis on December 29 were the empty docks his men had departed from, ten days ago under Sherman, and Grant's telegram, delayed eleven days in transmission. Nor did Grant's own plans, "all complete for weeks to come," work out as he had intended and predicted. In both cases—entirely in the former and largely in the latter—the cause could be summed up in three two-syllable nouns: Nathan Bedford Forrest.

"He was the only Confederate cavalryman of whom Grant stood in much dread," a friend of the Union general's once remarked. Then he told why. "Who's commanding?" Grant would ask on hearing that gray raiders were on the prowl. If it was some other rebel chieftain he would shrug off the threat with a light remark; "but if Forrest was in command he at once became apprehensive, because the latter was amenable to no known rules of procedure, was a law unto himself for all military acts, and was constantly doing the unexpected at all times and places."

Grant's apprehensions were well founded as he looked back over his shoulder in the direction of his main supply base at Columbus, Kentucky; or, more specifically, since the far-off river town was adequately garrisoned against raiders, as he traced on the map the nearly two hundred highly vulnerable, not to say frangible, miles of railroad which were his sole all-weather connection with the munitions and food his army in North Mississippi required if it was to continue to shoot and eat. Without that base and those railroads, once he had used up the reserve supplies already brought forward and stored at Holly Springs, his choice would lie between retreat on the one hand and starvation or sur-

render on the other. Just now, moreover, the reason his
apprehensions were so well founded was that Forrest
was looking—and not only looking, but moving—in
that direction, too: as Grant learned from a dispatch received December 15 from Jackson, Tennessee, a vital
junction about midway of his vulnerable supply line.
"Forrest is crossing [the] Tennessee at Clifton," the
local commander wired. Four days later, Jackson itself
was under attack by a mounted force which the Federal
defenders estimated at 10,000 men, with Forrest himself definitely in charge.

Pemberton had begun it by appealing to Braxton
Bragg in late November for a diversion in West Tennessee, which he thought might ease the pressure on his
front, and Bragg had responded by sending Forrest instructions to "throw his command rapidly over the
Tennessee River and precipitate it upon the enemy's
lines, break up railroads, burn bridges, destroy depots,
capture hospitals and guards, and harass him generally."
Receiving these orders December 10 at Columbia, forty
miles south of Nashville, Forrest was off next day with
four regiments of cavalry and a four-gun battery, 2100
men in all, mostly recruits newly brigaded under his
command and mainly armed with shotguns and flint-
lock muskets. Four days later and sixty miles away, he
began to cross the Tennessee at Clifton on two flatboats
which he had built for the emergency and which he afterwards sank in a nearby creek in case he needed them
coming back. Deep in enemy country, with the bluecoats warned of his crossing while it was still in progress, he encountered on the 18th, near Lexington, two
regiments of infantry, a battalion of cavalry, and a section of artillery, all under Robert G. Ingersoll, who had
been sent out to intercept him. The meeting engage-

ment was brief and decisive. Falling back on the town, Ingersoll took up what he thought was a good defensive position and was firing rapidly with his two guns at the rebels to his front, when suddenly he "found that the enemy were pouring in on all directions." The fight ended quite as abruptly as it had begun. "If he really believed that there is no hell," one grayback later said of the postwar orator-agnostic, "we convinced him that there was something mightily like it." Captured along with his two guns and 150 of his men, while the rest made off "on the full run" for Jackson, twenty-five miles to the west, the Illinois colonel greeted his captors with aplomb: "Is this the army of your Southern Confederacy for which I have so diligently sought? Then I am your guest until the wheels of the great Cartel are put in motion."

Following hard on the heels of the fugitives, who he knew would stumble into Jackson with exaggerated stories of his strength, Forrest advanced to within four miles of the place and began to dispose his "army" as if for assault, maneuvering boldly along the ridge-lines and beating kettledrums at widely scattered points to keep up the illusion, or, as he called it, "the skeer." It worked quite well. Convinced that he was heavily outnumbered, though in fact he had about four times as many troops inside the town as the Confederates had outside it, Jeremiah Sullivan prepared to make a desperate house-to-house defense. All next day the rebel host continued to gather, waxing bolder hour by hour. When dawn of the 20th showed the graybacks gone, the Federal brigadier took heart and set out after them, pushing eastward—into emptiness, as it turned out, for Forrest had swung north.

Today in fact, having thrown the Federal main body

off his trail, he began in earnest to carry out his primary assignment, the destruction of the sixty miles of the Mobile & Ohio connecting Jackson and Union City, up near the Kentucky line. The common complaint of army commanders, that cavalry could seldom be persuaded to get down off their horses for the hard work that was necessary if the damage to enemy installations was to be more than temporary, was never leveled against Forrest's men. Besides forcing the surrender of the several blue garrisons in towns along the line, they tore up track, burned crossties and trestles, and wrecked culverts so effectively that this stretch of the M&O was out of commission for the balance of the war.

In Union City on Christmas Eve, resting his troopers after their four-day rampage with axes and sledges, Forrest reported by courier to Bragg that, at a cost so far of 22 men, he had killed or captured more than 1300 of the enemy, "including 4 colonels, 4 majors, 10 captains, and 23 lieutenants." That he considered this no more than a respectable beginning was shown by his closing remark: "My men have all behaved well in action, and as soon as rested a little you will hear from me in another quarter."

His problem now, after paroling his captives and sending them north to Columbus to spread bizarre reports of his strength—reports that were based on bogus dispatches, which he had been careful to let them overhear while their papers were being made out at his headquarters—was, first, what further damage to inflict and, second, how to get back over the river intact before the various Federal columns, still chasing phantoms all over West Tennessee, converged on him with overwhelming numbers. The first was solved on Christmas Day, when he marched southeast out of Union City and spent the next two days administering to the Nashville & North-western the treatment already given the M&O. Reaching McKenzie on the 28th in an icy, pelting rain, he headed south across the swampy bottoms of the swollen Obion River, and now began his solution of the second part of his problem. Instead of trying to make a run for the Tennessee, with the chance of being caught half-over and hamstrung, he decided to brazen out the game by thrusting in among the Federals attempting a convergence, and by vigorous blows, struck right or left at whatever came within his reach, stun them into inaction or retreat, while he continued his movement toward the security of Middle Tennessee.

The fact was, he had little to fear from the direction of Columbus. Thomas A. Davies, commander of the 5000 bluecoats gathered there, had been so alarmed by demonstrations within ten miles of the town on Christmas Eve, as well as by the parolees coming in next day with reports of 40,000 infantry on the march from Bragg, that he had spiked the guns at New Madrid and Island Ten, throwing the powder into the Mississippi to keep it out of rebel hands, and now was concentrating everything in order to protect the $13,000,000 worth of supplies and equipment being loaded onto steamboats at the Columbus wharf for a getaway in case Forrest broke his lines. Conditions were scarcely better, from the Union point of view, 250 miles downriver at Memphis, where the citizens had become so elated over rumors that their former alderman was coming home, along with thousands of his troopers, that Stephen Hurlbut, perturbed by their reaction and the fact that his garrison was down to a handful since the departure of Sherman, telegraphed Washington: "I hold city by terror of heavy guns bearing upon it and the belief that an attack would cause its destruction."

Grant, however, was of a different breed. He was thinking not of his safety, but of the possible destruction of Forrest and his men. "I have directed such a concentration of troops that I think not many of them will get back to the east bank of the Tennessee," he informed a subordinate. Nor was this opinion ill-founded. One superior blue force was coming south from Fort Henry, another north from Corinth, and both were now much closer to the Clifton crossing than Forrest was. So, for that matter, were Jere Sullivan and his three brigades, two of which were back by now from their goose chase east of Jackson and headed north. Undiscouraged by his lack of luck so far, he believed he knew just where the raiders were, and he intended to bag them. "I have Forrest in a tight place," he wired Grant on December 29. "My troops are moving on him from three directions, and I hope with success."

Forrest was indeed in a tight place, and that place was about to get tighter. Emerging from the flooded Obion bottoms, which he had crossed by an abandoned causeway, he paused on December 30 to let Sullivan's unsuspecting lead brigade go by him, then resumed his march past Huntingdon and toward Clarksburg, nearing which place on the morning of the last day of the year he encountered the other brigade, forewarned and drawn up to meet him at Parker's Crossroads. By way of precaution he had sent four companies to guard the road from Huntingdon and warn him in case the lead brigade turned back, and now, secure in the belief that his rear was well protected against surprise, he settled down to a casualty-saving artillery duel with the blue force to his front. It lasted from about 9 o'clock until an hour past noon, by which time he had captured three of the enemy guns and 18 wagonloads of ammunition and had driven the skirmishers back on their supports. He had in fact ceased firing, in response to several white flags displayed along the Union line, and was sending in his usual demand for "unconditional surrender to prevent the further effusion of blood," when an attack exploded directly in his rear. For the first last only time in his career, Forrest was completely surprised in battle.

His reaction was immediate. Quickly resuming the fight to his front, he simultaneously charged rearward, stalling the surprise attackers with blows to the head and flanks, and withdrew sideways before his opponents recovered from the shock. It was smartly done—later giving rise to the legend that his response to a staff officer's flustered question, "What shall we do? What shall we do?" was: "Split in two and charge both ways!"—but not without sacrifice. The captured guns were abandoned, along with three of his own, for lack of horses to draw them, as well as the 18 wagonloads of ammunition. Three hundred men who had been fighting afoot were taken, too, while trying to catch their mounts, which had bolted at the sudden burst of gunfire from the rear. Sullivan, coming up from behind Jackson with his third brigade next day, was elated. "Forrest's army completely broken up," he wired Grant. "They are scattered over the country without ammunition. We need a good cavalry regiment to go through the country and pick them up."

So he said. But while he and his three brigades were waiting for that "good regiment," Forrest and his troopers were riding hard for the Tennessee and eluding the columns approaching cautiously from Corinth and Fort Henry. All in high spirits on New Year's Day —except possibly the captain who by now had been verbally blistered for taking yesterday's rear-guard companies up the wrong road and thus permitting the Federals to march past him unobserved—they reached Clifton about midday, raised the sunken flatboats, and were across the icy river before dawn.

The basis for their high spirits was a sense of accomplishment. They had gone out as green recruits, miserably armed, and had returned within less than three weeks as veterans, equipped with the best accouterments and weapons the U.S. government could provide. In the course of a brief midwinter campaign, which opened and closed with a pontoonless crossing of one of the nation's great rivers, and in the course of which they more than made up in recruits for what they lost in battle or on the march, they had killed or paroled as many men as they had in their whole command and had kept at least ten times their number of bluecoats frantically busy for a fortnight. Besides the estimated $3,000,000 they had cost the Federals in wrecked installations and equipment, they had taken or destroyed ten guns and captured 10,000 rifles and a million badly needed cartridges. Above all, they had accomplished their primary assignment by cutting Grant's lifeline, from Jackson north to the Kentucky border. They saw all this as Forrest's doing, and it was their pride, now and for all the rest of their lives—whether those lives were to end next week in combat or were to stretch on down the years to the ones they spent sunning their old bones on the galleries of crossroads stores throughout the Deep and Central South—that they had belonged to what in time would be known as his Old Brigade.

Pemberton was highly pleased, not only with the results of this cavalry action outside the limits of his department, but also with another which had been carried

out within those limits and which he himself had designed as a sort of companion piece or counterpart to
the raid-in-progress beyond the Tennessee line. Both
had a profound effect on the situation he had been facing ever since he called a halt and began intrenching
along the Yalobusha, preparatory to coming to grips
with Grant's superior army: so profound an effect, indeed, that it presently became obvious that if he and
Grant were to come to grips, it would be neither here
nor now. Like that of the first, the success of this second
horseback exploit—which in point of fact was simultaneous rather than sequential, beginning later and ending sooner—could also be summed up in three nouns,
though in this case the summary was even briefer, since
all three were single-syllabled: Earl Van Dorn.

"Buck" Van Dorn, as he had been called at West
Point and by his fellow officers in the old army, had
leaped at the chance for distinction, not only because it
was part of his nature to delight in desperate ventures,
but also because he was badly in need just now of personal redemption. After a brilliant pre-Manassas career
in Texas, he had been called to Virginia, then reassigned
to Arkansas, where his attempt at a double envelopment
had been foiled disastrously at Elkhorn Tavern. Crossing the Mississippi after Shiloh, he had suffered an even
bloodier repulse at Corinth in October, which gave him
so evil a reputation in his home state that a court had
been called to hear evidence of his bungling. Although
he was cleared by the court, the government soon afterwards promoted Pemberton over the head upon which
the public was still heaping condemnations. The accu-
sation that he was "the source of all our woes," an outraged senator wrote President Davis, was "so fastened

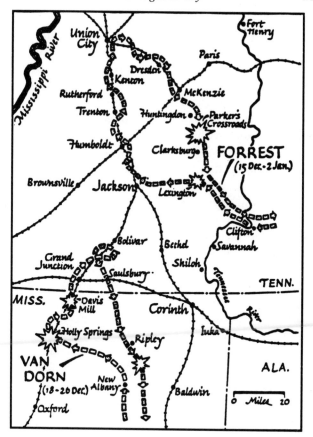

in the public belief that an acquittal by a court-martial of angels would not relieve him of the charge."

Van Dorn was depressed, but he was not without hope. A court-martial of angels was one thing; a brilliant military exploit, characterized by boldness and attended by great risk, was quite another. So when Pemberton

summoned him to army headquarters and gave him his
assignment—an all-out raid on Grant's communications and supply lines, including the great depot lately
established at Holly Springs—the Mississippian saw in
it the opportunity to retrieve his reputation and bask
once more in the warmth of his countrymen's affection.
Always one to grasp the nettle danger, he embraced the
offered chance without delay.

He left Grenada on December 18 with 3500 cavalry,
heading east at first to skirt Grant's flank, then north as
if for a return to Corinth. Next day, however, he turned
west beyond New Albany and came thundering into
Holly Springs at dawn, December 20. The Federal
commander there, R. C. Murphy, had been placed in a
similar uncomfortable position in September at Iuka,
which he had abandoned without a fight or even destruction of the stores to keep them from falling into
enemy hands. Grant had forgiven him then because of
his youth and inexperience, and now he was given another chance to prove his mettle. He did no better. In
fact, despite advance warning that a heavy column of
graybacks was moving in his direction, he did far worse.
This time, he lost not only the stores in his charge but
also the soldiers, 1500 of whom were captured and
paroled on the spot by the jubilant rebels, caracoling
their horses at the sight of the mountains of food and
equipment piled here for Grant's army. "My fate is
most mortifying," the young colonel reported that
night amid the embers which were all that remained of
the million-dollar depot of supplies. "I have done all in
my power—in truth, my force was inadequate."

Grant reacted "with pain and mortification" at the
news of his loss and ordered Murphy dismissed from the
service, as of "the date of his cowardly and disgraceful

conduct." With Forrest loose on the railroad north of Jackson that same day, and his own wife spared embarrassment at Holly Springs only because she had left to join him in Oxford the day before, Grant began to design combinations of forces in North Mississippi, not unlike those already sent out after Forrest in West Tennessee, to accomplish Van Dorn's destruction before he could return to safety behind the Yalobusha. "I want those fellows caught, if possible," he said.

The trouble with this was that by the time the various columns could be put in motion Van Dorn was no longer in North Mississippi. Instead of racing for home, and perhaps into the arms of superior forces already gathering in his rear, he pushed on northward into Tennessee. Before he left his native state, however, the commander of a small outpost at Davis Mill, twenty miles north of Holly Springs and just south of the Tennessee line, gave him—and, incidentally, Murphy—a lesson in how well an "inadequate" force could hold its own against "overwhelming" numbers. His name was W. H. Morgan and he had less than 300 men for the defense of a point made critical by the presence of a trestle by which the Mississippi Central crossed Wolf River. Hearing that the raiders were coming his way, he converted an old sawmill into a blockhouse, reinforcing its walls with cotton bales and crossties, and a nearby Indian mound into a moated earthwork, both of which covered the railroad approach with converging fire.

About noon of the 21st, the Confederates came up and launched a quick assault, which was repulsed. After a two-hour long-range skirmish, finding the fire too hot for a storming party to reach and ignite the trestle, let alone cross the river, the attackers sent forward, under a flag of truce, a note asking whether the defenders were ready to surrender. Morgan replied with what he later termed "a respectful but decided negative," and the Confederates withdrew, leaving 22 dead and 30 wounded on the field, along with another 20 prisoners who had ventured up too close to be able to pull back without exposing themselves to slaughter. Morgan's loss was 3 men slightly wounded.

Except for the further damage it did to his former opinion that one Southerner was worth ten Yankee hirelings in a scrap, Van Dorn was not greatly disturbed by this tactical upset. In the course of his approach to the fight, and even while it was in progress, he had done the railroad enough damage to be able to afford to let the trestle go. Bypassing Morgan's improvised blockhouse, he crossed upstream and pushed on northward between Grand Junction and LaGrange, where he tore up sections of the Memphis & Charleston for good measure. Near Bolivar on the 23rd, he circled Middleburg, still ripping up track and wrecking culverts, and headed back south on Christmas Eve, riding through Van Buren and Saulsbury to re-enter Mississippi. South of Ripley on Christmas Day, he had a brush with one of the converging Union columns, but pressed on without delay, through Pontotoc and thence on back to Grenada, which he reached by midafternoon of December 28.

He had carried out his mission in fine style, destroying Grant's reserve supplies of food, forage, and munitions. What was more, at least from a particular point of view, he had refurbished his tarnished reputation. Households which formerly had mentioned his name only with frowns of disapproval or downright scowls of condemnation now drank his health with shouts of joy and praised him to the skies.

Pemberton, then, was delighted at the manner in which Van Dorn had achieved redemption; but not Grant, who paid the bill which thus was added to all that Forrest was costing him simultaneously. With Columbus in a panic, Memphis cowed by heavy guns, his communications disrupted, and his supply line almost a continuous wreck from Holly Springs north to the Kentucky border, he was stymied and he knew it. Van Dorn having destroyed his supplies on hand and Forrest having made it impossible for him to bring up more, he could neither move forward nor stand still. There was no way he could go but back, and this he proceeded to do, meanwhile solving the problem of immediate subsistence by sending out "all the wagons we had, under proper escort, to collect and bring in all supplies of forage and food from a region of fifteen miles east and west of the road from our front back to Grand Junction."

At the news of this, the broad smiles caused by Van Dorn's coup faded from the faces of the people around Oxford. Their former mocking question, "What will you do now?" was changed to: "What are *we* to do?" Grant replied that he had done his best to feed his soldiers from their own northern resources, but now that these had been cut off "it could not be expected that men, with arms in their hands, would starve in the midst of plenty." In short, as he said later, "I advised them to emigrate east, or west, fifteen miles and assist in eating up what we left."

To his amazement—for he had thought the pickings would be slim and had lately advised his government that an army could not "subsist itself on the country except in forage"; "Disaster would result in the end," he had predicted—the wagons returned heavy-laden with hams, corn on the cob, field peas and beans, sweet and

Irish potatoes, and fowls of every description, accompanied by herds of beef on the hoof. "It showed that we could have subsisted off the country for two months instead of two weeks without going beyond the limits designated," he subsequently wrote, adding: "This taught me a lesson."

The knowledge thus gained might prove to be of great use in the future, but for the present one thing still bothered him beyond all others. This was the thought that, putting it baldly, he was leaving his friend Sherman in the lurch. He had promised to hold Pemberton in position, 150 miles from Vicksburg, while Sherman was storming its thinly held defenses; yet Pemberton was already hurrying troops in that direction, as Grant knew, and might well arrive in time to smother the attackers in the Yazoo bottoms. However, there was little he could do about it now, except depend on Sherman to work out his own salvation. Out of touch as he was, because of his ruptured communications, Grant did not even know whether Sherman had left Memphis yet—or, if so, whether he was still in command of the river expedition; McClernand, in event of delay, might have arrived in time to take over. All Grant could do was send a courier to Memphis with a message addressed to "Commanding Officer Expedition down Mississippi," advising him, whoever he was, "that farther advance by this route is perfectly impracticable" and that he and his men were falling back, while Pemberton did likewise. Whether this would arrive in time to forestall disaster, he did not know.

★   ★   ★

Sherman was already downriver, and so far his only thought of disaster had been the intention to inflict it. "You may calculate on our being at Vicksburg by Christmas," he wrote Grant's adjutant on December 19, the day he left Memphis. "River has risen some feet, and all is now good navigation. Gunboats are at mouth of Yazoo now, and there will be no difficulty in effecting a landing up Yazoo within twelve miles of Vicksburg." Two days later at Helena, where he picked up his fourth division, he received from upriver his first intimation that Grant might be having trouble in the form of rebel cavalry, which was reported to have captured Holly Springs. If this was so, then Sherman's first letter most likely had not got through to Oxford; nor would a second. Nevertheless, he refused to be disconcerted, and wrote again. "I hardly know what faith to put in such a report," he said, "but suppose whatever may be the case you will attend to it."

All was indeed "good navigation" for the fifty-odd army transports and the 32,500 soldiers close-packed on their decks, steaming rapidly toward their destiny below, as well as for the naval escort of three ironclads, two wooden gunboats, and two rams. But for the rest of Porter's fleet—three ironclads and two "tinclads," so called because their armor was no more than musket-proof—the going had been less easy. Sent downriver two weeks before, they had succeeded in clearing the Yazoo from its mouth upstream to Haines Bluff, where a stout Confederate battery defined the limit of penetration, 23 winding miles from the point of entrance.

This had not been accomplished without cost, however, for the defenses were in charge of Isaac Newton Brown, and Brown was known to be hungry for ven-

geance because of the recent loss above Baton Rouge of
the steam ram *Arkansas*, which he had built up this same
river the summer before and with which he had charged
and sundered the two flotillas then besieging Vicksburg.
He had no warship now, but he had notions about
torpedoes, five-gallon whiskey demijohns packed with
powder, fuzed with artillery friction tubes, and each suspended a few feet below a float on the muddy surface.
On December 12 the five-boat Union reconnaissance
squadron appeared up the Yazoo, shelling the banks and
fishing up Brown's torpedoes as it advanced. Approaching Haines Bluff, the ironclad *Cairo* made contact with
one of the glass demijohns at five minutes before noon,
and at 12.03 she was out of sight, all but the tips of her
stacks, in thirty feet of water.

Celerity and good discipline made it possible for the
crew to abandon ship within the allowed eight minutes.
No lives were lost, but the *Cairo*'s skipper, T. O. Selfridge, Jr., a young man with a lofty forehead and luxuri-
ant sideburns, was greatly disturbed by the loss of his
boat and the possible end of his career as well, depending on the admiral's reaction to the news. Steaming
back down the Yazoo aboard one of the tinclads, he
found Porter himself at the mouth of the river, just arrived from Memphis, and stiffly requested a court of inquiry. "Court!" the admiral snorted. "I have no time to
order courts. I can't blame an officer who puts his ship
close to the enemy. Is there any other vessel you would
like to have?" Without waiting for an answer he turned
abruptly to the flag captain standing beside him on the
bridge. "Breese, make out Selfridge's orders to the *Con-
estoga.*"

Porter was like that, when he chose to be. Just short
of fifty and rather hard-faced, with a hearty manner and

a full dark beard, he had been given his present assignment, together with the rank of acting rear admiral,
over the heads of eighty seniors. For the present,
though, despite this cause for self-congratulation, the
heartiness and bluster were cover for worry. Most of his
old sailors had broken down, with the result that his
heavy boats were half-manned, while ten light-draft
vessels were laid up for lack of crews, and he was complaining to Washington that a draft of new men, lately
arrived from New York, were "all boys and very ordinary landsmen." Characteristically, however, in a letter
written this week to Sherman, after protesting of these
and other matters, including a shortage of provisions,
fuel, medicines, and clothing—not to mention the loss
of the *Cairo*—he closed by observing: "I expected that
the government would send men from the East, but not
a man will they send or notice my complaints, so we will
have to go on with what we have."

Reaching Milliken's Bend, on the west bank of the
Mississippi ten miles above the mouth of the Yazoo,
Sherman landed a brigade on Christmas Day and sent
it out to wreck a section of the railroad connecting
Vicksburg and Monroe, Louisiana. Next morning,
while the brigade was returning, its mission accomplished, the rest of the armada proceeded downstream,
entered the Yazoo, and steamed up its intricate channel.
A light gunboat and an ironclad led the way, followed by
twenty transports, each with two companies of riflemen
charged with returning the fire of snipers. Then came
another ironclad and twenty more transports, similarly
protected. So it went, to the tail of the 64-boat column,
until a landing was made at Johnson's Farm, on the
Vicksburg shore of the Yazoo ten miles above its mouth.
Alertness had paid off, or else it had been unnecessary.

"Some few guerilla parties infested the banks," Sherman explained, "but did not dare to molest so strong a force as I commanded."

It occurred to some of his soldiers, though, that the rebels were going to let geography do their fighting for them. Wide-eyed as the Illinois and Indiana farmboys were in this strange land, that seemed altogether possible. First there had been the big river itself—or himself; the Old Man, natives called the stream, taking their cue from the Indians, who had named it the Father of Waters—the tawny, mile-wide Mississippi, so thick with silt that recruits could almost believe the steamboat hands who solemnly assured them that if you drank its water for as much as a week "you will have a sandbar in you a mile long." Then had come the smaller stream, with its currentless bayous and mazy sloughs, whose very name was the Indian word for death. And now there was this, the land itself, spongelike under their feet as they came ashore, desolate as the back side of the moon and brooded over by cypresses and water oaks with long gray beards of Spanish moss. North was only a direction indicated by a compass—if a man had one, that is, for otherwise there was no north or south or east or west; there was only the brooding desolation. If this was the country the rebs wanted to take out of the Union, the blue-coated farmboys were ready to say good riddance.

The molestation Sherman had said the Confederates did not dare to attempt began the following day, December 27, against the navy. William Gwin, a veteran of all the river fights since Fort Henry, took his ironclad *Benton* upstream to shell out some graybacks lurking in the woods on the left flank, but got caught in a narrow stretch of the river and was pounded by a battery on the bluffs. Three of the more than thirty hits came through the *Benton*'s ports, cutting her crew up badly, and Gwin, who refused to take cover in the shot-proof pilothouse —"A captain's place is on the quarterdeck," he protested when urged to step inside—was mortally wounded by an 8-inch solid that took off most of his right arm and breast, exposing the ribs and lung in a sudden flash of white and scarlet.

Moreover, the army was having its share of opposition, too, as it floundered about in the Yazoo bottoms and tried to get itself aligned for the assault on the Walnut Hills. The four division commanders, A. J. Smith, M. L. Smith, G. W. Morgan, and Frederick Steele, were in the thick of things next morning, dodging bullets like all the rest, when suddenly their number was reduced to three by a sniper who hit the second Smith in the hip joint and retired him from the campaign.

These two high-placed casualties only added to a confusion that was rife enough already. Johnson's Farm, which was little more than a patch of cleared ground in the midst of swampy woods, was separated from the hills ahead by a broad, shallow bayou, a former bed of the Yazoo, and hemmed in on the flanks by two others, Old River Bayou on the right and Chickasaw Bayou on the left. All three looked much alike to an unpracticed eye, so that there was much consequent loss of direction, misidentification of objectives, and countermarching of columns. A bridge ordered constructed over the shallow bayou to the front was built by mistake over one of the others, too late to be relaid. Whole companies got separated from their regiments and spent hours ricocheting from one alien outfit to another.

As a result of all this, and more, it was Monday morning, December 29, before the objectives could be assigned and pointed out on the ground rather than on the inadequate maps. Sherman's plan for overrunning the hilltop defenses was for all four divisions to make "a show of attack along the whole front," but to concentrate his main effort at two points, half a mile apart, which seemed to him to afford his soldiers the best chance for a penetration. One of these was in front of Morgan's division, and when Sherman pointed it out to him and told him what he wanted, Morgan nodded positively. "General, in ten minutes after you give the signal I'll be on those hills," he said.

His timing was a good deal off. Except for one brigade, which "took cover behind the [opposite] bank, and could not be moved forward," as Sherman later reported in disgust, Morgan not only did not reach "those hills," he did not even get across the bayou, in ten or any other number of minutes after the signal for attack was given by the batteries all along the Federal line. Presently, however, it was demonstrated that, all in all, this was perhaps the best thing to have done in the situation in which their red-headed commander had placed them. A brigade of Steele's division, led by Frank Blair, Jr., a former Missouri congressman and brother of the Postmaster General, got across in good order and excellent spirits, only to encounter a savage artillery crossfire that sent it staggering back, leaving 500 killed, wounded, and captured at the point where it had been struck. One regiment kept going but was stopped by the steepness of the bluff and a battery firing directly down the throats of the attackers. With their hands they began to scoop out burrows in the face of the nearly perpendicular hillside, seeking overhead cover from enemy riflemen who held their muskets out over the parapet and fired them vertically into the huddled, frantically digging mass below. Indeed, so critical was their position, as Sherman later said, "that we could not recall the men till after dark, and then one at a time." He added, in summation of the day's activities: "Our loss had been pretty heavy, and we had accomplished nothing, and had inflicted little loss on our enemy."

"Pretty heavy" was putting it mildly, as he would discover when he found time for counting noses, but the rest of this estimation was accurate enough. Federal losses reached the commemorative figure 1776, of whom 208 were killed, 1005 were wounded, and 563 were captured or otherwise missing. The Confederates lost 207 in all: 63 killed, 134 wounded, and 10 missing.

Unwilling to let it go at that—"We will lose 5000 men before we take Vicksburg," he had said, "and may as well lose them here as anywhere else"—Sherman decided to reload Steele's division aboard transports and move it upstream for a diversionary strike in the vicinity of Haines Bluff, which might induce the defenders to weaken their present line. Porter was no less willing than before. Moreover, by way of disposing of Brown's remaining torpedoes, he conceived the idea of using one of the rams to clear the path. "I propose to send her ahead and explode them," he explained. "If we lose her, it does not matter much." Colonel Charles R. Ellet, youthful successor to his dead father as commander of the former army vessels, did not take to this notion of a sacrificial ram. With Porter's consent, he added a 45-foot boom extending beyond the prow and equipped it with pulleys and cords and hooks for fishing up the floats and demijohns. Ram and transports set out by the dark of the moon on the last night of the year, while

Sherman alerted his other three divisions for a second all-out assault on the Walnut Hills as soon as they heard the boom of guns upstream.

What came instead, at 4 A.M. on New Year's Day, was a note from Steele, explaining that the boats were fogbound and could not proceed. So Sherman called a halt and took stock. He had been waiting all this time for some word from Grant, either on the line of the Yalobusha or here on the Yazoo, but there had been nothing since the rumor of the fall of Holly Springs. From Vicksburg itself, ten air-line miles away, its steeples visible from several points along his boggy front, he had been hearing for the past three days the sound of trains arriving and departing. It might be a ruse, as at Corinth back in May. On the other hand, it might signify what it sounded like: the arrival from Grenada or Mobile or Chattanooga, or possibly all three, of reinforcements for the rebel garrison. Also, rain had begun to fall by now in earnest, and looking up he saw watermarks on the trunks of trees "ten feet above our heads." In short, as he later reported, seeing "no good reason for remaining in so unenviable a position any longer," he "became convinced that the part of wisdom was to withdraw."

Withdraw he did, re-embarking his soldiers the following day and proceeding downriver without delay. There was more room on the decks of the transports now, and Sherman was low in spirits: not because he was dissatisfied with his direction of the attempt—"There was no bungling on my part," he wrote, "for I never worked harder or with more intensity of purpose in my life"—but because he knew that the journalists, whom he had snubbed at every opportunity since their spreading of last year's rumors that he was insane, would have a field day writing their descriptions of his repulse and retreat. Presently he was hailed by Porter, who signaled him to come aboard the flagship. Sherman did so, rain-drenched and disconsolate.

"I've lost 1700 men," he said, "and those infernal reporters will publish all over the country their ridiculous stories about Sherman being whipped."

"Pshaw," the admiral replied. "That's nothing; simply an episode of the war. You'll lose 17,000 before the war is over and think nothing of it. We'll have Vicksburg yet, before we die. Steward! Bring some punch."

When he got the red-head settled down he gave him the unwelcome news that McClernand was at hand, anchored just inside the mouth of the Yazoo and waiting to see him. Sherman, who could keep as straight a face as his friend Grant when so inclined, afterwards remarked of his rival's sudden but long-expected appearance on the scene: "It was rumored he had come down to supersede me."

McClernand, too, had news for him when they met later that day. Grant was not coming down through Mississippi; he had in fact been in retreat for more than a week, leaving Pemberton free to concentrate for the defense of Vicksburg. Sherman suggested that this meant that any further attempt against the town with their present force was hopeless. Indeed, in the light of this disclosure, he began to consider himself most fortunate in failure, even though it had cost him a total of 1848 casualties for the whole campaign. "Had we succeeded," he reasoned, "we might have found ourselves in a worse trap, when General Pemberton was at full liberty to turn his whole force against us."

Dark-bearded McClernand agreed that the grapes were sour, at least for now. Next day, January 3, he and

Sherman withdrew their troops from the Yazoo and rendezvoused again at Milliken's Bend, where McClernand took command.

"Well, we have been to Vicksburg and it was too much for us and we have backed out," Sherman wrote his wife from the camp on the west bank of the Mississippi. Reporting by dispatch to Grant, however, he went a bit more into detail as to causes. "I attribute our failure to the strength of the enemy's position, both natural and artificial, and not to his superior fighting," he declared; "but as we must all in the future have ample opportunities to test this quality, it is foolish to discuss it."

Pemberton would have agreed that it was foolish to discuss it, not for the reason his adversary gave, but because he considered the question already settled. The proof of the answer, so far as he was concerned, had been demonstrated in the course of the past two weeks, during which time he had stood off and repulsed two separate Union armies, each superior in numbers to his own. What was more, he had gained new confidence in his top commanders: in Van Dorn, whose lightning raid, staged in conjunction with Forrest's in West Tennessee, had abolished the northward menace: in the on-the-spot Vicksburg defenders, Martin L. Smith and Stephen D. Lee, who with fewer than 15,000 soldiers, most of whom had arrived at the last minute from Grenada, had driven better than twice as many bluecoats out of their side yard, inflicting in the process about nine times as many casualties as they suffered: and in himself, who had engineered the whole and had been present for both repulses. Not that he did not expect to have to fight a return engagement. He did. But he considered that this would be no more than an occasion for redemonstrating what had been proved already.

"Vicksburg is daily growing stronger," he wired Richmond soon after New Year's. "We intend to hold it."

★ 2 ★

McClernand, conferring with Sherman at Milliken's Bend on the day after his arrival from upriver—it was January 3; the two were aboard the former Illinois politician's headquarters boat, the *Tigress*, tied up to bank twenty-odd miles above Vicksburg—did not blame the red-haired Ohioan for the repulse suffered earlier that week at Chickasaw Bluffs; Sherman, he said in a letter to Stanton that same day, had "probably done all in the present case anyone could have done." The fault was Grant's, and Grant's alone; Grant had designed the operation and then, taking off half-cocked in his eagerness for glory that was rightfully another's, had failed to cooperate as promised, leaving Sherman to hold the bag and do the bleeding. So McClernand said, considerably embittered by the knowledge that a good part of the nearly two thousand casualties lost up the Yazoo were recruits he had been sending down from Cairo for the past two months, only to have them snatched from under him while his back was turned.

"I believe I am superseded. Please advise me," he had

wired Lincoln as soon as he got word of what was afoot. But permission to go downriver had not come in time for him to circumvent the circumvention; the fighting was over before he got there. He took what consolation he could from having been spared a share in a fiasco. At least he was with his men again—what was left of them, at any rate—and ready to take over. "Soon as I shall have verified the condition of the army," he told Stanton, "I will assume command of it."

He did so the following day. Christening his new command "The Army of the Mississippi" in nominal expression of his intentions, or at any rate his hopes, he divided it into two corps of two divisions each, the first under George Morgan and the second under Sherman —which, incidentally, was something of a bitter pill for the latter to swallow, since he believed a large share of the blame for the recent failure up the Yazoo rested with Morgan, who had promised that in ten minutes he would "be on those hills," but who apparently had forgot to wind his watch.

However that might be, McClernand now had what he had been wanting all along: the chance to prove his ingenuity and demonstrate his mettle in independent style. His eyes brightened with anticipation of triumph as he spoke of "opening the navigation of the Mississippi," of "cutting my way to the sea," and so forth. For all the expansiveness of his mood, however, the terms in which he expressed it were more general than specific; or, as Sherman later said, "the *modus operandi* was not so clear."

In this connection—being anxious, moreover, to balance his recent defeat with a success—the Ohioan had a suggestion. During the Chickasaw Bluffs expedition the packet *Blue Wing*, coming south out of Memphis with a

cargo of mail and ammunition, had been captured by a
Confederate gunboat that swooped down on her near
the mouth of the Arkansas and carried her forty miles
up that river to Arkansas Post, an outpost established by
the French away back in 1685, where the rebels had
constructed an inclosed work they called Fort Hindman, garrisoned by about 5000 men. So long as this
threat to the main Federal supply line existed, Sherman
said, operations against Vicksburg would be subject to
such harassment, and it was his belief that, by way of
preamble to McClernand's larger plans—whatever
they were, precisely—he ought to go up the Arkansas
and abolish the threat by "thrashing out Fort Hindman."

McClernand was not so sure. He had suffered no defeat that needed canceling, and what was more he had
larger things in mind than the capture of an obscure and
isolated post. However, he agreed to go with Sherman
for a discussion of the project with Porter, whose cooperation would be required. They steamed downriver
and found the admiral aboard his headquarters boat, the
Black Hawk, anchored in the mouth of the Yazoo. It was
late, near midnight; Porter received them in his night-
shirt. He too was not so sure at first. He was short of
coal, he said, and the ironclads, which would be needed
to reduce the fort, could not burn wood. Presently,
though, as Sherman continued to press his suit, asking
at least for the loan of a couple of gunboats, which he
offered to tow up the river and thus save coal, Porter—
perhaps reflecting that he had on his record that same
blot which a victory would erase—not only agreed to
give the landsmen naval support; "Suppose I go along
myself?" he added.

Suddenly, on second thought, McClernand was con-

vinced: so much so, indeed, that instead of merely sending Sherman to do the job with half the troops, as Sherman had expected, he decided it was worth the
undivided attention of the whole army and its commander, whose record, if blotless, was also blank. With
no minus to cancel, this plus would stand alone, auspi-
cious, and make a good beginning as he stepped off on
the road that led to glory and the White House.

He took three days to get ready, then (but not until
then) sent a message by way of Memphis to notify Grant
that he was off—one of his purposes being, as he said,
"the counteraction of the moral effect of the failure of
the attack near Vicksburg and the reinspiration of the
forces repulsed by making them the champions of new,
important, and successful enterprises."

He left Milliken's Bend that same day, January 8, his
30,000 soldiers still aboard their fifty transports, accompanied by 13 rams and gunboats, three of which were
ironclads and packed his Sunday punch. By way of
deception the flotilla steamed past the mouth of the Arkansas, then into the White, from which a cutoff led
back into the bypassed river. Late the following afternoon the troops began debarking three miles below
Fort Hindman, a square bastioned work set on high
ground at the head of a horseshoe bend, whose dozen
guns included three 9-inch Columbiads, one to each
riverward casemate, and a hard-hitting 8-inch rifle. A
good portion of the defending butternut infantry, supported by six light pieces of field artillery, occupied a
line of rifle-pits a mile and a half below the fort, but
these were quickly driven out when the gunboats forged
ahead and took them under fire from the flank. Late the
following afternoon, when the debarkation had been
completed and the four divisions were maneuvering for

positions from which to launch an assault, the ironclads took the lead. The *Louisville*, the *De Kalb*, and the *Cincinnati* advanced in line abreast to within four hundred yards of the fort, pressing the attack bows on, one to each casemate, while the thinner-skinned vessels followed close behind to throw in shrapnel and light rifled shell. It was hot work for a time as the defenders stood to their guns, firing with precision; the *Cincinnati*, for example, took eight hits from 9-inch shells on her pilot house alone, though Porter reported proudly that they "glanced off like peas against glass"; the only naval casualties were suffered from unlucky shots that came in through the ports.

When the admiral broke off the fight because of darkness, the fort was silent, apparently overwhelmed. But when Sherman, reconnoitering by moonlight, drew close to the enemy outposts he could hear the Confederates at work with spades and axes, drawing a new line under cover of their heavy guns and preparing to continue to resist despite the long numerical odds. Crouched behind a stump in the predawn darkness of January 11 he heard a rebel bugler sound what he later called "as pretty a reveille as I ever listened to."

Shortly before noon he sent word that he was ready. His corps was on the right, Morgan's on the left; both faced the newly drawn enemy line which extended across the rear of the fort, from the river to an impassable swamp one mile west. McClernand, having established a command post in the woods and sent a lookout up a tree to observe and report the progress of events, passed the word to Porter, who ordered the ironclads forward at 1.30 to renew yesterday's attack. Sherman heard the clear ring of the naval guns, the fire increasing in volume and rapidity as the range was closed. Then he and Morgan went forward, the troops advancing by rushes across the open fields, "once or twice falling to the ground," as Sherman said, "for a sort of rest or pause."

As they approached the fort they saw above its parapet the pennants of the ironclads, which had smothered the heavy guns by now and were giving the place a close-up pounding. Simultaneously, white flags began to break out all along the rebel line. "Cease firing! Cease firing!" Sherman cried, and rode forward to receive the fort's surrender.

But that was not to be: not just yet, at any rate, and not to Sherman. John Dunnington, the fort's commander, a former U.S. naval officer but now an army colonel, insisted on surrendering to Porter, and Thomas J. Churchill, a brigadier in command of the field force, did not want to surrender at all. As Sherman approached, Churchill was arguing with his subordinates, wanting to know by whose authority the white flags had been shown. (He had received an order from Little Rock the night before, while there was still a chance to get away, "to hold out till help arrives or until all dead"—which Theophilus Holmes, the district chief, later explained with the comment: "It never occurred to me when the order was issued that such an overpowering command would be devoted to an end so trivial.") One brigade commander, James Deshler of Alabama, a fiery West Pointer in his late twenties— "small but very handsome," Sherman called him—did not want to stop fighting even now, with the Yankees already inside his works. When Sherman, wishing as he said "to soften the blow of defeat," remarked in a friendly way that he knew a family of Deshlers in his home state and wondered if they were relations, the Al-

abamian hotly disclaimed kinship with anyone north of
the Ohio River; whereupon the red-headed general
changed his tone and, as he later wrote, "gave him a
piece of my mind that he did not relish."

However, all this was rather beside the point. The
fighting was over and the butternut troops stacked arms.
The Federals had suffered 31 navy and 1032 army casualties, for a total of 140 killed and 923 wounded. The
Confederates, on the other hand, had had only 109 men
hit; but that left 4791 to be taken captive, including a
regiment that marched in from Pine Bluff during the
surrender negotiations.

McClernand, who had got back aboard the *Tigress*
and come forward, was tremendously set up. "Glorious!
Glorious!" he kept exclaiming. "My star is ever in the
ascendant." He could scarcely contain himself. "I had a
man up a tree," he said. "I'll make a splendid report!"

Grant by now was in Memphis. He had arrived the
day before, riding in ahead of the main body, which was
still on the way under McPherson, near the end of its
long retrograde movement from Coffeeville, northward
through the scorched wreckage of Holly Springs, then
westward by way of Grand Junction and LaGrange.
Having heard no word from Sherman, he knew nothing
of his friend's defeat downriver—optimistic as always,
he was even inclined to credit rumors that the Vicksburg defenses had crumbled under assault from the
Yazoo—until the evening of his arrival, when he received McClernand's letter from Milliken's Bend informing him of the need for "reinspiration of the forces
repulsed."

This was something of a backhand slap, at least by
implication—McClernand seemed to be saying that he

would set right what Grant had bungled—but what disturbed him most was the Illinois general's expressed intention to withdraw upriver for what he called "new, important, and successful enterprises." For one thing, if Nathaniel Banks and his army were on the way up from New Orleans in accordance with the instructions for a combined assault on Vicksburg, it would leave them unsupported when they got there. For another, any division of effort was wrong as long as the true objective remained unaccomplished, and Grant said so in no uncertain terms next morning when he replied to McClernand's letter: "I do not approve of your move on the Post of Arkansas while the other is in abeyance. It will lead to the loss of men without a result. . . . It might answer for some of the purposes you suggest, but certainly not as a military movement looking to the accomplishment of the one great result, the capture of Vicksburg. Unless you are acting under authority not derived from me, keep your command where it can soonest be assembled for the renewal of the attack on Vicksburg. . . . From the best information I have, Milliken's Bend is the proper place for you to be, and unless there is some great reason of which I am not advised you will immediately proceed to that point and await the arrival of reinforcements and General Banks' expedition, keeping me fully advised of your movements."

He expressed his opinion more briefly in a telegram sent to Halleck that afternoon: "General McClernand has fallen back to White River, and gone on a wild-goose chase to the Post of Arkansas. I am ready to reinforce, but must await further information before knowing what to do." The general-in-chief replied promptly the following morning, January 12: "You are hereby authorized to relieve General McClernand from com-

mand of the expedition against Vicksburg, giving it to
the next in rank or taking it yourself."

Grant now had what he wanted. Formerly he had
moved with caution in the prosecution of his private
war, by no means sure that in wrecking McClernand he
would not be calling down thunder on his own head; but
not now. Halleck almost certainly would have discussed
so important a matter with Lincoln before adding this
ultimate weapon to Grant's arsenal and assuring him
that there would be no restrictions from above as to its
use. In short, Grant could proceed without fear of retal-
iation except from the victim himself, whom he outranked.

However, two pieces of information that came to
hand within the next twenty-four hours forestalled delivery of the blow. First, he learned that Port Hudson—
another stalwart river-bend bluff, 240 winding miles
below Vicksburg and about the same distance above
New Orleans, occupied and fortified by the Confederates after their retreat from nearby Baton Rouge in August of the previous year, but unsuspected by the
Federals until a gunboat probing upstream in September came under plunging fire from its high-sited guns
and withdrew in haste to spread word of this new problem—was a more formidable obstacle than he had formerly supposed, which meant that it was unlikely that
Banks's upriver thrust would reach Vicksburg at any
early date. And, second, he received next day from
McClernand himself the "splendid report" announcing
the fall of Arkansas Post and the capture of "a large
number of prisoners, variously estimated at from 7000
to 10,000, together with all [their] stores, animals, and
munitions of war." Not only was the urgency for a
hookup with Banks removed, but to proceed against

McClernand now would be to attack a public hero in his first full flush of victory; besides which, Grant had also learned that the inception of what he had called the "wild-goose chase" had been upon the advice of his friend Sherman, and this put a different complexion on his judgment as to the military soundness of the expedition.

All that remained was to play the old army game — which Grant well knew how to do, having had it played against him with such success, nine years ago in California, that he had been nudged completely out of the service. When the time came for pouncing he would pounce, but not before. Meanwhile he would wait, watching and building up his case as he did so.

This did not mean that he intended to sit idly by while McClernand continued to gather present glory; not by a long shot. Four days later, January 17 — McClernand having returned as ordered to the Mississippi, awaiting further instructions at Napoleon, just below the mouth of the Arkansas — Grant got aboard a steamboat headed south from the Memphis wharf. Before leaving he wired McPherson, who had called a halt at LaGrange to rest his troops near the end of their long retreat from Coffeeville: "It is my present intention to command the expedition down the river in person."

Banks was going to be a lot longer in reaching Vicksburg than Grant knew, and more was going to detain him than the guns that bristled atop the bluff at Port Hudson. After a sobering look at this bastion he decided that his proper course of action, before attempting a reduction of that place or a sprint past its frowning batteries, would be a move up the opposite bank of the big river, clearing out the various nests of rebels who otherwise would interfere with his progress by harassing his flank as he moved upstream. Godfrey Weitzel, a twenty-eight-year-old West Pointer who already had been stationed in that direction by Ben Butler, was reinforced by troops from the New Orleans and Baton Rouge garrisons and told to make the region west of those two cities secure from molestation. He built a stout defensive work at Donaldsonville, commanding the head of Bayou La Fourche, and threw up intrenchments at Brashear City, blocking the approach from Berwick Bay. Then, crossing the bay with his mobile force on January 13, he entered and began to ascend the Teche, accompanied by three gunboats.

This brought him into sudden contact next morning with Richard Taylor, the Confederate district commander, who fought briefly and fell back, sinking the armed steamer *Cotton* athwart the bayou as he did so, corking it against farther penetration. Weitzel, who had lost 33 killed and wounded, including one of the navy skippers picked off by a sniper, reported proudly as he withdrew: "The Confederate States gunboat *Cotton* is one of the things that were. . . . My men behaved magnificently. I am recrossing the bay."

As a successful operation—the first of what he intended would be many—this was unquestionably gratifying to Banks, who made the most of it in reporting the action to Washington as a follow-up to the bloodless reoccupation of the Louisiana capital. Yet even as he tendered his thanks to Weitzel for "the skillful manner in which he has performed the task confided to him," he could also see much that was foreboding in this small-scale expedition up the Teche. For one thing, the rebels were very much there, though in what numbers he did not know, and for another they would fight, but only as it suited them, choosing the time and place that gave them the best advantage, fading back into the rank undergrowth quite as mysteriously as they had appeared, and then moving forward again as the bluecoats withdrew from what Taylor himself, who knew all its crooks and byways, called "a region of lakes, bayous, jungle, and bog."

How long it might take to clear such an army of phantoms from the district, or whether indeed it could ever be done, Banks could not tell. By mid-January, however, he had decided that it would have to be done. His expectations, described in mid-December as "most sanguine," were tempered now by prudence and better acquaintance with the peculiar factors involved. He perceived that they would have to be refashioned to conform to a different schedule before he attempted the reduction of Port Hudson and the eventual link-up with Grant in front of Vicksburg, all those devious hundreds of miles up the tawny Mississippi.

★   ★   ★

After an all-night boat ride down the Mississippi, from Memphis past the mouth of the Arkansas, Grant reached Napoleon on January 18 to find McClernand, Porter, and Sherman awaiting his arrival with mixed emotions—mixed, that is, so far as McClernand's were concerned; Porter and Sherman were united, if by nothing more than a mutual dislike of the congressman-turned-commander. To them, Grant came as something of a savior, since he outranked the object of their scorn. To McClernand, on the other hand, he seemed

nothing of the sort; McClernand plainly suspected another attempt to steal his thunder, if not his army. He
had enlarged his Arkansas Post exploit by sending a pair
of gunboats up White River to drive the rebels from St
Charles and wreck their installations at De Valls Bluff,
terminus of the railroad running east from Little Rock
toward Memphis. It was smartly done, accomplishing at
the latter place the destruction of the depot and some
rolling stock, as well as the capture of two 8-inch guns
which the flustered garrison was trying to load aboard
the cars for a getaway west. Still at Fort Hindman while
this was in progress, McClernand received Grant's curt
and critical letter ordering him back to the Mississippi
at once, and he bucked it along to Lincoln with a covering letter of his own.

"I believe my success here is gall and wormwood to
the clique of West Pointers who have been persecuting
me for months," he wrote, imploring his friend and fellow townsman not to "let me be clandestinely destroyed, or, what is worse, dishonored, without a
hearing." He asked, "How can General Grant at a distance of 400 miles intelligently command the army with
me?" and answered his own question without a pause:
"He cannot do it. It should be made an independent
command, as both you and the Secretary of War, as I
believe, originally intended."

Grant was about to get in some licks of his own in this
regard, if not through out-of-channels access to Lincoln
—whom he had not only never met, but had never even
seen, despite the fact that both had gone to war from
Illinois—then at any rate through Halleck, which was
the next-best thing. For the present he merely conferred with the three officers, collectively and singly,
and ordered the return of the whole expedition to Mil-

liken's Bend for a renewal of the drive on Vicksburg by the direct route. By now, however, as a result of his talk with these men who had been there, he was beginning to see that the only successful approach, after all, might have to be roundabout. "What may be necessary to reduce the place I do not yet know," he wired the general-in-chief, "but since the late rains [I] think our troops must get below the city to be used effectually."

He spent the night ashore at Napoleon, whose partial destruction by incendiaries the day before caused Sherman to declare that he was "free to admit we all deserve to be killed unless we can produce a state of discipline when such disgraceful acts cannot be committed unpunished." One solution, he decided, would be "to assess the damages upon the whole army, officers included," but no such drastic remedy was adopted. The following morning Grant saw the transports and their escort vessels steam away south, in accordance with his orders, and returned that evening to Memphis.

Next day, January 20, he sent Halleck a long dispatch explaining the tactical situation as he saw it and announcing that, by way of a start, he intended to try his hand at redigging the canal across the base of the hairpin bend in front of Vicksburg, abandoned the previous summer by Benjamin Butler's men when the two Union fleets were sundered and repulsed by the rebel warship *Arkansas*, now fortunately at the bottom of the river. Grant suggested that, in view of the importance of the campaign he was about to undertake, it would be wise to combine the four western departments, now under Banks, Samuel Curtis, William Rosecrans, and himself, under a single over-all commander in order to assure cooperation. "As I am the senior department commander in the West," he wrote—apparently unaware that Banks was nine months his senior and in point of fact had been a major general before Grant himself was even a brigadier—"I will state that I have no desire whatever for such combined command, but would prefer the command I now have to any other than can be given."

From this disclaimer he passed at once to the subject of John McClernand: "I regard it as my duty to state that I found there was not sufficient confidence felt in General McClernand as a commander, either by the Army or Navy, to insure him success. Of course, all would cooperate to the best of their ability, but still with a distrust. This is a matter I made no inquiries about, but it was thrust upon me." (As a later observer pointed out, there was "a touch of artfulness" in this; Grant "elevated Sherman and Porter to speak for entire branches of the service, then sought audiences with them so that the issue might be forced upon him!") However, he continued, "as it is my intention to command in person, unless otherwise directed, there is no special necessity of mentioning this matter; but I want you to know that others besides myself agree in the necessity of the course I had already determined upon pursuing."

His belief that Old Brains was on his side was strengthened the following day by a quick reply to his suggestion that "both banks of the Mississippi should be under one command, at least during the present operations." "The President has directed that so much of Arkansas as you may desire to control be temporarily attached to your department," Halleck wired. "This will give you control of both banks of the river." Pleased to learn of Lincoln's support, even at second hand, Grant kept busy with administrative and logistical matters preparatory to his departure from Memphis at the earliest possible date. McPherson was marching in from LaGrange with two divisions to accompany him downriver; these 14,979, added to the 32,015 already there, would give him an "aggregate present" of 46,994 in the vicinity of Vicksburg, with more to follow, not only from his own Department of the Tennessee, which included a grand total of 93,816 of all arms, but also from the Department of Missouri, now under Curtis and later under John M. Schofield.

On January 25 he received further evidence of Lincoln's interest in the campaign for control of the Lower Mississippi, whose whimsical habit of carving itself new channels the Chief Executive knew from having made two flatboat voyages down it to New Orleans as a youth. "Direct your attention particularly to the canal proposed across the point," Halleck urged. "The President attaches much importance to this."

Grant himself was about ready to embark by now, wiring the general-in-chief this same day: "I leave for the fleet . . . tomorrow." Last-minute details held him up an extra day, but on the 27th he was off. "The work of reducing Vicksburg will take time and men," he had told Halleck the week before, "but can be accomplished."

Sherman was already hard at work on the project which had drawn Lincoln's particular attention, and with his present arduous endeavor—in effect a gigantic wrestling match with Mother Nature herself, or at any rate with her son the Father of Waters—added to his previous bloody experience up the Yazoo, he could testify as to the validity of Grant's long-range observation that the conquest of Vicksburg would "take time and men." In fact, he was inclined to think it might require so much of both commodities as to prove impossible. Both were expendable in the ordinary sense, but after all there were limits.

He was discouraged, he wrote his senator brother John this week, by the lack of substantial progress by Union arms, East and West, and by the unexpected resilience of the Confederates, civilian as well as military: "Two years have passed and the rebel flag still haunts our nation's capital. Our armies enter the best rebel territory and the wave closes in behind. The utmost we can claim is that our enemy respects our power to do them physical harm more than they did at first; but as to loving us any more, it were idle even to claim it. . . . I still see no end," he added, "or even the beginning of the end."

Perhaps the senseless burning of Napoleon the week before was on his mind or conscience, but the truth was he had enough on his hands to distress him here and now. The rain continued to come down hard—even harder, perhaps, than it was falling along the Rappahannock, where Ambrose Burnside's Mud March was coming to its sticky close and the soldiers were composing a parody of a bedtime prayer:

> Now I lay me down to sleep
> In mud that's many fathoms deep.
> If I'm not here when you awake
> Just hunt me up with an oyster rake

—with the result that Sherman's men, in addition to having to widen and deepen the old canal, which was little more than a narrow ditch across the base of the low-lying tongue of land, had to work day and night at throwing up a levee along its right flank in order not to be washed away by water from the flooded bayous in their rear. Besides, even if the river could be persuaded to scour out a new channel along this line and thus "leave Vicksburg out in the cold," as Sherman said, it would be no great gain so far as he could see. The Confederates would merely shift their guns southward along the bluff to command the river at and below the outlet, leaving the shovel-weary Federals no better off than before.

So he told his senator brother John. And Porter, watching his red-haired friend slosh around in the mud and lose his temper a dozen times a day—"half sailor, half soldier, with a touch of the snapping turtle," he called him—once more found it necessary to bolster Sherman's spirits with hot rum and rollicking words. "If this rain lasts much longer we will not need a canal," he ended a note to the unhappy general on January 27. "I think the whole point will disappear, troops and all, in which case the gunboats will have the field to themselves."

Next day, however, Grant arrived, and Porter, reporting the fact to Welles, could say: "I hope for a better state of things."

★   ★   ★

Along toward sunset of January 28, completing a 400-mile overnight trip from Memphis down the swollen, tawny, mile-wide Mississippi, a stern-wheel packet warped in for a west-bank landing at Young's Point, just opposite the base of the long hairpin bend in front of Vicksburg and within half a dozen air-line miles of the guns emplaced along the lip of the tall clay bluff the city stood on. First off the steamboat, once the deck hands had swung out the stageplank, was a slight man, rather stooped, five feet eight inches in height and weighing less than a hundred and forty pounds, who walked with a peculiar gait, shoulders hunched "a little forward of the perpendicular," as one observer remarked, so that each step seemed to arrest him momentarily in the act of pitching on his face. He had on a plain blue suit and what the same reporter called "an indifferently good 'Kossuth' hat, with the top battered in close to his head." Forty years old, he looked considerably older, partly because of the crow's-feet crinkling the outer corners of his eyes—the result of intense concentration, according to some, while others identified them as whiskey lines, plainly confirming rumors of overindulgence and refuting the protestations of friends that he never touched the stuff—but mainly because of the full, barely grizzled, light brown beard, close-cropped to emphasize the jut of a square jaw and expose a mouth described as being "of the letterbox shape," clamped firmly shut below a nose that surprised by contrast, being delicately chiseled, and blue-gray eyes that gave the face a somewhat out-of-balance look because one was set a trifle lower than the other. Wearing neither sword nor sash, and indeed no trappings of rank at all, except for the twin-starred straps of a major general tacked to the weathered shoulders of his coat, he was reading a newspaper as he came down the plank to the Louisiana shore, and he chewed the unlighted stump of a cigar, which not only seemed habitual but also appeared to be a more congruous facial appendage than the surprisingly aquiline nose.

"There's General Grant," an Illinois soldier told a
comrade as they stood watching this unceremonious arrival.

"I guess not," the other replied, shaking his head.
"That fellow don't look like he has the ability to command a regiment, much less an army."

It was not so much that Grant was unexpected; he
had a habit of turning up unannounced at almost any
time and place within the limits of his large department.
The trouble was that he bore such faint resemblance to
his photographs, which had been distributed widely
ever since Donelson and which, according to an acquaintance, made him look like a "burly beef-contrac-
tor." In person he resembled at best a badly printed
copy of one of those photos, with the burliness left out.
Conversely, the lines of worry—if his friends were right
and that was what they were—were more pronounced,
as was perhaps only natural when he had more to fret
about than the discomfort of holding still for a camera.
Just now, for instance, there was John McClernand,
who persisted in considering the river force a separate
command and continued to issue general orders under
the heading, "Headquarters, Army of the Mississippi."

Before Grant had been downriver two days he received a letter from McClernand, noting "that orders
are being issued directly from your headquarters directly to army corps commanders, and not through
me." This could only result in "dangerous confusion,"
McClernand protested, "as I am invested, by order of
the Secretary of War, indorsed by the President, and by
order of the President communicated to you by the
General-in-Chief, with the command of all the forces
operating on the Mississippi River. . . . If different views
are entertained by you, then the question should be im-

mediately referred to Washington, and one or the other, or both of us, relieved. One thing is certain; two generals cannot command this army, issuing independent and direct orders to subordinate officers, and the public service be promoted."

Grant agreed at least with the final sentence—which he later paraphrased and sharpened into a maxim: "Two commanders on the same field are always one too many"—but he found the letter as a whole "more in the nature of a reprimand than a protest." The fact was, it approached outright insubordination, although not quite close enough to afford occasion for the pounce Grant was crouched for. "I overlooked it, as I believed, for the good of the service," he subsequently wrote.

By way of reply, instead of direct reproof, he issued orders announcing that he was assuming personal command of the river expedition and instructing all corps commanders, including McClernand, to report henceforth directly to him; McClernand's corps, he added by way of a stinger, would garrison Helena and other west-bank points well upriver.

Outraged at being the apparent victim of a squeeze play, the former congressman responded by asking whether, "having projected the Mississippi River expedition, and having been by a series of orders assigned to the command of it," he was thus to be "entirely withdrawn from it." Grant replied to the effect that he would do as he saw fit, since "as yet I have seen no order to prevent my taking command in the field." McClernand acquiesced, as he said, "for the purpose of avoiding a conflict of authority in the presence of the enemy," but requested that the entire matter be referred to their superiors in Washington, "not only in respect for the President and Secretary, under whose authority I claim the right to command the expedition, but in justice to myself as its author and actual promoter."

Grant accordingly forwarded the correspondence to Halleck, saying that he had assumed command only because he lacked confidence in McClernand. "I respectfully submit the whole matter to the General-in-Chief and the President," he ended his indorsement. "Whatever the decision made by them, I will cheerfully submit to and give a hearty support."

In bucking all this up to the top echelon Grant was on even safer ground than he supposed. Just last week McClernand had received, in reply to a private letter to Lincoln charging Halleck "with wilful contempt of superior authority" because of his so-far "interference" in the matter, "and with incompetency for the extraordinary and vital functions with which he is charged," a note in which the President told him plainly: "I have too many *family* controversies (so to speak) already on my hands to voluntarily, or so long as I can avoid it, take up another. You are now doing well—well for the country, and well for yourself—much better than you could possibly be if engaged in open war with General Halleck. Allow me to beg that for your sake, for my sake, and for the country's sake, you give your whole attention to the better work."

So it was: McClernand already had his answer before he filed his latest appeal. Lincoln would not interfere. The army was Grant's, and would remain Grant's, to do with as he saw fit in accomplishing what Lincoln called "the better work."

His problem was how best to go about it. Now that he had inspected at first hand the obstacles to success in this swampy region, much of which was at present under water and would continue to be so for months to come, he could see that the wisest procedure, from a strategic point of view, "would have been to go back to Memphis, establish that as a base of supplies, fortify it so that the storehouses could be held by a small garrison, and move from there along the line of the railroad, repairing as we advanced to the Yalobusha," from which point he would have what he now so gravely lacked: a straight, high-ground shot at the city on the rebel bluff.

So he wrote, years later, having gained the advantage of hindsight. For the present, however, he saw certain drawbacks to the retrograde movement, which in his judgment far outweighed the strictly tactical advantages. For one thing, the November elections had gone against the party that stood for all-out prosecution of the war, and this had turned out to be a warning of future trouble, with the croakers finding encouragement in the reverse. There was the question of morale, not only in the army itself, but also on the home front, where even a temporary withdrawal would be considered an admission that Vicksburg was too tough a nut to crack. At this critical juncture, both temporal and political, with voluntary enlistment practically at a standstill throughout much of the North and the new conscription laws already meeting sporadic opposition, such a discouragement might well prove fatal to the cause.

"It was my judgment at the time," Grant subsequently wrote, "that to make a backward movement as long as that from Vicksburg to Memphis, would be interpreted, by many of those yet full of hope for the preservation of the Union, as a defeat, and that the draft would be resisted, desertions ensue, and the power to capture and punish deserters lost. There was nothing left to be done but to *go forward to a decisive victory*. This was in my mind from the moment I took command in person at Young's Point."

In his own mind at least that much was settled. He would stay. But this decision only brought him face to face with the basic problem, as he put it, of how "to secure a footing upon dry ground on the east side of the river, from which the troops could operate against Vicksburg . . . without an apparent retreat." Aside from a frontal assault, either against the bluff itself or against the heights flanking it on the north—which Sherman, even if he had done nothing more last month, had proved would not only be costly in the extreme but would also be fruitless, and which Grant said "was never contemplated; certainly not by me"—the choice lay between whether to cross upstream or down, above or below the rebel bastion.

One seemed about as impossible as the other. Above, the swampy, fifty-mile-wide Delta lay in his path, practically roadless and altogether malarial. Even if he were able to slog his foot soldiers across it, which was doubtful, it was worse than doubtful whether he would be able to establish and maintain a vital supply line by that route. On the other hand, to attempt a crossing below the city seemed even more suicidal, since this would involve a run past frowning batteries, not only at Vicksburg itself, but also at Warrenton and Grand Gulf, respectively seven and thirty-five miles downriver. Armored gunboats—as Farragut had demonstrated twice the year before, first up, then down, with his heavily gunned salt-water fleet—might run this fiery gauntlet, taking their losses as they went, but brittle-skinned transports and supply boats would be quite another matter, considering the likelihood of their being reduced to kindling in short order, with much attendant loss of life and goods. . . . In short, the choice seemed to lie between two impossibilities, flanking a third which had been rejected before it was even considered.

Two clear advantages Grant had, however, by way of helping to offset the gloom, and both afforded him comfort under the strain. One was the unflinching support of his superiors; the other was an ample supply of troops, either downstream with him or else on call above. "The eyes and hopes of the whole country are now directed to your army," Halleck presently would tell him. "In my opinion, the opening of the Mississippi River will be to us of more advantage than the capture of forty Richmonds. We shall omit nothing which we can do to assist you." Already, before Grant left Memphis, Old Brains had urged him: "Take everything you can dispense with in Tennessee and [North] Mississippi. We must not fail in this if within human power to accomplish it."

His total effective strength within his department, as of late January, was approximately 103,000 officers and men, and of these, as a result of abandoning railroads and other important rear-area installations, Grant had been able to earmark just over half for the downriver expedition: 32,000 in the two corps under McClernand and Sherman, already at hand, and 15,000 in McPherson's corps, filing aboard transports southbound from Memphis even now. In addition to these 47,000—the official total, "present for duty, equipped," was 46,994 —another 15,000 were standing by under Stephen Hurlbut, who commanded the Memphis-based fourth corps, ready to follow McPherson as soon as they got the word.

Just now, though, there not only was no need for them; there actually was no room. Because of the high water and the incessant rain overflowing the bayous, there was no place to camp on the low-lying west bank except upon the levee, with the result that the army was strung out along it for more than fifty miles, north and south, under conditions that were anything but healthy. As morale declined, the sick-lists lengthened; desertions were up; funerals were frequent. "Go any day down the levee," one recruit wrote home, "and you could see a squad or two of soldiers burying a companion, until the levee was nearly full of graves and the hospitals still full of sick. And those that were not down sick were not well by a considerable."

Pneumonia was the chief killer, with smallpox a close second. Some regiments soon had more men down than up. The food was bad. Paymasters did not venture south of Helena, which increased the disaffection, and the rumor mills were grinding as never before. When the mails were held up, as they frequently were, it was reported from camp to camp, like a spark moving along a fifty-mile train of powder, that the war was over but that the news was being kept from the troops "for fear we could not be held in subjection if we knew the state of affairs." They took out at least a share of their resentment on such rebel property as came within their reach. "Farms disappear, houses are burned and plundered, and every living animal killed and eaten," Sherman informed his senator brother. "General officers make feeble efforts to stay the disorder, but it is idle." Then when the mail came through at last they could read in anti-administration newspapers of the instability and incompetence of the West Pointers responsible for their welfare, including Sherman—"He hates reporters, foams at the mouth when he sees them, snaps at them; sure symptoms of a deep-seated mania"—and the army commander himself: "The confidence of the army is greatly shaken in General Grant, who hitherto undoubtedly depended more upon good fortune than upon military ability for success."

The wet season would continue for months, during which all these problems would be with him. As Grant said in retrospect, "There seemed to be no possibility of a land movement before the end of March or later." Yet "it would not do to lie idle all this time. The effect would be demoralizing to the troops and injurious to their health. Friends in the North would have grown more and more insolent in their gibes and denunciations of the cause and those engaged in it." So he launched (or rather, continued) what he called "a series of experiments," designed not only "to consume time," but also to serve the triple purpose of diverting "the attention of the enemy, of my troops, and of the public generally."

Two failures were already behind him in his campaign against Vicksburg: the advance down the Mississippi Central and the assault on the Chickasaw Bluffs, both of which had ended in retreat. Now there followed five more failures, bringing the total to seven. Looking back on them later he was to say—quite untruthfully, as the record would show—that he had "never felt great confidence that any of the experiments resorted to would prove successful," though he had always been "prepared to take advantage of them in case they did."

The third of these seven "experiments"—the attempt, by means of a canal across the base of the tongue of land in front of Vicksburg, to divert the channel of the river and thus permit the column of warships, transports, and supply boats to bypass the batteries on the bluff—had been in progress ever since the return of the army from Arkansas Post, but Sherman, who had assigned a thousand men a day to the digging job, was not sanguine of results. "The river is about full and threatens to drown us out," he was complaining as he sloshed about in a waste of gumbo, with the rain coming down harder every week. "The ground is wet, almost water, and it is impossible for wagons to haul stores from the river to camp, or even horses to wallow through."

Conversely, as if to preserve a balance of optimism, Grant's expectations rose with the passage of time. In early March he wired Halleck: "The canal is near completion. . . . I will have Vicksburg this month, or fail in the attempt."

This was the signal for disaster. "If the river rises 8 feet more, we would have to take to the trees," Sherman had said, and presently it did. The dam at the upper end of the cut gave way, and the water, instead of scouring out a channel—as had been expected, or anyhow intended—spread all over the lower end of the peninsula, forcing the evacuation of the troops from their flooded camps, with the resultant sacrifice of many horses and much equipment. "This little affair of ours here on Vicksburg Point is labor lost," Sherman reported in disgust, announcing the unceremonious end of the third experiment.

But Grant already had a fourth in progress. Fifty-odd miles above Vicksburg, just west of the river and south of the Arkansas line, lay Lake Providence, once a bend of the Mississippi but long since abandoned by the Old Man in the course of one of his cataclysmic whims. Though the lake now was land-locked, separated moreover from the river by a levee, Bayou Baxter drained it sluggishly westward into Bayou Macon, which in turn flowed into the Tensas River, just over a hundred winding miles to the south. Still farther down, the Tensas joined the Ouachita to form the Black, and the Black ran into the Red, which entered the Mississippi a brief stretch above Port Hudson. Despite its roundabout meandering, a distance of some 470 miles, this route seemed to Grant to offer a chance, once the levee had been breached to afford access to Lake Providence and the intricate system of hinterland bayous and rivers, for a naval column to avoid not only the Vicksburg batteries but also those below at Warrenton and Grand Gulf.

Accordingly, two days after his arrival at Young's Point, he sent an engineer detail to look into the possibilities indicated on the map, and the following week, in early February, he went up to see for himself. It seemed to him that "a little digging"—"less than one-quarter," he said, of what Sherman had done already on the old canal—"will connect the Mississippi and Lake, and in all probability will wash a channel in a short time." If so, the way would be open for a bloodless descent, at the end of which he would join Banks for a combined attack on Port Hudson, and once that final bastion had been reduced the Confederacy would have been cut in two and the Great Lakes region would have recovered its sorely missed trade connection with the Gulf. Impressed by this vista, Grant sent at once for McPherson to come down with a full division and get the project started without delay. "This bids fair to be the most practicable route for turning Vicksburg," he told him in the body of the summons.

He could scarcely have assigned the task to an officer better prepared to undertake it. McPherson, who was thirty-three and a fellow Ohioan, had been top man in the West Point class of '53 and had returned to the

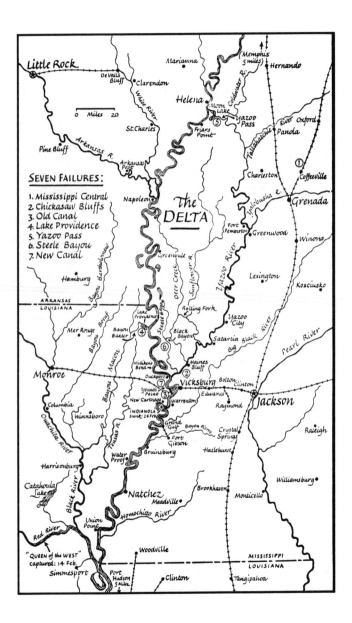

academy as an engineering instructor; he also had
worked on river and harbor projects in the peacetime
army, and had served at the time of Shiloh, when he was
a lieutenant colonel, as chief engineer on Grant's staff.
His advancement since then had been rapid, though not
without some grousing, on the part of line officers he
passed on his way up the ladder, that a man who had
never led troops in a major action should be given command of a corps. Sherman, on the other hand, considered him the army's "best hope for a great soldier," not
excepting Grant and himself; "if he lives," he added. A
bright-eyed, pleasant-faced young man, alternately
bland and impulsive, McPherson came quickly down
from Memphis with one of his two divisions and set to
work at once.

Without waiting for the levee to be cut, he horsed a
small towboat overland, launched it on the lake, and got
aboard for a reconnaissance—with the result that his
high hopes took a sudden drop. The Bayou Baxter outlet led through an extensive cypress brake, and what
could be found of its channel, which was but little at the
present flood stage, was badly choked with stumps and
snags that threatened to knock or rip the bottom out of
whatever came their way. He put his men to work with
underwater saws, but it was clear that at best the job
would be a long one, if not impossible. Besides, Grant
now saw that, even if a passage could be opened in time
to be of use, he would never be able to get together
enough light-draft boats to carry his army down to the
Red River anyhow. McPherson and his staff meanwhile
enjoyed something of a holiday, taking a regimental
band aboard the little steamer for moonlight excursions,
to and from the landing at one of the lakeside plantation
houses which turned out to have a well-stocked cellar.

Soldiers too found relaxation in this quiet backwater of the war, mainly in fishing, what time they were not taking turns on the underwater saws.

By early March it was more or less obvious that nothing substantial was going to come of this fourth attempt to take or bypass Vicksburg, but Grant declared, later and rather laconically: "I let the work go on, believing employment was better than idleness for the men."

All seven of these experiments, four of which by now had gone by the board, anticipated some degree of co-operation from the navy. For the most part, indeed, they were classically amphibious, depending as much on naval as on army strength and skill. But if Porter, whatever his other shortcomings—one acquaintance called him "by all odds the greatest humbug of the war"—was not the kind of man to withhold needed help, neither was he the kind to be satisfied with a supporting role if he saw even an outside chance at stardom. And he believed he saw one now: had seen it, in fact, from the outset, and had already made his solo entrance on the stage.

One of the two main reasons for attempting the reduction of Vicksburg and Port Hudson—in addition, that is, to opening a pathway to New Orleans and the Gulf—was to choke off rebel traffic along and across the nearly three hundred miles of river that flowed between them, particularly that segment of it tangent to the mouth of Red River, the main artery of trade connecting the goods-rich Transmississippi's far-west region with the principal Confederate supply depots in Georgia and Virginia. To accomplish this, the admiral perceived, it would not be absolutely necessary to capture either of the two bastions anchoring opposite ends of the long stretch of river. All that was needed, really, was to control what lay between them, and this could be done by sending warships down to knock out whatever vestiges of the rebel fleet remained and to establish a sort of internal blockade by patrolling all possible crossings. In early February, accordingly, while Sherman's men were still digging their way across soggy Vicksburg Point and Grant was steaming upriver for a preliminary look at cypress-choked Lake Providence, Porter gave orders which put his plan in the way of execution.

First off, this would require a run past the batteries on the bluff, and he gave the assignment to the steam ram *Queen of the West*, which had done it twice before, back in July, in an unsuccessful attempt to come to grips with the *Arkansas*. She was one of the navy's best-known vessels, having led the ram attack at the Battle of Memphis, where she had been commanded by her designer and builder, Charles Ellet, Jr., who had died of the only wound inflicted on a Northerner in that one-sided triumph. His son, nineteen-year-old Charles R. Ellet— who, as a medical cadet, had gone ashore in a rowboat, accompanied by three seamen, to complete the Memphis victory by raising the Stars and Stripes over the post office—had succeeded his uncle A. W. Ellet, who had succeeded the first Ellet as commander of the ram fleet, as skipper of the *Queen*. Patched up from the two poundings she had taken from Vicksburg's high-perched guns, and fitted out now with guns of her own for the first time—previously she had depended solely on her punch—she made her run at daybreak, February 4, taking an even dozen hits, including two in the hull but none below the water line, and pulled up at a battery Sherman had established on the west bank, just around the bend, for the protection of his diggers.

Above the town, two nights later, Porter set adrift a

barge loaded with 20,000 bushels of coal, which made it downstream on schedule and without mishap, apparently not having been spotted by the lookouts on the bluff. "This gives the ram nearly coal enough to last a month," the admiral proudly informed Secretary Welles, "in which time she can commit great havoc, if no accident happens to her."

Though at first it seemed an unnecessary flourish— he knew the rebels had nothing afloat to match the *Queen*—that final reservation was prophetic. Setting out on the night of February 10, accompanied by an ex-Confederate steamboat, the *DeSoto*, which had been captured by the army below Vicksburg, Ellet began his career as a commerce raider in fine style, slipping past the Warrenton batteries undetected and going to work at once on enemy shipping by destroying skiffs and flatboats on both banks. He burned or commandeered hundreds of bales of cotton, taking some aboard for "armoring" the wheelhouse, destroyed supply trains heavily loaded with grain and salt pork being sent to collection points, and in reprisal for a sniper bullet, which struck one of his sailors in the leg, burned no less than three plantation houses, together with their outbuildings, apparently undismayed even when one planter's daughter sang "The Bonny Blue Flag" full in his face as the flames crackled.

His greatest single prize, however, was the corn-laden packet *Era No. 5*, which he captured after passing Natchez and entering the Red River. But at that point, or just beyond it—seventy-five miles from the mouth of the river and with Alexandria in a turmoil less than half that far ahead—he and the *Queen* ran out of luck. On Valentine's Day, approaching Gordon's Landing, where a battery of guns had been reported, the ram stuck fast on a mud flat and was taken suddenly under fire by enemy gunners who yelled with delight at thus being offered a stationary target at a range of four hundred yards. In short order the boat's engine controls were smashed, her escape-pipe shot away, her boiler fractured. As she disappeared in hissing clouds of steam— one survivor later claimed to have avoided scalding his lungs because "I had sufficient presence of mind to cram the tail of my coat into my mouth"—officers and men began to tumble bales of cotton over the rail, then leap after them into the river, clinging to them in hope of reaching the *DeSoto* or the *Era*, a mile below. By now it was every man for himself, including the wounded, and the youthful skipper was not among the last to abandon the *Queen* in favor of a downstream ride astride a bale of cotton.

Picked up by the *DeSoto*, Ellet and the others were alarmed to discover that in the excitement she had unshipped both rudders and become unmanageable; so they set her afire and abandoned her, too, in favor of the more recently captured *Era*. Their career as raiders had lasted just four days. From now on, their only concern was escape, which seemed unlikely because of reports that the Confederates had at Alexandria a high-speed steamboat, the *William H. Webb*, which would surely be after them as soon as the news arrived upriver. She mounted only one gun, they had heard, and would never have dared to tackle the *Queen*, but now the tables were more or less turned; the pursuers became the pursued. "With a sigh for the poor fellows left behind, and a hope that our enemies would be merciful," a survivor wrote, "the prow of the *Era* was turned toward the Mississippi."

They made it by daylight, after a race through stormy

darkness unrelieved except for blinding flashes of lightning, and started north up the big river, heaving overboard all possible incidentals, including rations, in an attempt to coax more speed from their unarmed boat. Next morning, February 16, just below Natchez, with the *Webb* reportedly closing fast on their stern, they were startled to see an enormous, twin-stacked vessel bearing down on them from dead ahead. Their dismay at the prospect of being ground between two millstones was relieved, however, when the lookout identified her as the *Indianola*. The latest addition to the ironclad fleet and the pride of the Federal inland-waters navy, she mounted two great 11-inch smoothbores forward and a pair of 9-inch rifles amidships, casemated between her towering sidewheel-boxes, while for power she boasted four engines, driving twin screws in addition to her paddles, and she had brought two large barges of coal along, one lashed to starboard and one to port, to insure a long-term stay on the previously rebel-held 250-mile stretch of river above Port Hudson. Porter had sent her down past the Vicksburg batteries three nights ago, intending for her to support the *Queen* and thus, as he said, "make matters doubly sure."

Learning from Ellet that the *Queen* had been lost, George Brown, captain of the *Indianola*, decided at once to proceed downriver, accompanied by the *Era*. Presently they sighted the *Webb*, in hot pursuit, and once more the tables were turned; for the *Webb* took one quick look at the iron-clad monster and promptly made use of her superior speed to withdraw before coming within range of those 11-inch guns, two short-falling shots from which only served to hurry her along, as one observer said, "for all the world like a frightened racehorse." Brown gave chase as far as the mouth of Red

River, up which the rebel vessel disappeared, but there he called a halt, Porter having warned him not to venture up that stream without an experienced pilot, which he lacked.

While Brown continued on patrol, guarding against a re-emergence of the *Webb*, Ellet took off northward in the *Era* with the unpleasant duty of informing Porter that he had lost the *Queen*. Two days later, still on patrol at the mouth of the Red, Brown received astounding news. The Confederates had resurrected the *Queen of the West*, patching up her punctured hull and repairing her fractured steam drum. Even now, in company with the skittish *Webb* and two cottonclad boats whose upper decks were crowded with sharpshooters, she was preparing to come out after the *Indianola*. Brown thought it over and decided to retire.

He would have done better to leave without taking time to think it over; the fuze was burning shorter than he knew. However, he was in for a fight in any event because of the two coal barges, which he knew would decrease his upstream speed considerably, but which he was determined to hold on to, despite the fact that the *Indianola's* bunkers were chock-full. Partly this decision was the result of his ingrained peacetime frugality, but mostly it was because he wanted to have plenty of fuel on hand in case Porter complied with his request, forwarded by Ellet, that another gunboat be sent downriver as a replacement for the *Queen*. Brown left the mouth of the Red on Saturday, February 21, and stopped for the night at a plantation landing up the Mississippi to take on a load of cotton bales, which he stacked around the ironclad's low main deck to make her less vulnerable to boarders. Next morning he was off again in earnest, all four engines straining to offset the drag of the two barges lashed alongside. He did not know how much of a head start he had, but he feared it was not enough.

In point of fact, it was even less than he supposed; for the four-boat Confederate flotilla, including the resurrected *Queen*, set out after him at about the same hour that Sunday morning, ninety miles astern of the landing where the *Indianola* had commandeered the cotton. The race was on.

It was not really much of a race. Joseph L. Brent, an army major commanding the quartet of rebel warships, each of which was in the charge of an army captain, could have overtaken Brown at almost anytime Tuesday afternoon, the 24th, but he preferred to wait for darkness, which would not only make the aiming of the ironclad's big guns more difficult but would also give the Grand Gulf batteries a chance at her as she went by.

Held to a crawl though she was by the awkward burden of her barges, the *Indianola* got past that danger without mishap; but Brown could see the smoke from his pursuers' chimneys drawing closer with every mile as the sun declined, and he knew that he was in for a fight before it rose again. He also knew by now that no reinforcing consort was going to join him from the fleet above Vicksburg, in spite of which he held doggedly to his barges, counting on them to give him fender protection from ram attacks. As darkness fell, moonless but dusky with starlight, he cleared for action and kept half of his crew at battle stations: "watch and watch," it was called. At 9.30 he passed New Carthage, which put him within thirteen miles of the nearest west-bank Union battery, but by that time the rebel boats were in plain sight. Abreast of Palmyra Island, heading into Davis Bend—so called because it flowed past the Confederate

President's Brierfield Plantation—Brown swung his iron prow around to face his pursuers at last, thus bringing his heavy guns to bear and protecting his more vulnerable stern.

As the *Queen* and the *Webb* came at him simultaneously, the former in the lead, he fired an 11-inch shell point-blank at each. Both missed, and the *Queen* was on him, lunging in from port with such force that the barge on that side was sliced almost in two. Emerging unscathed from this, except for the loss of the barge, which was cut adrift to sink, the *Indianola* met the *Webb* bows on, with a crash that knocked most of both crews off their feet and left the Confederate with a gash in her bow extending from water line to keelson, while the Federal was comparatively unhurt. Nevertheless the *Webb* backed off and struck again, crushing the remaining barge so completely as to leave it hanging by the lashings.

Meanwhile the *Queen,* having run upstream a ways to gain momentum, turned and came charging down, striking her adversary just abaft the starboard wheelhouse, which was wrecked along with the rudder on that side, and starting a number of leaks along the shaft. Likewise the *Webb,* having gained momentum in the same fashion, brought her broken nose down hard and fair on the crippled ironclad's lightly armored stern, starting the timbers and causing the water to pour in rapidly. All this time the *Indianola* had kept throwing shells into the smoky darkness, left and right, but had scored only a single hit on the *Queen,* which did no considerable damage to the boat herself though it killed two and wounded four of her crew. Brown, having done his worst with this one shot, was now in a hopeless condition, scarcely able to steer and with both of his starboard engines flooded. After waiting a while in midstream until the water had risen nearly to the grate-bars of the ironclad's furnaces, planning thus to avoid her capture by making sure that she would sink, he ran her hard into the more friendly west bank and hauled down his colors just as the two cottonclads came alongside, crowded with yelling rebels prepared for boarding.

Quickly they leaped down and attached two ropes by which the steamers could haul the *Indianola* across the river to the Confederate-held east bank, barely making it in time for her to sink in ten feet of water. As soon as they got their prisoners ashore they went to work on the captured dreadnought, intending to raise her, as they had raised the *Queen of the West* the week before, for service under the Stars and Bars.

Though he had heard the heavy nighttime firing just downriver, Porter did not know for certain what had happened until two days later, when a seaman who had escaped from the *Indianola* during her brief contact with the western bank came aboard his flagship *Black Hawk* and gave him an eyewitness account of the tragedy. Coming as it did on the heels of news of the loss of the *Queen*—which in turn had been preceded, two months back, by the destruction of the *Cairo*—the blow was hard, especially since it included the information that the *Queen* had been taken over by the enemy and had played a leading part in the defeat of her intended consort, which was now about to be used in the same manner as soon as the rebels succeeded in getting her afloat. What made it doubly hard, for Porter at any rate, was the contrast between his present gloom and his recent optimism.

"If you open the Father of Waters," Assistant Navy Secretary G. A. Fox had wired the acting rear admiral in response to reports of his progress just two weeks ago, "you will at once be made an admiral; besides we will try for a ribboned star. . . . Do your work up clean," Fox added, "and the public will never be in doubt who did it. The flaming army correspondence misleads nobody. Keep cool, be very modest under great success, as a contrast to the soldiers."

At any rate, such strain as there had been on Porter's modesty was removed by the awareness that all he had really accomplished so far—aside from the capture of Arkansas Post, which had had to be shared with the army—was the loss of three of his best warships, two of which were now in enemy hands. What filled his mind just now was the thought of what this newest-model ironclad, the former pride of the Union fleet, could accomplish once she went into action on the Confederate side. Supported as she would be by the captured ram, she might well prove invincible in an upstream fight. In fact, any attempt to challenge her en masse would probably add other powerful units to the rebel flotilla of defected boats, since any disabled vessel would be swept helplessly downstream in such an engagement. Far from opening the Father of Waters, and gaining thereby a ribboned star and the permanent rank of admiral, Porter could see that he would be more likely to lose what had been won by his predecessors. Besides, even if he had wanted to launch such an all-out attack, he had no gunboats in the vicinity of Vicksburg now; they had been sent far upriver to co-operate in another of Grant's ill-fated amphibious experiments.

Porter was inventive in more ways than one, however, and his resourcefulness now stood him in good stead. If he had no available ironclad, then he would build one—or anyhow the semblance of one. Ordering every man off the noncombatant vessels to turn to, he took an old flat-bottomed barge, extended its length to three hundred feet by use of rafts hidden behind false bulwarks, and covered it over with flimsy decking to support a frame-and-canvas pilothouse and two huge but empty paddle-wheel boxes. A casemate was mounted forward, with a number of large-caliber logs protruding from its ports, and two tall smokestacks were erected by piling barrels one upon another. As a final realistic touch, after two abandoned skiffs were swung from un-workable davits, the completed dummy warship was given an all-over coat of tar. Within twenty-four hours, at a reported cost of $8.63, the navy had what appeared, at least from a distance, to be a sister ship of the *In-dianola*.

Belching smoke from pots of burning tar and oakum installed in her barrel stacks, she was set adrift the fol-lowing night to make her run past the Vicksburg batte-ries. They gave her everything they had, but to no avail; her black armor seemingly impervious to damage, she glided unscathed past the roaring guns, not even deign-ing to reply. At daybreak she grounded near the lower end of Sherman's canal, and the diggers pushed her off again with a cheer. As she resumed her course down-river, the *Queen of the West*, coming up past Warrenton on a scout, spotted the dark behemoth in the distance, bearing down with her guns run out and her deck appar-ently cleared for action. The ram spun on her heel and sped back to spread the alarm: whereupon—since nei-ther the *Queen* nor the broken-nosed *Webb* was in any condition for another fight just yet—all four of the Confederate vessels made off southward to avoid a clash with this second ironclad.

Aboard the *Indianola*, still immobile and now deserted by her new friends, the lieutenant in charge of salvage operations was for holding on to her and fighting it out, despite repeated orders for him to complete her destruction before she could be recaptured. At a range of about two miles, the dreadnought halted as if to look the situation over before closing in for the bloody work she was bent on. Still the lieutenant held his ground until nightfall, when he decided to comply with the instructions of his superiors. After heaving the 9-inch rifles into the river, he laid the 11-inch smooth-bores muzzle to muzzle and fired them with slow matches. When the smoke from this had cleared, he came back and set fire to what was left, burning the wreckage to the water line and ending the brief but stormy career of the ironclad *Indianola*.

Next morning, seeing the black monster still in her former position, some two miles upriver—one observer later described her as "terrible though inert"—a party of Confederates went out in a rowboat to investigate. Drawing closer they recognized her for the hoax she was, and saw that she had come to rest on a mudbank. Nailed to her starboard wheelhouse was a crudely lettered sign. "Deluded people, cave in," it read.

"Then, too," Grant added, continuing the comment on his reasons for keeping McPherson's men sawing away at the underwater stumps and snags clogging the Bayou Baxter exit from Lake Providence even after he knew that, in itself, the work was unlikely to produce anything substantial, "it served as a cover for other efforts which gave a better prospect of success." What he had in mind—in addition, that is, to Sherman's canal, which was not to be abandoned until March—was a fifth experimental project, whose starting point was four hundred tortuous miles upriver from its intended finish atop the Vicksburg bluff.

In olden days, just south of Helena and on the opposite bank, a bayou had afforded egress from the Mississippi; Yazoo Pass, it was called, because it connected eastward with the Coldwater River, which flowed south into the Tallahatchie, which in turn combined with the Yalobusha, farther down, to form the Yazoo. Steamboats once had plied this route for trade with the planters of the Delta hinterland. In fact, they still steamed up and down this intricate chain of rivers, but only by entering from below, through the mouth of the Yazoo River; for the state of Mississippi had sealed off the northern entrance, five years before the war, by constructing across the mouth of Yazoo Pass a levee which served to keep the low-lying cotton fields from going under water with every rise of the big river. Now it was Grant's notion that perhaps all he needed to do, in order to utilize this old peacetime trade route for his wartime purpose, was cut the levee and send in gunboats to provide cover for transports, which then could be unloaded on high ground—well down the left bank of the Yazoo but short of Haines Bluff, whose fortifications blocked an ascent of that river from below—and thus, by forcing the outnumbered defenders to come out into the open for a fight which could only result in their defeat, take Vicksburg from the rear. Accordingly, at the same time he ordered McPherson down from Memphis to Lake Providence, he sent his chief topographical engineer, James H. Wilson, to inspect and report on the possibility of launching such an attack by way of Yazoo Pass.

Wilson, described by a contemporary as "a slight person of a light complexion and with rather a pinched face," was enthusiastic from the start. An Illinois regular, only two years out of West Point and approaching his twenty-sixth birthday, he recently had been transferred from the East, where he had served as an aide to George McClellan at Antietam, and he had approached his western assignment with doubts, particularly in regard to Grant, whose "simple and unmilitary bearing," as the young man phrased it, made a drab impression by contrast with the recent splendor of Little Mac, whose official family had included an Astor and two genuine French princes of the blood. But in this case familiarity bred affection; Wilson soon was remarking that his new commander was "a most agreeable companion both on the march and in camp." What drew him more than anything, however, was the trust Grant showed in sending him to take charge of the opening phase of this fifth and latest project for the reduction of the Gibraltar of the West.

After a bit of preliminary surveying and shovel work, he wasted no time. On the evening of February 3 — while Ellet prepared to take the *Queen* past the Vicksburg bluff at daybreak and Grant himself was about to head upriver for a first-hand look at Lake Providence — Wilson mined and blew the levee sealing the mouth of Yazoo Pass. The result was altogether spectacular, he reported, "water pouring through like nothing else I ever saw except Niagara." After waiting four days for the surface levels to equalize, east and west of the cut, he boarded a gunboat, steamed "with great ease" into Moon Lake, a mile beyond, and "ran down it about five miles to where the Pass leaves it." Hard work was going to be involved, he wrote Grant's adjutant, but he was confident of a large return on such an investment.

Grant was infected at once with the colonel's enthusiasm. Wilson already had with him a 4500-man division from Helena; now a second division was ordered to join him from there. Presently, when he reported that he had got through to the Coldwater, McPherson was told to be prepared to follow with his whole corps. "The Yazoo Pass expedition is going to prove a perfect success," Grant informed Elihu B. Washburne, his home-state Representative and congressional guardian angel.

Hard work had been foreseen, and that was what it took. Emerging from Moon Lake, Wilson found the remaining twelve-mile segment of the pass sufficiently deep but so narrow in some places that the gunboat could not squeeze between giant oaks and cypresses growing on opposite banks. These had to be felled with axes, a patience-testing business but by no means the most discouraging he encountered. Warned of his coming, the Confederates had brought in working parties of slaves from surrounding plantations and had chopped down other trees, some of them more than four feet through the bole, so that they lay athwart the bayou, ponderous and apparently immovable. Undaunted, Wilson borrowed navy hawsers long enough to afford simultaneous handholds for whole regiments of soldiers, whom he put to work snaking the impediments out of the way. They did it with such ease, he later remarked, that he never afterwards wondered how the Egyptians had lifted the great stones in place when they built the Pyramids; enough men on a rope could move anything, he decided.

Still, he had no such span of time at his disposal as the Pharaohs had had, and this was at best a time-consuming process. February was almost gone before he reached the eastern end of the pass. South of there, however, he expected to find clear sailing. The Coldwater being "a considerable stream," he reported, vessels of almost any length and draft could be sent from the Mississippi into the Tallahatchie in just four days. And so it proved when a ten-boat flotilla, including two ironclads, two steam rams, and six tinclads—the 22 light transports were to come along behind—tried it during the first week in March. In fact, it was not until the warships were more than a hundred miles down the winding Tallahatchie, near its junction with the Yalobusha, that Wilson realized he was in for a great deal more trouble, and of a kind he had not encountered up to now.

The trouble now was the rebels themselves, not just the various obstructions they had left in his path before fading back into the swamps and woods. Five miles above Greenwood, a hamlet at the confluence of the rivers, they had improvised on a boggy island inclosed by a loop of the Tallahatchie a fort whose parapets, built of cotton bales and reinforced with sandbags, were designed not only to deflect heavy projectiles but also to keep out the river itself, which had gone well past the flood stage when the Yankees blew the levee far upstream. Fort Pemberton, the place was called, and it had as its commander a man out of the dim Confederate past: Lloyd Tilghman, who had fought unsuccessfully against Grant and the ironclads under similar circumstances at Fort Henry, thirteen months ago. Exchanged and reinstated, he was determined to wipe out that defeat, though the odds were as long and the tactical situation not much different. His immediate superior, W. W. Loring, was also a carry-over from the past, and as commander of the Delta subdepartment he intended to give the Federals even more trouble than he had given Lee and Jackson in Virginia the year before, which was considerable.

A third relic on the scene was the former U.S. ocean steamer *Star of the West*, whose name had been in the scareheads three full months before the war, when the Charleston batteries fired on her for attempting the relief of Sumter. Continuing on to Texas, she had been captured in mid-April by Van Dorn at Indianola and was in the rebel service as a receiving-ship at New Orleans a year later, when Farragut provoked her flight up the Mississippi and into the Yazoo to avoid recapture. Here above Greenwood she ended her days afloat, but not her career, for she was sunk in the Tallahatchie alongside Fort Pemberton, blocking the channel and thus becoming an integral part of the outer defenses of Vicksburg.

Three regiments, one from Texas and two from Mississippi, were all the high command could spare for manning the breastworks and the guns, which included one 6.4-inch rifle and half a dozen smaller pieces. This was scarcely a formidable armament with which to oppose 11-inch Dahlgrens housed in armored casemates, but on March 11—while northward a long column of approaching warships and transports sent up a winding trail of smoke, stretching out of sight beyond the heavy screen of woods—the graybacks were a determined crew as they sighted their guns up the straight stretch of river giving down upon the fort.

Watson Smith, a veteran lieutenant commander who had charge of the ten-boat Union flotilla, was by now in a state of acute distress; he had never experienced anything like this in all his years afloat. Coming through Yazoo Pass into the Coldwater and down the Tallahatchie, all of which were so narrow in places that the gunboats had to be warped around the sharper bends with ropes, one tinclad had shattered her wheel and was out of action, while another had lost both smokestacks. All the rest had taken similar punishment in passing over rafts of driftwood or under projecting limbs that came sweeping and crashing along their upper works. The most serious of these mishaps was suffered when the *Chillicothe*, one of the two ironclads, struck a snag and started a plank in her bottom, which had to be held in place by beams shored in from the deck above.

Smith's distress was greatly increased this morning, however, when this same unlucky vessel, at the head of the column, rounded the next-to-final bend leading down to the Yazoo and was struck hard twice on the turrets by high-velocity shells from dead ahead. She pulled back to survey the damage and fortify with cotton bales, then came on again that afternoon, accompanied by the other ironclad, the *De Kalb*. She got off four rounds at 800 yards and was about to fire a fifth—the loaders had already set the 11-inch shell in the gun's muzzle and were stripping the patch from the fuze—when a rebel shell came screaming through the port; both projectiles exploded on contact, killing 2 and wounding 11 of the gun crew. The two ironclads withdrew under urgent orders from Smith, whose distress had increased to the point where, according to Porter's subsequent report, he was showing "symptoms of aberration of mind."

Twice more, on the 13th and the 16th—without, however, attempting to close the range—the ironclads tried for a reduction of the fort at the end of that tree-lined stretch of river, as straight and uncluttered as a bowling alley: with similar results. Unable to maneuver in the narrow stream, the two boats took a terrible pounding, but could do little more than bounce their big projectiles off the resilient enemy parapet. The infantry, waiting rearward in the transports, gave no help at all; for the flooded banks made debarkation impossible, and any attempt at a small-boat attack—even if such boats had been available, which they were not— would have been suicidal. By the time the third day's bombardment was over, both ironclads were badly crippled; the *De Kalb* had lost ten of her gun-deck beams and her steerage was shot to pieces, while the luckless *Chillicothe* had more of her crew felled by armor bolts driven inward, under the impact of shells from the hard-hitting enemy rifle, to fly like bullets through the casemate.

On March 17, in an apparent moment of lucidity, Smith ordered the flotilla to withdraw. Everyone agreed that this was the wisest course: everyone but Wilson, who complained hotly to Grant that the issue had not been pressed. "To let one 6½-inch rifle stop our navy. Bah!" he protested, and put the blame on "Acting Rear Admiral, Commodore, Captain, Lieutenant-Commander Smith" and the other naval officers. "I've talked with them all and tried to give them backbone," he said, "but they are not confident."

Returning up the Coldwater two days later—while Loring and Tilghman were celebrating the repulse in victory dispatches sent downriver to Vicksburg—the disconsolate Federals met the second Helena division on its way to reinforce them under Isaac Quinby, a hard-handed brigadier who outranked all the brass on the scene and was unwilling to retreat without so much as a look at what stood in the way of an advance. So the expedition turned around and came back down again.

Stopping short of the bend leading into the bowling alley, the men aboard the transports and gunboats slapped at mosquitoes and practiced their marksmanship on alligators, while Quinby conducted a boggy twelve-day reconnaissance which finally persuaded him that Smith had been right in the first place. Besides, even Wilson was convinced by now that the game was not worth the candle, for the rebels had brought up another steamboat which they were "either ready to sink or use as a boarding-craft and ram," and it seemed to the young colonel that they were "making great calculations 'to bag us' entire." He agreed that the time had come for a final departure.

This began on April 5 and brought the Yazoo Pass experiment to a close. Being, as he said, "solicitous for my reputation at headquarters," Wilson ended a letter to Grant's adjutant with a request for the latest staff gossip, and thought to add: "Remember me kindly to the general."

His fears, though natural enough in an ambitious young career officer who had failed in his first independent assignment, were groundless. For unlike Porter, who no sooner learned the details of the Tallahatchie nightmare than he relieved Watson Smith of duty with the fleet and sent him North—where presently, by way of proving that his affliction had been physical as well as mental, he died in a delirium of fever and chagrin—Grant did not hold the collapse of this fifth experiment against his subordinate, but rather, when Wilson returned at last to Young's Point after an absence of more than two months, welcomed him back without reproach into the fold. By then the army commander had a better appreciation of the problems that stood in the way of an

amphibious penetration of the Delta, having been involved simultaneously in a not unsimilar nightmare of
his own.

In point of fact, no matter how little he chose to bring
it to bear, Porter had even greater occasion for such
charity, since he had been more intimately involved, not
only as the author but also as the on-the-scene director
of still another fiasco, the sole result of which had been
the addition of a sixth to the sequence of failures designed for the reduction of Vicksburg.

Left with time more or less on his hands after the
downriver loss of two of his best warships, and being
anxious moreover to offset the damage to his reputation
with an exploit involving something less flimsy than a
dummy ironclad, the admiral pored over his charts and
made various exploratory trips up and down the network of creeks and bayous flowing into the Yazoo River
below Haines Bluff, whose guns he had learned to respect back in December. Five miles upstream from its
junction with the Mississippi, the Yazoo received the
sluggish waters of Steele Bayou, and forty miles up
Steele Bayou, Black Bayou connected eastward with
Deer Creek, which in turn, at about the same upstream
distance and by means of another stream called Rolling
Fork, connected eastward with the Sunflower River.
That was where the payoff came within easy reach; for
the Sunflower flowed into the Yazoo, fifty miles below,
offering the chance for an uncontested high-ground
landing well above the Haines Bluff fortifications,
which then could be assaulted from the rear or bypassed
on the way to the back door of Vicksburg.

Though the route was crooked and the distance great

—especially by contrast; no less than two hundred roundabout miles would have to be traversed by the column of gunboats and transports in order to put the troops ashore no more than twenty air-line miles above their starting point—Porter was so firmly convinced he had found the solution to the knotty Vicksburg problem that he called at Young's Point and persuaded Grant to come aboard the *Black Hawk* for a demonstration. Steaming up the Yazoo, the admiral watched the tree-fringed north bank for a while, then suddenly to his companion's amazement signaled the helm for a hard turn to port, into brush that was apparently impenetrable. So far, high water had been the curse of the campaign, but now it proved an asset. As the boat swung through the leafy barrier, which parted to admit it, the leadsman sang out a sounding of fifteen feet—better than twice the depth the ironclads required. Formerly startled, Grant was now convinced, especially when Porter informed him that they were steaming above an old road once used for hauling cotton to the river.

Practically all the lower Delta was submerged, in part because of the seasonal rise of the rivers, but mostly because of the cut Wilson had made in the levee, four hundred miles upstream at Yazoo Pass; a tremendous volume of water had come down the various tributaries and had spread itself over the land. It was Porter's contention, based on limited reconnaissance, that as a result all those creeks and bayous would be navigable from end to end by vessels of almost any size, including the gunboats and transports selected to thread the labyrinth giving down upon the back-door approach to Vicksburg. Infected once more with contagious enthusiasm, Grant returned without delay to Young's Point, where he issued orders that same night for the army's share in what was known thereafter as the Steele Bayou expedition.

Sherman drew the assignment, along with one of his two divisions of men who just that week had been flooded out of their pick-and-shovel work on the doomed canal, and went up the Mississippi to a point where a long bend swung eastward to within a mile of Steele Bayou. On the afternoon of March 16, after slogging across this boggy neck of land, he made contact with the naval units, which had come up by way of the Yazoo that morning. As soon as he got his troops aboard the waiting transports the column resumed its progress northward, five ironclads in the lead, followed by four all-purpose tugs and a pair of mortar boats which Porter, not knowing what he might encounter in the labyrinth ahead, had had "built for the occasion." With his mind's eye fixed on permanent rank and the ribboned star Fox had promised to try for, the admiral was taking no chances he could avoid.

All went well—as he had expected because of his preliminary reconnaissance—until the gunboats approached Black Bayou, where the unreconnoitered portion of the route began. This narrow, four-mile, time-forgotten stretch of stagnant water was not only extremely crooked, it was also filled with trees. Porter used his heavy boats to butt them down, bulldozer style, and hoisted them aside with snatch blocks. This was heavy labor, necessarily slow, and as it progressed the column changed considerably in appearance. Overhead branches swept the upper decks of the warships, leaving a mess of wreckage in the place of boats and woodwork. Occasionally, too, as Porter said, "a rude tree would throw Briarean arms" around the stacks of the slowly passing vessels, "and knock their bonnets sideways." After about a mile of this, Sherman's men were put to work with ropes and axes, clearing a broader passage for the transports, while the sturdier ironclads forged ahead, thumping and bumping their way into Deer Creek, where they resumed a northward course next morning.

But this was worse in several ways, one of them being that the creek was even narrower than the bayou. If the trees were fewer, they were also closer together, and vermin of all kinds had taken refuge in them from the flood; so that when one of the gunboats struck a tree the quivering limbs let fall a plague of rats, mice, cockroaches, snakes, and lizards. Men were stationed about the decks with brooms to rid the vessels of such unwelcome boarders, but sometimes the sweepers had larger game to contend with, including coons and wildcats. These last, however, "were prejudiced against us, and refused to be comforted on board," the admiral subsequently wrote, "though I am sorry to say we found more Union feeling among the bugs."

To add to the nightmare, Deer Creek was the crookedest stream he had ever encountered: "One minute an ironclad would apparently be leading ahead, and the next minute would as apparently be steering the other way." Along one brief stretch, less than half a mile in length, the five warships were steaming in five quite different directions. Moreover, this was a region of plantations, which meant that there were man-made obstacles such as bridges, and though these gave the heavy boats no real trouble—they could plow through them as if they were built of matchsticks—other impediments were more disturbing. For example, hearing of the approach of the Yankees, the planters had had

their baled cotton stacked along both creekbanks and
set afire in order to keep it out of the hands of the invaders: with the result that, from time to time, the gunboats
had to run a fiery gauntlet. The thick white smoke sent
the crews into spasms of coughing, while the heat
singed their hair, scorched their faces, and blistered the
paint from the vessels' iron flanks.

So far, despite the crowds of field hands who lined
the banks to marvel at the appearance of ironclads
where not even flat-bottomed packets had ventured
before, Porter had not seen a single white man. He
found this odd, and indeed somewhat foreboding.

Presently, however, spotting one sitting in front of a
cabin and smoking a pipe as if nothing unusual was
going on around him, the admiral had the flagship
stopped just short of another bridge and summoned the
man to come down to the landing; which he did—a
burly, rough-faced individual, in shirt sleeves and bare-
headed; "half bulldog, half bloodhound," Porter called
him. When the admiral began to question him he identified himself as the plantation overseer. "I suppose you
are Union, of course?" Porter said. "You all are so when
it suits you." "No, by God, I'm not, and never will be,"
the man replied. "As to the others, I know nothing
about them. Find out for yourself. I'm for Jeff Davis
first, last, and all the time. Do you want any more of
me?" he added; "for I am not a loquacious man at any
time." "No, I want nothing more with you," Porter
said. "But I am going to steam into that bridge of yours
across the stream and knock it down. Is it strongly
built?" "You may knock it down and be damned," the
overseer told him. "It don't belong to me." Catching
something in his accent, Porter remarked: "You're a
Yankee by birth, are you not?" "Yes, damn it, I am," the

man admitted. "But that's no reason I should like the institution. I cut it long ago." And with this he turned on his heel and walked away.

Porter had the skipper ring "Go ahead fast," and the ironclad smashed through the bridge about as easily as if it had not been there. When he looked back, however, to see what impression this had made on the overseer, he saw him seated once more in front of the cabin, smoking his pipe, not having bothered even to turn his head and watch. Deciding that the fellow "was but one remove from a brute," Porter was disturbed by the thought that "there were hundreds more like him" lurking somewhere in the brush. At any rate, he fervently hoped that Sherman's men—particularly one regiment, which had the reputation of being able to "catch, scrape, and skin a hog without a soldier leaving the ranks"—would "pay the apostate Yankee a visit, if only to teach him good manners."

Under the circumstances, even aside from the necessary halts, half a mile an hour was the best speed the ironclads could make on this St Patrick's Day. Nightfall overtook them a scant eight miles from the morning's starting point. Twelve miles they made next day, but the increased speed increased the damage to the boats, including the loss of all the skylights to falling debris, and when they stopped engines for the night, Porter heard from up ahead the least welcome of all sounds: the steady chuck of axes, informing him that the rebels were warned of his coming. He wished fervently for Sherman, whose men were still at work in Black Bayou, widening a pathway for their transports, and consoled himself with the thought that the red-haired general would be along eventually; "there was only one road, so he couldn't have taken the wrong one."

For the present, however, Porter did what he could
with what he had, sending the mortar boats forward in
the darkness; and when their firing stopped, so had the
axes. Next morning, March 19, he pushed on. Despite
the delay involved in hoisting the felled trees aside, he
made such good progress that by nightfall he was within
half a mile of the entrance to Rolling Fork. At daybreak
he steamed north again, but the flagship had gone
barely two hundred yards when, just ahead and extending all the way across the creek, the admiral saw "a large
green patch . . . like the green scum on ponds."

He shouted down from the bridge to one of the admiring field hands on the bank: "What is that?"

"It's nuffin but willers, sah," the Negro replied, explaining that in the off season the plantation workers
often went out in skiffs and canoes to cut the willow
wands for weaving baskets. "You kin go through dat lak
a eel."

That this last was an overstatement—based on a failure to realize that, unlike skiffs and canoes, the gunboats
moved *through* rather than *over* the water, and what was
more had paddle wheels and overlapping plates of
armor—Porter discovered within a couple of minutes
of giving the order to go ahead. Starting with a full head
of steam, the ironclad made about thirty yards before
coming to a dead stop, gripped tightly by the willow
withes, not unlike Gulliver when he woke to find himself in Lilliputian bonds. The admiral called for hard
astern; but that was no good either; the vessel would not
budge. Here was a ticklish situation. The high creekbanks rendered the warships practically helpless, for
their guns would not clear them even at extreme ele-
vation. Not knowing what he would do if the Confederates made a determined boarding attack, Porter

fortified a nearby Indian mound* with four smoothbore howitzers and put the flagship's crew over the side with knives and hooks and orders to cut her loose, twig by twig. It was slow work; "I wished ironclads were in Jericho," he later declared.

Just then his wish seemed about to be fulfilled. The shrill shrieks of two rifle shots, which he recognized as high-velocity Whitworths, were followed at once by a pair of bursts, abrupt as blue-sky thunder and directly over the mound. Suddenly, in the wake of these two ranging shots—within six hundred yards of Rolling Fork and less than ten miles from clear sailing down the broad and unobstructed Sunflower River—two six-gun rebel batteries were firing on the outranged smoothbores from opposite directions, and the naval commander was shocked to see his cannoneers come tumbling down the rearward slope of the mound, seeking cover from the rain of shells. Continuing to hack at the clinging willows, he got his mortars into counter-battery action and, with the help of half a dollar, persuaded a "truthful contraband" (so Porter termed him later, but just then he called him Sambo; which drew the reply, "My name aint Sambo, sah. My name's Tub") to attempt to get a message through to Sherman and his soldiers, wherever downstream they might be by now. "Dear Sherman," the note began: "Hurry up, for Heaven's sake."

Tub reached Sherman on Black Bayou late that night, having taken various short cuts, and Sherman

---

*My father was born in a house later built on this mound, and was buried alongside *his* father in a cemetery less than a quarter mile away. I expect to join them there in the not-too-distant future. . . . This, I promise, is not only the first but also the last footnote in this work. —S.F.

started northward before daylight, accompanied by all the troops on hand. Retracing the messenger's route through darkness, they carried lighted candles in their hands as they slogged waist-deep through swamps and canebrakes. "The smaller drummer boys had to carry their drums on their heads," the general afterwards recalled, "and most of the men slung their cartridge boxes around their necks." All the following day they pushed on, frequently losing their way, and into darkness again. At dawn Sunday, March 22, they heard from surprisingly close at hand the boom of Porter's mortars, punctuated by the sharper crack of the Whitworths. Presently they encountered rebels who had got below the ironclads and were felling trees to block their escape downstream. Sherman chased them from their work and pushed on.

Soon he came within sight of the beleaguered flotilla, but found it woefully changed in appearance. After finally managing to extricate the willow-bound flagship with winches, Porter had unshipped the rudders of all five gunboats and was steaming backward down the narrow creek, fighting as he went. He had not only heard the sound of axes in his rear; what was worse, he had suddenly realized that the Confederates might dam the creek upstream with cotton bales and leave him stranded in the mud. The arriving bluecoats ran the snipers off—they were not actually so numerous as they seemed; just industrious—and came up to find the admiral on the deck of the flagship, directing the retreat from behind a shield improvised from a section of smokestack. "I doubt if he was ever more glad to meet a friend than he was to see me," Sherman later declared. For the present, though, he asked if Porter wanted him to go ahead and "clean those fellows out" so the navy could resume its former course. "Thank you, no," the admiral said.

He had had enough, and so had Sherman, who complained hotly that this was "the most infernal expedition I was ever on." As Porter subsequently put it, "The game was up, and we bumped on homeward."

All the way downstream, from Deer Creek through Black Bayou, the sailors took a ribbing from the soldiers who stood along the banks to watch them go by, in reverse and rudderless. "Halloo, Jack," they would call. "How do you like playing mud turtle?" "Where's all your masts and sails, Jack?" "By the Widow Perkins, if Johnny Reb hasn't taken their rudders away and set them adrift!" But an old forecastleman gave as good as he got. "Dry up!" he shouted back at them. "We wa'n't half as much used up as you was at Chickasaw Bayou."

So it went until the gunboats regained Steele Bayou and finally the mouth of the Yazoo, where they dropped anchor—those that still had them—and were laid up for repairs. Within another week they were supplied with new chimneys and skylights and woodwork; they glistened with fresh coats of paint, and according to Porter, "no one would have supposed we had ever been away from a dock-yard." By then, too, the officers had begun to discuss their share in this sixth of Grant's Vicksburg failures with something resembling nostalgia. There was an edge of pride in their voices as they spoke of the exploit, and some even talked of being willing to go again. But they did so, the admiral added, much "as people who have gone in search of the North Pole, and have fared dreadfully, wish to try it once more."

Despite the high hopes generated during the preliminary reconnaissance up Steele Bayou, Grant was no more discouraged by this penultimate failure, reported in no uncertain terms by a disgusted Sherman, than he had been by the preceding five. Now as before, he already had a successive experiment in progress, which served to distract the public's attention and occupy his mind and men. Besides, for once, he had good news to send along to Washington with the bad—the announcement of the first real success achieved by Federal arms on the river since his arrival in late January—although his pleasure in reporting it was considerably diminished by the fact that it had been accomplished not in his own department but in Banks's, not by the army but by the navy, and not by Porter but by Farragut.

Banks himself had been having troubles that rivaled Grant's, if not in number—being limited by a lack of corresponding ingenuity and equipment in his attempts to come to grips with the problem—then at any rate in thorniness. Port Hudson was quite as invulnerable to a frontal assault as Vicksburg, so that here too the solution was restricted to two methods: either to attack the hundred-foot bluff from the rear or else to go around it. He worked hard for a time at the latter, seeking a route up the Atchafalaya, into the Red, and thence into the Mississippi, fifty miles above the Confederate bastion. At first this appeared to be ready-made for his use, but it turned out to be impractical on three counts. 1) He had only one gunboat designed for work on the rivers; 2) a large portion of the Atchafalaya basin was under water as a result of breaks in the neglected levees; and 3) he became convinced that to leave the rebel garrison alive and kicking in his rear would be to risk, if not invite, the recapture of New Orleans.

This last was so unthinkable that it no sooner occurred to him than he abandoned all notion of such an attempt. As for attacking Port Hudson from the rear, he perceived that this would be about as risky as attacking it from the front. Knowing nothing of Grant's success or failure upriver, except the significant fact that something must have happened to delay him, Banks did not know but what the Confederates would be free to concentrate against him from all directions, including the north, as soon as he got his troops ashore; which would mean, at best, that he would lose his siege train in a retreat from superior numbers, and at worst that he would lose his army. Thus both methods of approaching a solution to the problem seemed to him likely to end in disaster; he did not know what to do, at least until he could get in touch with Grant upstream. Consequently, he did nothing.

This reverse approach, with its stress on what the enemy might do to him, rather than on what he intended to do to the enemy, had not been Grant's way of coming to grips with the similar problem, nearly three hundred miles upstream; nor was it Farragut's. The old sea dog—approaching sixty-two, he was Tennessee-born and twice married, both times to Virginians, which had caused some doubt as to his loyalty in the early months of the war—had surmounted what had seemed to be longer odds below New Orleans the year before, and he was altogether willing to try it again, "army or no army."

In early March, when he received word that the rebels, by way of reinforcing their claim to control of the

whole Red River system, along with so much of the
Mississippi as ran between Vicksburg and Port Hudson,
had captured the steam ram *Queen of the West*, he took
the action as a challenge to personal combat; especially
when they emphasized it by sinking and seizing the
ironclad *Indianola*, which for all he knew was about to
join the *Queen* in defying the flag she once had flown.
He promptly assembled his seven wooden ships off
Profit's Island, seven miles below Port Hudson, intending to take them past the fortified heights for a showdown with the renegade boats upriver.

He had with him the three heavy sloops-of-war *Hartford, Richmond*, and *Monongahela*, the old side-wheeler
Mississippi, and three gunboats. All were ocean-going
vessels, unarmored but mounting a total of 95 guns,
mostly heavy—the flagship *Hartford* alone carried two
dozen 9-inch Dahlgrens—with which to oppose the 21
pieces manned by the Confederates ashore. This advantage in the weight of metal would be offset considerably,
however, by the plunging fire of the guns on the hundred-foot bluff and by the five-knot current, which
would hold the ships to a crawl as they rounded the
sharp bend at its foot. In an attempt to increase the
speed and power of his slower and larger ships, Farragut
gave instructions for the three gunboats to be lashed to
the unengaged port sides of the three sloops; the *Mississippi*, whose paddle boxes would not allow this, would
have to take her chances unassisted. It was the admiral's
hope that the flotilla would steam past undetected in the
moonless darkness, but a greenhorn chaplain, watching
the gun crews place within easy reach "little square,
shallow, wooden boxes filled with sawdust, like the spi-
toons one used to see in country barrooms," was
shocked to learn that the contents were to be scattered

about the deck as "an absorbent" to keep the men from slipping in their own blood, when and if the guns began to roar and hits were scored.

At 9.30 P.M. March 14, the prearranged signal—two red lights described by the same impressionable chaplain as "two distinct red spots like burning coals"—appeared just under the stern of the flagship in the lead, and the run began.

At first it went as had been planned and hoped for. Undetected, unsuspected, the *Hartford* led the way up the long straight stretch of river leading due north into the bend that would swing the column west-southwest; she even cleared the first battery south of town, her engines throbbing in the darkness, her pilot hugging the east bank to avoid the mudflat shallows of the point across the way. Then suddenly the night was bright with rockets and the glare of pitch-pine bonfires ignited by west-bank sentinels, who thus not only alerted the gun crews on the bluff, but also did them the service of illuminating their targets on the river down below.

The fight began with a full-voiced roar. Still holding so close to the east bank that the men on her deck could hear the shouts of the enemy cannoneers, the flagship opened a rolling fire which was taken up in turn by the ships astern. The night was misty and windless; smoke settled thick on the water, leaving the helmsmen groping blindly and the gunners with nothing to aim at but the overhead muzzle flashes. In this respect the *Hartford* had the advantage, steaming ahead of her own smoke, but even she had her troubles, being caught by the swift current and swept against the enemy bank as she turned into the bend. Helped by her gunboat tug, she backed off and swung clear, chugging upstream at barely three knots, much damaged about her top and spars, but with

only three men hit. Attempting to follow, the *Richmond*
was struck by a plunging shot that crashed into her engine room and caromed about, cracking both port and
starboard safety valves and dropping her boiler pressure
below ten pounds. Too weak to make headway, even
with the assistance of the gunboat lashed to her flank,
she went with the current and out of the fight, leaking
steam from all her ports, followed presently by the
Monongahela, which suffered the same fate when her escort's rudder was wedged by an unlucky shot, one of her
own engines was disabled by an overheated crankpin,
and her captain was incapacitated by a shell that cut the
bridge from under him and pitched him headlong onto
the deck below. Between them, the two sloops and their
escorts lost 45 killed and wounded before they veered
out of range downriver.

But the veteran frigate *Mississippi*—Commodore
Matthew Perry's flagship, ten years ago, when he
steamed into Tokyo Bay and opened Japan to the Western world—took the worst beating of the lot, not only
from the Confederates on the bluff, but also from the
gunners on the *Richmond*, who, not having gotten the
word that the sloop had turned in the opposite direction, fired at the flashes of the side-wheeler's guns as
they swept past her. Blind in the smoke, pounded alike
by friend and foe, the pilot went into the bend and put
the ship hard to larboard all too soon: with the result
that she ran full tilt onto the mudflats across the way
from the fuming bluff. Silhouetted against the glare of
bonfires and taking hit after hit from the rebel guns, she
tried for half an hour to pull loose by reversing her engines, but to no avail. Her captain ordered her set afire
as soon as the crew—64 of whom were casualties by
now—could be taken off in boats, and it was only

through the efforts of her executive, Lieutenant George Dewey, that many of her wounded were not roasted, including a badly frightened ship's boy he found hiding under a pile of corpses. Burning furiously, the *Mississippi* lightened before dawn and drifted off the flats of her own accord, threatening to set the other repulsed vessels afire as she passed unmanned among them and piled up at last on the head of Profit's Island, where she exploded with what an observer called "the grandest display of fireworks I ever witnessed, and the costliest."

It had been quite a costly operation all around. Thirty-five of the flotilla's 112 casualties were dead men —only two less than had been killed in the venture below New Orleans by a force almost three times as large—and of the seven ships that had attempted to run Port Hudson, one was destroyed and four had been driven back disabled. As a box score, this gave the Confederates ample claim to the honors of the engagement; but the fact remained that, whatever the cost, Farragut had done what he set out to do. He had put warships north of the bluff on the Mississippi, and he was ready to use them to dispute the rebel claim to control of the 240 miles of river below Vicksburg.

Dropping down at dawn to just beyond range of Port Hudson's upper batteries, he fired the prearranged three-gun signal to let the rest of the flotilla know that he was still afloat, then set out upriver and anchored next morning off the mouth of the Red, up which he learned that the renegade *Queen* and the fast-steaming *Webb* had taken refuge after their flight from Porter's dummy ironclad.

Both were too heavily damaged, as a result of their ram attacks on the *Indianola*, to be able to fight again without extensive repairs. So he heard; but he was taking no chances. Lowering the *Hartford*'s yards to the deck, he lashed them there and carried a heavy anchor chain from yard tip to yard tip, all the way round, to fend off attackers. Still unsatisfied, he improvised waterline armor by lashing cypress logs to the sides of the vessel and slung hawsers from the rigging, thirty feet above the deck, with heavy netting carried all the way down to the rail to frustrate would-be boarders. Then, accompanied by her six-gun escort *Albatross*, the *Hartford*—whose own builders would scarcely have recognized her, dressed out in this manner—set out northward, heading for Vicksburg in order to open communications with the upper fleet.

Passing Grand Gulf on March 19 the two ships came under fire that cost them 2 more killed and 6 more wounded, almost three times the number they had lost five nights ago; otherwise they encountered no opposition between Port Hudson and the point where they dropped anchor next morning, just beyond range of the lower Vicksburg batteries. Porter was up Steele Bayou, but conferring that afternoon with Grant and A. W. Ellet, the ram fleet commander, Farragut asked that he be reinforced by units from the upper flotilla. Ellet volunteered to send two of his boats, the *Switzerland* and the *Lancaster*, respectively under C. R. Ellet, the former captain of the *Queen*, and his uncle J. A. Ellet.

They made their run at first light, March 25. The *Lancaster* was struck repeatedly in her machinery and hull, but she made it downstream, where a week's patchwork labor would put her back in shape to fight again. Not so the *Switzerland*; she received a shell in her boilers and others which did such damage to her hull that she went to pieces and sank, affording her nineteen-year-old skipper another ride on a bale of cotton. Unperturbed, Grant reported her loss as a blessing in disguise, since it served to reveal her basic unfitness for combat: "It is almost certain that had she made one *ram* into another vessel she would have closed up like a spyglass, encompassing all on board."

In point of fact, whatever the cost and entirely aside from his accustomed optimism, he and all who favored the Union cause had much to be joyful about. As a result of this latest naval development, which would establish a blockade of the mouth of the Red and deny the rebels the use of their last extensive stretch of the Mississippi, Farragut had cut the Confederacy in two. The halves were still unconquered, and seemed likely to remain so for no one knew how long, but they were severed one from the other. When the *Hartford* and the *Albatross* passed Port Hudson and were joined ten days later below Vicksburg by the steam ram *Lancaster*, the cattle and cereals of the Transmississippi, together with the goods of war that could be smuggled in through Mexico from Europe, became as inaccessible to the eastern South as if they were awaiting shipment on the moon.

This was not to say, conversely, that the Mississippi was open throughout its length to Federal commerce or even to Federal gunboats; that would not be the case, of course, until Vicksburg and Port Hudson had been taken or abolished. Continuing his efforts to accomplish this end, or anyhow his half of it, Grant was already engaged in the seventh of his experiments—which presently turned out to be the seventh of his failures. Work on the canal across the base of Vicksburg Point having been abandoned, he sent an engineering party out to find a better site for such a project close at hand. Receiving a report that a little digging south of Duckport, just above Young's Point, would give the light-draft vessels access to Roundaway Bayou, which entered the main river at New Carthage, well below the Vicksburg and Warrenton batteries, Grant gave McClernand's men a turn on the picks and shovels.

For once, however, he had no great hope that much would come of the enterprise, even if it went as planned —only the lightest-draft supply boats would be able to get through; besides, there would still be the Grand Gulf batteries to contend with—and for once he was right. Even this limited success depended on a rise of the river; whereupon the river, perverse as always, began to fall, leaving Grant with a seventh failure on his hands.

★   ★   ★

"This campaign is being badly managed," Cadwallader Washburn, a brigadier in McPherson's corps, informed his congressman brother Elihu in Washington. "I am sure of it. I fear a calamity before Vicksburg. All Grant's schemes have failed. He knows that he has got to do something or off goes his head. My impression is that he intends to attack in front."

(Washburn's fears were better founded than he knew. Grant had just written a long letter to Banks, reviewing his lack of progress up to now, and in it he had stated flatly: "There is nothing left for me but to collect my strength and attack Haines Bluff. This will necessarily be attended with much loss, but I think it can be done." On April Fools' Day, however, accompanying Porter up the Yazoo for a reconnaissance of the position, he decided that such an attack "would be attended with immense sacrifice of life, if not defeat," and abandoned the notion, adding: "This, then, closes out the last hope of turning the enemy by the right.")

Nor were others, farther removed from the scene of action, more reticent in giving their opinion of the disaster in store for the Army of the Tennessee. For example Marat Halstead, editor of the *Cincinnati Commercial*, addressed his friend the Secretary of the Treasury on the matter: "You do once in a while, don't you, say a word to the President, or Stanton, or Halleck, about the conduct of the war? Well, now, for God's sake say that Genl Grant, entrusted with our greatest army, is a jackass in the original package. He is a poor drunken imbecile. He is a poor stick sober, and he is most of the time more than half drunk, and much of the time idiotically drunk. . . . Grant will fail miserably, hopelessly, eternally. You may look for and calculate his failures, in every position in which he may be placed, as a perfect certainty. Don't say I am grumbling. Alas! I know too well I am but feebly outlining the truth."

Alarmed, Salmon Chase passed the letter on to Lincoln with the reminder that the *Commercial* was an influential paper, and the indorsement: "Reports concerning General Grant similar to the statements made by Mr Halstead are too common to be safely or even prudently disregarded." Lincoln read it with a sigh. "I think Grant has hardly a friend left, except myself," he told his secretary, and when a delegation came to protest Grant's alleged insobriety he reportedly put these civilians off with the remark, "If I knew what brand of whiskey he drinks I would send a barrel or so to some other generals."

About this time a Nebraska brigadier, in Washington on leave from Vicksburg, called on the President and the two men got to talking. "What I want, and what the people want, is generals who will fight battles and win victories," Lincoln said. "Grant has done this, and I propose to stand by him."

The evidence was conflicting. Some said the general never touched a drop; others declared that he was seldom sober; while still others had him pegged as a spree drinker. "He tries to let liquor alone but he cannot resist the temptation always," a Wisconsin brigadier wrote home. "When he came to Memphis he left his wife at LaGrange, and for several days after getting here was beastly drunk, utterly incapable of doing anything. Quinby and I took him in charge, watching him day and night and keeping liquor away from him." According to this witness, the bender was only brought to an end when "we telegraphed to his wife and brought her on to take care of him." On the other hand, Mary Livermore —later famous as a suffragette—led a Sanitary Commission delegation down to Young's Point to investigate the rumors, and it was her opinion that the general's "clear eye, clean skin, firm flesh, and steady nerves . . . gave the lie to the universal calumnies then current concerning his intemperate habits."

Still unsatisfied, Stanton sent the former Brook Farm colonist and Greeley journalist Charles Dana down the Mississippi, ostensibly as an inspector of the pay service, but actually as a spy for the War Department. He arrived in early April, became in effect a member of the general's military family, and soon was filing reports that glowed with praise not only of Grant but also of Sherman and McPherson, declaring that in their "unpretending simplicity" the three Ohioans were "as alike as three peas." McClernand did not fare so well in these dispatches; for if Dana acquired a fondness for the army commander's friends, he also developed a dislike for his enemies. Later he summed up his findings by describing Grant as "the most modest, the most disinterested, and the most honest man I ever knew, with a temper that nothing could disturb and a judgment that was judicial in its comprehensiveness and wisdom. Not a great man except morally; not an original or brilliant man, but sincere, thoughtful, deep, and gifted with courage that never faltered."

Aside from the rhetoric here included, practically all of the general's soldiers would have agreed with this assessment of his character and abilities, even though it was delivered in the wake of seven failures. "Everything that Grant directs is right," one declared. "His soldiers believe in him. In our private talks among ourselves I never heard a single soldier speak in doubt of Grant." According to a New York reporter, this was not only because of "his energy and disposition to do something," it was also because he had "the remarkable tact of never spoiling any mysterious and vague notions which [might] be entertained in the minds of the privates as to the qualities of the commander-in-chief. He confines himself to saying and doing as little as possible before his men." Another described him as "a man who could be silent in several languages," and it was remarked that, on the march, he was more inclined to talk of "Illinois horses, hogs, cattle, and farming, than of the business actually at hand." In general he went about his job, as one observer had stated at the outset, "with so little friction and noise that it required a second look to be sure he was doing anything at all."

One of his staff officers got the impression that he was "half a dozen men condensed into one," while a journalist, finding him puzzling in the extreme because he seemed to amount to a good deal more than the sum of all his parts, came up with the word "unpronounceable" as the one that described him best. Grant, he wrote, "has none of the soldier's bearing about him, but is a man whom one would take for a country merchant or a village lawyer. He has no distinctive feature; there are a thousand like him in personal appearance in the ranks. . . . A plain, unpretending face, with a comely, brownish-red beard and a square forehead, of short stature and thick-set. He is we would say a good liver, and altogether an unpronounceable man; he is so like hundreds of others as to be only described in general terms."

His soldiers appreciated the lack of "superfluous flummery" as he moved among them, "turning and chewing restlessly the end of his unlighted cigar." They almost never cheered him, and they did not often salute him formally; rather, they watched him, as one said, "with a certain sort of familiar reverence." Present discouragements were mutual; so, someday, would be the glory. Somehow he was more partner than boss; they were in this thing together. "Good morning, General," "Pleasant day, General," were the usual salutations, more fitting than cheers or hat-tossing exhibitions; "A pleasant salute to, and a good-natured nod from him in return, seems more appropriate."

All these things were said of him, and this: "Here was no McClellan, begging the boys to allow him to light his cigar on theirs, or inquiring to what regiment that exceedingly fine-marching company belonged. . . . There was no nonsense, no sentiment; only a plain business man of the republic, there for the one single purpose of getting that command over the river in the shortest time possible."

Yet the fact remained that he and they were into their third month of camping almost within the shadow of the Vicksburg bluff, and all they had accomplished so far was the addition of five to their previous two failures; they were still not "over the river." However, as the flood waters receded, defining the banks of the bayous and even the network of greasy-looking roads hub-deep in mud, there were rumors that Grant was evolving an entirely new approach to the old problem. "As one after another of his schemes fail," Congressman Washburne heard from his brigadier brother—who had dropped the final euphonious "e" from his surname, presumably as superfluous baggage for a soldier—"I hear that he says he has a plan of his own which is yet to be tried [but] in which he has great confidence."

Just what this was Grant would not say, either to subordinates or superiors, but his staff observed that he spent long hours in the former ladies' cabin of his headquarters boat the *Magnolia*, blueing the air with cigar smoke as he pored over maps and tentative orders, not so much inaccessible ("I aint got no business with you, General," they heard one caller tell him; "I just wanted to have a little talk with you, because folks will ask me if I did") as removed, withdrawn behind a barrier of intense preoccupation.

After several days of this, McPherson came into the cabin one evening, glass in hand, and stood facing Grant across the work-littered desk. "General, this won't do," he said. "You are injuring yourself. Join us in a few toasts, and throw this burden off your mind." Mrs Livermore, for one, would have been horrified, but what followed would have quickly reassured her. Grant looked up, smiled, and replied that whiskey was not the answer; if McPherson really wanted to help him, he said, he could give him a dozen cigars and leave him alone. McPherson did so, and Grant returned to brooding over his papers, still seeking a way to come to grips with the Confederates in their hilltop citadel.

★ 3 ★

While Joe Hooker, up in Virginia, was crossing the Rappahannock, unaware as yet that he would come to grief at Chancellorsville within a week, Grant, having caught what he believed was a gleam of victory through the haze of cigar smoke in the former ladies' cabin of the *Magnolia*, was putting the final improvisatorial touches to a plan of campaign that would open, two days later, with a crossing of the greatest river of them all. He too might come to grief, as two of his three chief lieutenants feared and even predicted, but he was willing to risk it for the sake of the prize, which had grown in value with every sore frustration. As spring advanced and the roads emerged from the drowned lands adjacent to the Mississippi—although so far they were little more than trails of slime through the surrounding ooze, not quite firm enough for wagons nor quite wet enough for boats—the Illinois general, with seven failures behind him in the course of the three months he had spent attempting to take or bypass Vicksburg, reverted in early April to what he had told Halleck in mid-

January, before he left Memphis to assume command in person of the expedition four hundred miles downriver: "[I] think our troops must get below the city to be used effectively."

His plan, in essence, was to march his army down the Louisiana bank to a position well south of the fortified bluff, then cross the river and establish a bridgehead from which to assail the Confederate bastion from the rear. The Duckport canal, designed to give his transports access to Walnut and Roundaway bayous, and thus allow them to avoid exposure to the plunging fire of the batteries at Vicksburg and Warrenton, had failed; only one small steamer had got through before the water level fell too low for navigation; but exploration of the route had shown that, by bridging those sloughs that could not be avoided by following the crests of levees flanking the horseshoe curves of the several bayous, it might be practicable to march dry-shod all the way from Milliken's Bend to New Carthage, a west-bank hamlet about midway between Warrenton and Grand Gulf, third of the rebel east-bank strongholds. In late March, by way of preparation, Grant had assigned McClernand the task of putting this route into shape for a march by his own corps as well as the two others, which would follow. This, if it worked, would get the army well south of its objective.

Getting the troops across the river was quite another matter, however, depending as it did on the cooperation of the navy, which, as Grant said, "was absolutely essential to the success (even to the contemplation) of such an enterprise." For the navy to get below, in position to ferry the men across and cover the east-bank landing, it would have to run the batteries, and this had been shown in the past to be an expensive proposition even

for armored vessels, let alone the brittle-skinned transports which would be required for the ferrying operation. Moreover, Porter was no more under Grant's
command than Grant was under Porter's. The most
Grant could do was "request" that the run be made. But
that was enough, as it turned out. The admiral—who
had returned only the week before from the near-disas-
trous Steele Bayou expedition, considerably the worse
for wear and with his boats still being hammered back
into shape—expressed an instant willingness to give the

thing a try, though not without first warning of what the consequences would be, not only in the event of initial failure but also in the event of initial success, so far at least as the navy was concerned. He could make a downstream run, he said, and in fact had proved it twice already with the ill-fated *Queen of the West* and the equally ill-fated *Indianola*, but his underpowered vessels could never attempt a slow-motion return trip, against the four-knot current, until Vicksburg had been reduced.

"You must recollect that when these gunboats once go below we give up all hopes of ever getting them up again," he replied, wanting it understood from the start that this would be an all-or-nothing venture. Moreover: "If I do send vessels below, it will be the best vessels I have, and there will be nothing left to attack Haines Bluff, in case it should be deemed necessary to try it."

Grant replied on April 2 that McClernand's men were already at work on the circuitous thirty-mile road down to New Carthage; he had no intention of turning back, even if that had been possible; and in any case Haines Bluff had cost the army blood enough by now. "I would, Admiral, therefore renew my request to prepare for running the blockade at as early a day as possible."

Two days later he wrote Halleck: "My expectation is for a portion of the naval fleet to run the batteries of Vicksburg, whilst the army moves through by this new route [to New Carthage]. Once there, I will move either to Warrenton or Grand Gulf; most probably the latter. From either of these points there are good roads to Vicksburg, and from Grand Gulf there is a good road to Jackson and the Black River Bridge without crossing the Black River."

Much could be said for making the landing at either

place. Warrenton, for example, was some fifteen air-line miles closer to his objective. But he knew well enough that a straight line was not always the surest connection between two military points. A Grand Gulf landing, in addition to giving him access to Vicksburg's main artery of supply, would also afford him a chance to supplement his own. By holding the newly established bridgehead with part of his army and sending the balance downstream to assist in the reduction of Port Hudson by Banks, who presumably was working his way upstream at the same time, he then would have an un-broken, all-weather connection with New Orleans and would no longer be exclusively and precariously depen-dent on what could be brought down from Memphis, first by steamboat, then by wagon over the new road skirting the west-bank complex of bayous across from the fortified bluff, and then again by steamboat in order to get the supplies over the river and into the east-bank bridgehead. Grant pondered the alternatives, and by April 11, a week after the dispatch giving Halleck a brief statement of the problem, he had made his choice: "Grand Gulf is the point at which I expect to strike, and send an army corps to Port Hudson to cooperate with General Banks."

He did not know how Old Brains, whose timidity had been demonstrated in situations far less risky than this one, would react to a plan of campaign that involved 1) exposing the irreplaceable Union fleet to instantaneous destruction by batteries that had been sited on com-manding and impregnable heights with just that end in mind, 2) crossing a mile-wide river in order to throw his troops into the immediate rear of a rebel force of un-known strength which, holding as it did the interior lines, presumably could be reinforced more quickly than his own, and 3) remaining dependent all the while, or at least until the problematical capture of Port Hudson, on a supply line that was not only tenuous to the point of inadequacy, but was also subject to being cut by enemy intervention or obliterated by some accident of nature, by no means unusual at this season, such as a week of unrelenting rain, a sudden rise of the river, and a resultant overflow that would re-drown the west-bank lowlands and the improvised road that wound its way around and across the curving bayous and treacherous morasses into which a wagon or a gun could disappear completely, leaving no more trace than a man or a mule whose bones had been picked clean by gars and crawfish.

Whether Halleck would approve the taking of all these risks, Grant did not know; but he was left in no such doubt as to the reaction closer at hand. So far, of his three corps commanders, only his archrival McClernand had indicated anything resembling enthusiasm for the plan. Hard at work constructing makeshift bridges from materials found along the designated route to New Carthage, which he reached before mid-April, the former Illinois politician was in high spirits and predicted great results, for both the country and himself, because his corps had been assigned to lead the way. By contrast, though perhaps for the same reason—that is, because the nonprofessional McClernand had the lead —Sherman and McPherson, along with Dana and practically every member of Grant's own staff, considered the proposed operation not only overrisky and unwise, but also downright unmilitary. Sherman in fact was so alarmed at the prospect that he sat down and wrote Grant a long letter, insisting that the proper course would be for the army to return at once to Memphis and resume from there the overland advance along the Mississippi Central, abandoned in December.

When his friend and chief replied that he had no intention of canceling his plans, Sherman had no choice except to go along with them, although he still did not approve. "I confess I don't like this roundabout project," he told one of his division commanders, "but we must support Grant in whatever he undertakes." He was loyal and he would remain so, but he also remained glum, writing home even as he ordered his men out of their camps at Milliken's Bend to join the movement: "I feel in its success less confidence than in any similar undertaking of the war."

Porter too had doubts as to the over-all wisdom of Grant's plan, as well as fears in regard to the specific risk the plan required the navy to assume, but he took no counsel of them aside from the more or less normal precautions the prospect of such exposure always prompted, as in the case of a farmer sending eggs to market in a springless wagon over a bumpy road. Unlike Sherman, he wrote no Cassandran letters and made no protest after his initial warning that once the fleet had gone below it could not come back up again until the batteries had been silenced in its rear. Instead, he kept busy preparing his crews and vessels for the passage of bluffs that bristled with 40-odd pieces of artillery, light and heavy, manned by cannoneers whose skill had improved with every chance to show it.

By April 16 he was ready. Seven armored gunboats, mounting a total of 79 guns, were assigned to make the run, accompanied by three army transports, loaded with commissary stores instead of troops, and a steam ram captured the year before at Memphis when the Confederate flotilla was abolished in a brief half-morning's fight. At 9.30, two hours after dusk gave way to a starry but moonless night, the column cleared the mouth of the Yazoo, Porter leading aboard the flagship *Benton*.

The "run," so called, was in fact more creep than sprint, however, at least in its early stages; stealth was the watchword up and down the line of eleven boats steaming southward in single file on the dark chocolate surface of what one observer called "the great calm river, more like a long winding lake than a stream." Furnaces had been banked in advance, so as to show a minimum of smoke. All ports were covered and all deck lights doused, except for hooded lanterns visible only from dead astern for guidance. It was hoped that such precautions would hide the column from prying eyes. To reduce the likelihood of noise, which also might give the movement away, low speed was prescribed and exhaust pipes were diverted from the stacks to the paddle boxes, where the hiss of steam would be muffled. Pets and poultry were put ashore, moreover, lest a sudden mewing or cackling alert the rebel sentries. The admiral was leaving as little as possible to chance; but in the event of discovery he was prepared to shift at once from stealth to boldness. Coal-laden barges were lashed to the starboard flanks of the warships, leaving their portside weapons free to take up any challenge from the high-sited batteries on the Mississippi shore, and water-soaked bales of hay were stacked around the otherwise unprotected boilers and pilot houses of the transports. Instructed to maintain a fifty-yard interval, each helmsman was also told to steer a little to one side of the boat he followed, so as not to have to slow engines or change course to avoid a collision in case of a breakdown up ahead. Thus, though he wanted no trouble he could avoid, Porter was prepared to give as well as receive it in the event that his carefully woven veil of secrecy was ripped away.

Passing Young's Point at about 10.30, the dark and silent column swung north as it approached the mouth of Sherman's abandoned canal, then rounded the final turn at 11 sharp, altering course again from north to south, and headed down the straightaway eastern shank of the hairpin bend that led past Vicksburg's dark and silent bluff. Ten minutes later all hell broke loose.

Grant was there to see the show, and he had his two families with him, one military and the other personal, the former consisting of his staff, the latter of his wife and their two sons, who had come downriver from Illinois to afford him a sort of furlough-in-reverse. Both were gathered tonight on the upper deck of the *Magnolia*, which was anchored three miles below Young's Point, just beyond range of the heaviest enemy guns, so that they watched as if from a box in a darkened theater, awaiting the raising of the curtain. The general and Mrs Grant occupied deck chairs near the starboard rail—front row center, as it were—with twelve-year-old Fred beside them; Ulysses Junior, who was ten, sat nearby in young Colonel Wilson's lap. Behind and on both sides of them stood twenty-odd men in uniform, staff officers and two high-ranking observers. One was Dana, who had been sent by Stanton to watch Grant, and the other was no less a personage than Adjutant General Lorenzo Thomas, who had arrived five days ago, five days after Dana, to watch them both. Or so it was said at any rate, so deep was the supposed mistrust the War Department felt.

Just now though, whatever truth there was to the rumored assignment, there was a good deal more to watch than the unimpressive-looking department command-

er. First there was the passage of the hooded and muffled warships, disappearing northward in the direction
of the bend that swung them south toward the rebel batteries; then a long wait in the blackness; then, eastward
—across the narrow tongue of land called Vicksburg
Point, beyond which the dark loom of bluff reared up to
blot out the low-hanging stars—a sudden burgeoning
incandescence, exposed as if by a rapid lifting of the
awaited curtain. The show was on.

It began, so to speak, in mid-crescendo as the guns
came alive on the bluff and were replied to by those
down on the brightly lighted river, growling full-
throated, jarring the earth and water for miles around,
and adding their muzzle flashes to the vivid illumination
of the scene. "Magnificent, but terrible," Grant later
called the sight. For the present, however, aside from
ordering the younger boy to bed when he heard him
whimper and saw him press his face against Wilson's
chest in terror at the holocaust of flame and thunder, he
said nothing. He merely smoked and watched the fireworks, holding all the while to his wife's hand.

After ninety minutes of uproar, during which Dana
tallied 525 shots fired by the Confederates, the bluff was
once more dark and silent except for the reflection of
fires still burning fitfully on the lower level where the
boats had been. How much damage had been done and
suffered, no one aboard the *Magnolia* could tell, although presently it was clear that some at least of the
vessels had got past, for the Warrenton batteries came
alive downstream, reproducing in miniature the earlier
performance. Finally these too fell silent; which told the
watchers exactly nothing, save that the final curtain had
come down. Near and far, the fires burned out and the
former blackness returned to the bluff and the river.

Unable to wait for word from below—news, perhaps, that the indispensable fleet had gone out of existence—Grant went ashore, got on his horse, and rode south under the paling stars, galloping along the crude and pot-holed road McClernand's corps had spent the past three weeks constructing. This was quite unlike the old Grant, who had never seemed in a hurry about anything at all. Something had come over him, here lately. "None who had known him the previous years could recognize him as being the same man," one officer observed. He had never seen the general ride at even a fast trot, let alone a gallop; but now, he said, "[Grant's] energies seemed to burst forth with new life," with the result that he rode at top speed practically all the way and "seemed wrought up to the last pitch of determination and energy."

Shiloh and the long hot unproductive summer of 1862, the ill-wind fiasco near Iuka and the fruitless victory at Corinth, the period of indecision in Memphis and the recent seven failures above Vicksburg, all were behind him now; he was launched at last on an all-or-nothing effort, a go-for-broke campaign, of which the passage of the batteries by the fleet was the first stage. If this failed, all failed; he would never get his troops across the mile-wide Mississippi. It was no wonder he rode fast.

Near New Carthage about midday he drew rein and breathed a sigh of relief at the sight of the fleet riding at anchor, apparently intact. Closer inspection showed that the boats had been knocked about considerably, however. All were damaged to various degrees, some in their hulls and others in their machinery. One was missing altogether: a transport, as it turned out, set afire by repeated hits and sunk to the accompaniment of cheers from the rebel batteries. But all the rest were seaworthy, or soon would be, after the completion of repairs already under way by bluejackets swarming over their ripped-up decks and pounded bulwarks.

Porter and his captains were in excellent spirits, though they were frank to admit that last night's experience had been little short of horrendous. For one thing, all their precautions involving stealth and secrecy had availed them nothing. As they proceeded, dark and silent, down the straightaway eastern shank of the hairpin bend, Confederate sentries posted in skiffs on the river spotted them quickly; whereupon some rowed eastward to give the alarm to the Vicksburg cannoneers, while others, risking capture, crossed to the opposite bank, where they set fire to prepared stacks of pitch-soaked wood, as well as to the abandoned De Soto railroad station midway up the point. Quick-leaping flames floodlighted the approaching Yankee gunboats and the alerted rebel gunners promptly took these well-defined targets under fire. Another difficulty was that the prescribed low speed left the vessels to the mercy of the eddying current, which caught them alternately on the bow and quarter, swinging them broadside to the stream and in some cases even spinning them halfway around, so that they were obliged to come full circle under the plunging fire, as if responding to cruel encores that held them on the brightly lighted stage for further pelting by an irate audience. Clear at last, they played a brief epilogue at Warrenton, then swept on south to anchor above New Carthage in the predawn darkness.

Assessing damages, Porter was grateful to discover that, despite a total of 68 hits received, the transport *Henry Clay* was the flotilla's only loss. Not a man had been killed, even aboard the missing boat, and only 13

—in this case a decidedly lucky number—had been wounded. Give him a couple of days in which to complete repairs, he said, and he would be quite ready to cooperate with the army.

Grant returned to Milliken's Bend, much pleased with the outcome, and prepared for another run within the week, this time by transports alone, in order to provide more ferries for the crossing. "If I do not underestimate the enemy," he wrote Halleck on April 21, "my force is abundant, with a foothold once obtained, to do the work."

Next night six river steamers, loaded with rations, forage, and medical supplies, attempted the second run under instructions "to drop noiselessly down with the current . . . and not show steam until the enemy's batteries began firing, when the boats were to use all their legs."

This was an all-army show, the steamers being army-owned and manned by army volunteers, since the civilian crews had balked at exposing their persons to what they had watched six nights ago from a safe distance. Now as then, Grant was there to see the show; an Illinois private later told how he "saw standing on the upper deck of his headquarters boat a man of iron, his wife by his side. He seemed to me the most immovable figure I ever saw." Then came the fireworks across the way, the sudden illumination and the uproar of the guns on the fuming bluff. Grant took it calmly, the soldier recalled; "No word escaped his lips, no muscle of his earnest face moved."

Presently the batteries fell silent and word arrived from below that, now as before, only a single vessel had failed to survive the run—the steamer *Tigress*, McClernand's former headquarters boat, which Grant had ridden to Shiloh a year ago. Loaded with medicines and surgical equipment, she was hulled a dozen times or more and broke in two and sank, her skeleton crew floating downstream to safety on bits of wreckage. Once more not a man had been killed and the wounded were only a handful. Half the steamers had their engines permanently smashed, but that was no real drawback, since they would hold as many troops as ever and could be pushed or towed across the river as barges. As Grant saw it, this second run had been quite as successful as the first, and he was twice as pleased.

Belittling the loss of the *Tigress* and her cargo, which he said amounted to nothing more than "little extras for the men," he set off southward again on horseback to join Porter for a naval reconnaissance of Grand Gulf, designated as the point where the army would obtain a foothold once the navy had blasted its batteries out of existence. Porter was experiencing misgivings, and Grant, looking the place over from just beyond range of its guns on the 24th, saw that he had indeed given the navy a tough nut to crack. Its batteries were sited high, as at Donelson and Vicksburg, and what was more they seemed altogether ready for whatever came their way. "I foresee great difficulties in our present position," he informed Sherman on his return from the exploratory boat ride, "but it will not do to let these retard any movements."

In this connection it seemed to him there might be a chance for an assault to succeed at last up the Yazoo, despite the previous fiasco. "It may possibly happen," he wrote Sherman, "that the enemy may so weaken his forces about Vicksburg and Haines Bluff as to make the latter vulnerable, particularly with a fall of water to give you an extended landing." However: "I leave the man-

agement of affairs at your end of the line to you," he
added by way of making it clear that he was not definitely ordering an assault.

Monday, April 27, was Grant's forty-first birthday. It
also marked the completion of his first-stage preparations for getting his troops across the river in order to
come to grips with the rebels on dry ground, which was
what he had been after from the start. By now all four
divisions of McClernand's corps, having extended their
march southward around Bayou Vidal and Lake Saint
Joseph, were at Hard Times, Louisiana, the designated
point of embarkation for the landing at Grand Gulf, five
miles downstream. One of McPherson's divisions was
also there and the other two were closing fast, while
Sherman's three remained at Young's Point, on call to
follow but held in place for the present so as to confuse
the lookouts on the Vicksburg bluff. Seven warships and
seven transports were available below, and though Porter was still troubled by misgivings—he thought his
gunboats could suppress the Grand Gulf batteries, all
right, but he warned that they might get so knocked
about in the process that they would not be able to provide adequate cover for the crossing that would follow
—Grant himself, as usual, expressed no doubt as to the
outcome. He foresaw "great difficulties," but he did not
admit that they were any occasion for delay. All he asked
of the navy was that the rebel guns be silenced, after
which there would be no need for cover.

Before the anniversary was over, he sent McClernand
word to go ahead: "Commence immediately the embarkation of your corps, or so much of it as there is transportation for."

————

The showdown was unquestionably at hand; but Grant was disclosing nothing he could avoid disclosing until the final moment. He had, in fact, devised three separate feints or demonstrations, two of them designed to mislead the enemy as to his chosen point of attack, well downstream, and a third whereby he hoped not only to distract his opponent by diverting his attention from front to rear, but also to add to his confusion, throughout this critical period, by disrupting the lines of supply and communication leading back into the interior of the state whose welfare and defense were the southern commander's assigned concern.

Sherman was organically involved in two of these, one of which had already been accomplished during the first ten days of April. Lest Pemberton call in the troops disposed to guard against a penetration of the Delta, and thereby strengthen the Vicksburg garrison in time for the showdown fight now imminent, Fred Steele's division was sent a hundred miles up the Mississippi to Greenville, where the men went ashore and thrashed about for a week in the interior, giving the impression that they were merely the advance contingent for another major drive on the Gibraltar of the West. Having done so—to the extreme alarm of the local planters, who bemoaned the attendant loss of cotton, cattle, and Negroes, and the home-guard commanders, who called loudly for reinforcements—they got back aboard their transports and rejoined Sherman at Young's Point for a share in the second and more important feint, this time against Haines Bluff.

Grant had suggested it in his letter of the 24th, after a look at the Grand Gulf defenses, but now on his birthday he returned to the matter in more persuasive terms.

"The effect of a heavy demonstration in that direction would be good so far as the enemy are concerned," he wrote Sherman from Hard Times, where McClernand's men were preparing to embark, "but I am loth to order it, because it would be hard to make our own troops understand that only a demonstration was intended and our people at home would characterize it as a repulse. I therefore leave it to you whether to make such a demonstration."

In referring thus to the probable adverse reaction by "our people at home," who of course would get their information from the papers, many of which were hostile—particularly toward Sherman, who returned the hostility in full measure—Grant may or may not have intended to use psychology on his journalist-hating friend. But at any rate it worked. "Does General Grant think I care what the newspapers say?" Sherman exclaimed as soon as he read the letter. And despite his growing antipathy for the strategy his superior had evolved ("I tremble for the result," he wrote his wife that week; "I look upon the whole thing as one of the most hazardous and desperate moves of this or any other war") he replied at once with a pledge of full co-operation.

"We will make as strong a demonstration as possible," he declared. "The troops will all understand the purpose and not be hurt by the repulse. The people of the country must find out the truth as best they can; it is none of their business. You are engaged in a hazardous enterprise, and for good reason wish to divert attention; that is sufficient for me, and it shall be done." Warming as he wrote, the red-haired general bristled with contempt for public opinion. "The men have sense, and will trust us. As to the reports in newspapers, we must scorn them, else they will ruin us and our country. They are as much enemies to good government as the secesh, and between the two I like the secesh best, because they are a brave, open enemy and not a set of sneaking, croaking scoundrels."

Accordingly, he spent the next two days in preparation, and on the final day of April—previously designated by Lincoln, at the request of Congress, "as a day of national humiliation, fasting, and prayer" because, in the words of the proclamation, the people had "forgotten God" and become "too proud to pray"—set off up the Yazoo with ten regiments from Frank Blair's division, escorted by the flotilla remnant Porter had left behind, three gunboats, four tinclads, and three mortars, under K. R. Breese. Intent on making the greatest possible show of strength, Sherman spread his troops over the transport decks with orders for "every man [to] look as numerous as possible."

Short of Haines Bluff and near the scene of their December repulse, the bluecoats went ashore; marching and countermarching, banners flying and bands playing for all they were worth in the boggy woodland, they demonstrated in sight of the fortified line of hills, while the gunboats closed to within point-blank range of the bluff itself. For three hours the naval attack was pressed, as if in preparation for an infantry assault. However, the defenders clearly had their backs up; nor was there anything wrong with their marksmanship. The overaged *Tyler*, a veteran of all the fights since Henry, retired early with a shot below the water line, and the other two hauled off at 2 P.M. roughly handled, one having taken a total of forty-six hits.

Sherman might have let it go at that, but he was determined to play out the game to full advantage. May

Day morning he wrote Grant: "At 3 P.M. we will open another cannonade to prolong the diversion, and keep it up till after dark, when we shall drop down to Chickasaw and go on back to camp."

The other two divisions, waiting at Young's Point under Steele and James M. Tuttle, were alerted for the long march to Hard Times, while Blair was told to keep up the pretense of attack until darkness afforded cover for withdrawal, at which time he would "let out for home," meaning Milliken's Bend, where he was to shield the rear of the two divisions moving southward to join Grant. Meanwhile, Sherman told him, "I will hammer away this P.M. because Major Rowley, [a staff observer] now here, says that our diversion has had perfect success, great activity being seen in Vicksburg, and troops pushing up this way. By prolonging the effort, we give Grant more chance." The infantry continued to mass as if for attack, and the gunboats moved again within range of Haines Bluff, keeping up the action until 8 o'clock that evening. Then Blair's men got back aboard their transports and withdrew, returning to the west bank of the Mississippi, followed by the somewhat battered but undaunted ten-boat flotilla, which dropped anchor off the mouth of the Yazoo.

Steele and Tuttle took up the march for Hard Times at first light next morning, accompanied by Sherman himself, who sent a courier ahead with a full account of the two-day affair. Casualties had been negligible, he reported, afloat and ashore. Whether matters had gone as well for Grant, far downriver at Grand Gulf, he did not know; but he was satisfied that the feint from above had held a considerable portion of the Vicksburg garrison in position north of the city, away from the simultaneous main effort to the south. "We will be there as soon as possible," he assured his friend and superior.

★ ★ ★

Such were the first two of the three diversions intended to confuse and distract the Confederate defenders in the course of this highly critical span of time during which Grant was preparing to launch, and indeed was launching, his main effort a good forty miles downriver from the bluff that was his goal. Though both appeared to have exceeded strategic expectations, the third, while altogether different in scope and composition, was even more successful, and in fact was referred to afterwards by Sherman, who had no direct connection with the venture, as nothing less than "the most brilliant expedition of the war." Grant was as usual more restrained in judgment, qualifying his praise by calling the exploit "one of the most brilliant," but he added that it would "be handed down in history as an example to be imitated."

In point of fact, it was itself an imitation. For two years now, in the West as in the East, the Federal cavalry had suffered from a well-founded inferiority complex: Jeb Stuart and John Morgan and Bedford Forrest had quite literally ridden rings around the awkward blue squadrons and the armies in their charge. Now, perhaps, the time had come for them to emulate the example set by the exuberant gray riders. Hooker thought so, in Virginia, and so did Grant in Mississippi. Back in February he had suggested to Hurlbut, commanding in Memphis, that a cavalry force, "with about 500 picked men, might succeed in making [its] way south and cut the railroad east of Jackson, Miss. The undertaking would be a hazardous one," he added, "but would pay well if carried out. I do not direct that this shall be done, but leave it for a volunteer enterprise." A month later, in mid-March, his instructions were more specific. The conception had been enlarged, tripling the strength of the force to be employed, and the volunteer provision had been removed. Hurlbut was to have all "the available cavalry put in as good condition as possible in the next few weeks for heavy service. . . . The date when the expedition should start will depend upon movements here. You will be informed of the exact time for them to start."

In early April the date was set and a leader chosen: Benjamin H. Grierson, of Grant's home state of Illinois. Hurlbut saw to it that the raiders got away on schedule, April 17, riding south out of La Grange, forty miles east of Memphis, into the dawn that saw Porter's battered gunboats drop anchor near New Carthage after their fiery run past the Vicksburg bluff. "God speed him," Hurlbut said of Grierson, who led the 1700-man column in the direction of the Mississippi line, "for he has started gallantly on a long and perilous ride. I shall anxiously await intelligence of the result."

The wait would necessarily be a long one. Before the raid was over, the blue riders would have covered more than six hundred miles of road and swamp, through hostile territory. At the outset, however, none of the troopers in the three regiments, two from Illinois and one from Iowa, nor of the cannoneers in the attached six-gun battery of 2-pounders, suspected that the warning order, "Oats in the nosebag and five days rations in haversacks, the rations to last ten days," was prelude to so deep a penetration. "We are going on a big scout to

Columbus, Mississippi, and play smash with the railroads," one predicted. Only Grierson himself, riding at the head of the column, knew that the true objective was Pemberton's main supply line, the Southern Railroad east of Jackson, connecting Vicksburg with Meridian and thence with Mobile and the arsenals in Alabama, Georgia, and the East.

Pennsylvania-born and just short of thirty-seven years of age, with a spade beard and an acquired mistrust of horses dating back to a kick received from a pony in childhood, which smashed one of his cheekbones, split his forehead, and left him scarred for life — he had protested his assignment to the cavalry in the first place, though to no avail; Halleck, who made the appointment, insisted that he looked "active and wiry enough to make a good cavalryman" — Grierson eighteen months ago had been a music teacher and bandmaster at Jacksonville, Illinois, but all that was left to remind him or anyone else of that now was a jew's-harp he carried inside his blouse, along with a pocket compass and a small-scale map of the region he and his men would be traversing in the course of their strike at the railroad some two hundred air-line miles away.

Riding where no bluecoat had ever been before, he could expect to be surrounded en route by small bodies of home guardsmen, who would outnumber him badly if they were consolidated, as well as by sizable detachments of regulars, horse and foot, which Pemberton would certainly send to oppose him, front and rear, once his presence and intention became known. Even if he succeeded in his mission — that is, reached and wrecked an appreciable stretch of the railroad between Jackson and Meridian, temporarily severing the one connection by which reinforcements could reach Vicksburg swiftly from outside Mississippi—he would then be deep in the heart of a land where every man's hand would be raised against him.

One suggestion, included in his orders, was that he return to Tennessee by swinging east, then north through Alabama; another was that he plunge on south and west for a hookup with Grant in the vicinity of Grand Gulf, anticipating a successful crossing by McClernand and McPherson at that point, or else take sanctuary within Banks's outpost lines at Baton Rouge, which would give him about as far to go from the railroad south as he would have come already in order to reach it. In any case, whatever escape plan he adopted as a result of the unfolding course of events, the tactical requisites were vigilance, speed, boldness, and deception. Without any one of these four, he and his troopers, in the cavalry slang of the time, would be "gone up."

Across the Mississippi line by sunup, they made thirty miles the first day—a good average march for cavalry, though Grant himself covered nearly as great a distance before noon, galloping south from Milliken's Bend at dawn to check on the condition of Porter's gunboats at New Carthage—and called a halt that night just short of Ripley, which they passed through next morning, brushing aside the few startled gray militia they encountered, to camp beyond New Albany at sundown. On the third day, April 19, they continued due south through Pontotoc. Eighty miles from base, with rebel detachments no doubt alerted in his front and rear, Grierson began his fourth day with an inspection, culled out 175 victims of dysentery, chills and fever, and saddle galls—"the Quinine Brigade," the rejected troopers promptly dubbed themselves—and sent them back, under a staff major, with one of the 2-pounders and instructions to "pass through Pontotoc in the night, marching by fours, obliterating our tracks, and producing the impression that we have all returned."

He himself continued south with the main body, to Houston and beyond. Deciding to throw a still larger tub to the Confederate whale, he detached Edward Hatch's regiment of Iowans next morning, along with another of the guns, and gave its commander orders to strike eastward for the Mobile & Ohio, inflicting what damage he could to that vital supply line before heading north in the wake of the Quinine Brigade, thus spreading the scare and increasing the impression that all the raiders were returning. Hatch, a transplanted New Englander hungry for fame and advancement—tomorrow would be his thirty-second birthday—now began a five-day adventure on his own. Though he did not succeed in breaking the well-guarded railroad to the east, he fought two severe skirmishes—one at the outset, a delaying action which allowed Grierson to get away southward, the other near the finish, which allowed his own getaway northward—burned several cotton-stocked warehouses in Okolona, and succeeded handsomely in his primary mission of drawing most of the North Mississippi home guardsmen pell-mell after him and away from Grierson. At a cost of ten men lost en route, he reported that he had inflicted ten times as many casualties on the enemy and "accumulated 600 head of horses and mules, with about 200 able-bodied negroes to lead them." Returning to La Grange on Sunday morning, April 26, he brought Hurlbut the first substantial news of the raiders' progress since their departure, nine days back.

The unavailable news was a good deal better; Grierson by then had not only reached his objective, he was already forty hours beyond it, having formulated and put into execution his tactics for escape. Relieved of the threat to his rear on the 21st by Hatch's decoy action south of Houston, he and his 1000 troopers—all Illinoisans now, including the fifty cannoneers with the four remaining guns—rode on past Starkville, where he detached one company for a strike at Macon, twenty-odd miles southeast on the M&O, then took up the march at dawn and cleared Louisville by sundown. Beyond Philadelphia on the 23d he called a halt at nightfall, and made an early start next morning in order to reach the Southern Railroad before noon.

Preceded by scouts who seized the telegraph office and thus kept the alarm from being spread—"Butternut Guerillas," these outriders called themselves, for they wore Confederate uniforms, risking hanging for the advantage gained—the raiders burst into Newton Station, a trackside hamlet twenty-five miles west of Meridian and about twice as far east of Jackson, where they at once got down to the work for which they had ridden all this way. Two locomotives were captured and wrecked, along with three dozen freight cars loaded with ordnance and commissary supplies, including artillery ammunition on consignment for Vicksburg, which afforded a rackety fireworks display when set aflame. Meantime other details were ripping up miles of track and crossties, burning trestles and bridges, tearing down telegraph wires all the way to the Chunky River, and setting fire to a government building stocked with 500 small arms and a quantity of new gray uniforms. By 2 o'clock the destruction was complete; Grierson had his bugler sound the rally to assemble the smoke-grimed raiders, some of whom were showing the effects of rebel whiskey they had "rescued" from the flames,

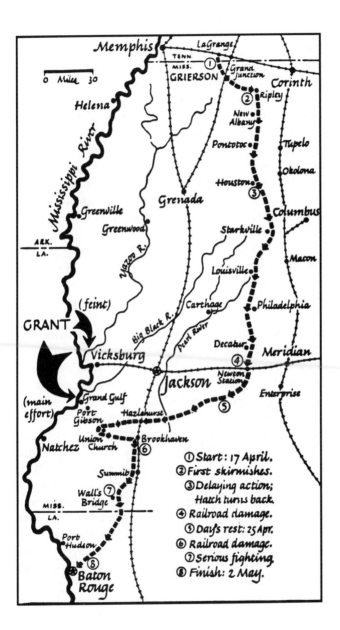

Memphis · LaGrange
TENN.
MISS.
GRIERSON
Grand Junction ①
Corinth

Helena

② Ripley
New Albany
Pontotoc · Tupelo
Houston ③ Okolona
Columbus

Greenville
Greenwood
Grenada
Starkville
ARK.
LA.
Macon
Louisville

Yazoo R.
Carthage
Philadelphia

(feint)

GRANT
Big Black R.
Pearl River
Decatur
Meridian

Vicksburg
④
Newton Station
Jackson
⑤ Enterprise

(main effort)
Grand Gulf
Port Gibson
Hazlehurst
Natchez
Union Church
Brookhaven ⑥

Summit
Wall's Bridge ⑦

MISS.
LA.

Port Hudson
⑧ Baton Rouge

① Start: 17 April.
② First skirmishes.
③ Delaying action;
   Hatch turns back.
④ Railroad damage.
⑤ Day's rest: 25 Apr.
⑥ Railroad damage.
⑦ Serious fighting.
⑧ Finish: 2 May.

0 Miles 30

then took his accustomed post at the head of the column and led them away from the charred and smoldering evidence of their efficiency as wreckers.

Now as before, the march was south. They did not bivouac till near midnight, having covered a good fifty miles of road despite the arduous delay at Newton Station. Next day, April 25, was the easiest of the raid, however, since the blue raiders spent most of it on a plantation in the piny highlands just short of the Leaf River valley, resting their mounts, gorging themselves on smokehouse ham, and presumably nursing their hangovers. Sunday followed, and while Hatch was riding into La Grange at the end of his five-day excursion through North Mississippi, the raiders turned west. In time, according to Grierson's calculations, this would bring them either to Grand Gulf, in case Grant had effected a crossing as planned, or some forty miles downriver to Natchez, which had been under intermittent Federal occupation for nearly a year.

Either place would afford refuge for his saddle-weary troopers if all went as he hoped and planned, but he knew well enough that the most dangerous part of the long ride lay before him. By now, doubtless, every grayback in the state would have learned of the presence of his two regiments at Newton Station two days ago, with the result that a considerable number of them must be hot on his trail or lying in wait for him in all directions. However, this had its compensations as well as its drawbacks. Scarcely less important than the temporary severing of Vicksburg's main supply line was the disruption of its defenses, preventing the hasty concentration of its outlying forces against Grant in the early stages of his river crossing.

In point of fact, Grierson was more successful in this

regard than he had any way of knowing. Orders flew thick and fast from Pemberton's headquarters in the Mississippi capital, directing all units within possible reach to concentrate on the capture of the ubiquitous blue column. An infantry brigade, en route from Alabama to reinforce Vicksburg, was halted at Meridian to protect that vital intersection of the Southern Railroad and the Mobile & Ohio, while another moved east from Jackson in the direction of the break at Newton Station. Forces at Panola and Canton, under James Chalmers and Lloyd Tilghman, were shifted to Okolona and Carthage to block the northern escape route. All of these troops, amounting to no less than a full division, not counting the various home-guard units caught up in the swirl, were thus effectively taken out of the play and removed from possible use at this critical time against either Grant or Grierson, who were off in the opposite corner of the map. Not that Pemberton was neglecting matters in that direction, at least so far as Grierson was concerned. Detachments of fast-riding cavalry were ordered eastward from Port Hudson and Port Gibson— the latter a scant half dozen miles from Grant's intended point of landing at Grand Gulf—in case the marauders tried for a getaway to the south or the southwest. In short, Pemberton's reaction to the widespread confusion in his rear and along his lines of supply and communication, while altogether commendable from a limited point of view, amounted to full cooperation with the raiders in the accomplishment of their secondary mission, which was to divert his attention, as well as his reserves, away from the point at which Grant was preparing to hurl two thirds of the blue army.

Grierson wasted no time. Monday, April 27— Grant's birthday; Sherman prepared for his feint up the

Yazoo, and McClernand was told to get his troops aboard the transports at Hard Times—the blue riders pushed westward across Pearl River, aided considerably by the capture of a ferryboat by scouts who masqueraded as Confederates. While the crossing was in progress the company detached five days ago near Starkville rejoined the main body, reporting that in addition to throwing a scare into the defenders of Macon, as instructed, it had also made a feint at Enterprise, twelve miles below Meridian, thus adding to the difficulties of the rebel high command's attempt to pinpoint the location of the invaders.

Safely across the Pearl, the reunited 1000-man column pressed on west to Hazlehurst, where a string of boxcars was set afire on a siding of the New Orleans, Jackson & Great Northern Railroad. Flames spreading to a nearby block of buildings, the erstwhile incendiaries turned firemen and worked side by side with the citizens in preventing the loss of the whole town. At dusk, in a driving rain which had helped to contain the fire, the colonel ordered his troopers to remount. The march was west; Grand Gulf was only forty miles away and he hoped to make it there tomorrow, in case Grant had crossed the Mississippi. However, morning brought no indication that any part of the Army of the Tennessee was on this side of the river, so Grierson veered a bit to the south for Natchez, his alternate sanctuary, which was only twenty miles farther away than Grand Gulf. But that too was not to be. Beyond Union Church that afternoon, the raiders were enjoying a rest halt when they were charged by what one of them called "a crowd of graylooking horsemen galloping and shooting in a cloud of dust and smoke." The result at first was panic and the beginning of a rout, but presently they stiffened and repulsed the attackers, who turned out to be nothing more than a couple of understrength companies on the prowl.

The colonel prepared to push on next day to Natchez, but was warned that night by one of the Butternut Guerillas, who had ridden ahead and struck up a conversation with a rebel outpost group, that seven companies of cavalry from Grand Gulf were planning to ambush him when he moved westward in the morning. So Grierson once more changed his plans, abandoning Natchez as his destination. Determined now to press on down to Baton Rouge, though this added another hundred miles to the distance his weary men would have to ride, he turned back east at dawn of April 29, avoiding the ambush laid so carefully in what was now his rear.

By early afternoon they were in Brookhaven, twenty-five miles east, astride the railroad they had crossed two days ago, twenty miles to the north, when the march was west. "There was much running and yelling" on the part of the startled citizens, Grierson later reported, "but it soon quieted into almost a welcome." Here, as at Hazlehurst on Monday, sparks from the burning railroad station and another string of boxcars set a section of the town ablaze, and the troopers once more turned firemen to help the natives keep the flames from spreading. Meantime, however, a wrecking crew kept busy tearing up track and burning crossties, thus abolishing the possibility of a locomotive pursuit by troops from Jackson. Back in the saddle, the raiders moved south along the railroad and made camp that night, eight miles below Brookhaven and just over a hundred miles from Baton Rouge.

At Summit before sundown of the last day of April, the colonel spared the depot lest his men have to turn firefighters again to save the town, but there was another unfortunate—or fortunate, depending on the point of view—encounter with rebel spirits when the troopers uncovered a cache of rum in fifty-gallon barrels. Grierson broke up the binge, got the revelers mounted at last, drunk or sober, and pressed on south another half dozen miles before stopping for the night. Dawn of May Day completed two full weeks the men had spent in the saddle, with only a half day's rest aside from the minimal halts for sleep and food. Once more the march was west. "A straight line for Baton Rouge, and let speed be our safety," Grierson told his officers as the column was put in motion.

Speed there was—the raiders covered no less than seventy-five miles of road in the following twenty-eight hours—but there was fighting, too, the first and only serious opposition the main body encountered in the course of the long raid. Even so, it was not much. At Wall's Bridge, which spanned the Tickfaw River just north of the Louisiana line, three companies of Confederates from Port Hudson laid a noonday ambush that cost the leading Union company eight casualties. Grierson promptly brought his artillery to the front, shelled the opposite bank, and ordered a charge that not only cleared the bridge but threw the rebels into headlong flight.

Riding south all night, with no time out for rest or food, the blue column reached and crossed the Amite River, the last unfordable stream this side of Baton Rouge, before the aroused graybacks could bar the way. Six miles short of the Louisiana capital next morning, his troopers reeling in their saddles from lack of sleep, Grierson called a halt at last.

The men tumbled from their mounts and slept where

they fell, along the roadside, but the colonel himself, as befitted a former music teacher with an ingrained mistrust of horses, was refreshing himself by playing the piano in the parlor of a nearby plantation house when a picket burst in with news that they were about to be overwhelmed and captured. A rebel force was approaching from the west, he said, with skirmishers out! Grierson, knowing better, rode out to meet the reported enemy, who turned out to be members of the blue garrison at Baton Rouge, sent to investigate an improbable-sounding rumor "that a brigade of cavalry from General Grant's army had cut their way through the heart of the rebel country, and were then only five miles outside the city."

Somewhat restored by their naps, the men remounted and rode into the capital that afternoon. Cheered by spectators, civilians as well as soldiers, the two-mile-long procession of road-worn men and animals, so weathered and dust-caked that they could scarcely be distinguished from the prisoners and Negroes they had gathered along the way, wound slowly around the public square, then south out of town to a grove of magnolias two miles south, where they dismounted, unsaddled, and fell so soundly asleep that they could not be roused to accept hot coffee.

They had cause for weariness, having covered more than six hundred miles in less than sixteen days, and for thankfulness as well: thankfulness that Pemberton had lost Van Dorn to Bragg three months before, along with nearly all his cavalry, and that it was Abel Streight and not themselves who had been made the prime concern of Bedford Forest. Streight had left Fort Henry on the day they left La Grange, and was surrendering in East Alabama while Grierson's men, having caught up on

their sleep at last, were enjoying their first midday meal
in the magnolia grove just south of the Louisiana capital. Different circumstances might well have led to different results, including perhaps a reversal of their
current roles as prisoners on the one hand and heroes
on the other, but the fact remained that the Illinois
troopers had dealt with conditions as they found them.

And having done so, they had cause for pride. At a
total cost of barely two dozen casualties—"3 killed, 7
wounded, 5 left on the route sick . . . and 9 men missing,
supposed to have straggled"—they had "killed and
wounded about one hundred of the enemy, captured
and paroled over 500 prisoners, many of them officers,
destroyed between fifty and sixty miles of railroad and
telegraph, captured and destroyed over 3000 stand of
arms, and other army stores and government property
to an immense amount." So Grierson later reported,
adding as if by afterthought, despite his continued mistrust of all equine creatures: "We also captured 1000
horses and mules."

Within three days the colonel was on a steamboat for
New Orleans, where he was feted and presented with a
horse by the admiring citizenry. "My dear Alice," he
wrote his wife that night, "I like Byron have had to wake
up one morning and find myself famous. Since I have
been here it has been one continuous ovation."

In early June, with his picture on the covers of both
Harper's Weekly and *Leslie's Illustrated,* he was promoted
to brigadier general. But perhaps the finest tribute of all
came from a man by no means given to using superla-
tives, on or off the record. Assessing the value of the raid
in its relation to the over-all campaign for the taking of
Vicksburg, of which it was very much a part, Grant said
flatly: "It was Grierson who first set the example of what

might be done in the interior of the enemy's country
without any base from which to draw supplies."

★　　★　　★

For the present, however, Grant at Hard Times had no
more knowledge of Grierson's progress, across the way,
than Grierson had had of Grant's while riding west
from Hazlehurst. All the cavalryman learned for certain
as he pressed on toward the river was that the army had
not crossed as planned, which meant that something
must have gone awry. Something had indeed. When the
raiders turned back east from Union Church at dawn of
April 29, avoiding the ambush laid in what had been
their front, they missed hearing the guns of the attackers and defenders at Grand Gulf, less than thirty air-line
miles away. It was just as well, for otherwise they might
have been lured into what would have been a trap. Except for the rather negative advantage of proving that
this was no place to attempt an east-bank landing, the
attack was an utter failure, and an expensive one at that.

Porter's doubts had been increasing all week, ever
since his April 22 reconnaissance of the stronghold on
the bluff across the way. Though he had kept up a show
of confidence in his talks with Grant, privately he was
airing his misgivings in dispatches to his Washington
superiors, not only by way of preparing them for bad
news, but also by way of divesting himself in advance of
any responsibility for the failure he saw looming. "I am
quite depressed with this adventure," he wrote Fox,
"which as you know never met with my approval."

This last was something less than strictly true,
though when he signaled the flotilla captains to move
against Grand Gulf at 8 o'clock next morning, April 29,

his forebodings soon turned out to have been well founded. The navy's task was to silence the rebel batteries, then cover the crossing by the transports bringing the army over to take the place by storm; but when four of the seven ironclads closed to within pistol shot of the 75-foot bluff—so at least it seemed to Grant, who watched the contest from aboard a tug—they were severely mauled. The flagship *Benton* took 70 hits, the *Tuscumbia* 81; the *Lafayette* took 45, the *Pittsburg* 35. The other three boats, *Carondelet*, *Mound City*, and *Louisville*, all veterans of the river war from its beginning, did their fighting at long range, lobbing shells into the blufftop works, and consequently suffered little damage. Even so, when Porter hoisted the pennant for the flotilla to drop back out of action at 12.30—all but the *Tuscumbia*, which had been struck in her machinery and swept powerless downstream until she fetched up short against the Louisiana bank—a total of 75 casualties, including 18 dead, had been subtracted from its crews. By contrast, although time would disclose that they had lost 3 killed and 15 wounded, the defenders seemed unhurt behind their earthwork fortifications. Grand Gulf was as much a failure for the Union navy as Fort Donelson had been, just over a year ago. Porter frankly admitted as much. A crossing might be managed elsewhere, he told Grant, but not here, under the muzzles of those guns across the way.

Grant had not expected a repulse, but he was prepared for what he considered the outside chance of one. Now that a repulse had been encountered, an alternate plan was put into execution without delay. McClernand's men would debark at Hard Times, march south across the point of land to De Shroon's, a plantation landing some four miles downstream, and be ready before dawn to get back aboard the transports, which were to steal past Grand Gulf under cover of darkness, hugging the western bank while the gunboats re-engaged the batteries. All this went as planned, afloat and ashore. The navy lost only one man in its renewal of the duel with the blufftop cannoneers, and the army made its night march unobserved, to find the transports waiting unscathed in the predawn darkness at De Shroon's. "By the time it was light," Grant later wrote, "the enemy saw our whole fleet, ironclads, gunboats, river steamers, and barges, quietly moving down the river three miles below them, black, or rather blue, with National troops."

Accomplishing this he showed the flexibility that would characterize his planning throughout the various stages of the campaign which now was under way in earnest. Other characteristics he also showed. An officer was to remember seeing the general sitting his horse beside the road at a point where a narrow bridge had been thrown across a bog. "Push right along, men," he told the marchers, speaking in almost a conversational tone. "Close up fast and hurry over." The soldiers recognized him and were obviously pleased to see their commander sharing their exertions, but the officer noted that their only reply was to do as he directed. They did not cheer him; they just "hurried over." It was as if, in the course of the long winter of repeated failures, they had caught his quality of quiet confidence.

Charles Dana, for one, had begun to think so. He had come down here three weeks ago to report on Grant's alleged bad habits. So far, though, he not only had detected none of these; he had never even heard him curse or seen him lose his temper. Dana was puzzled. "His equanimity was becoming a curious spectacle to me," the former journalist later recalled. Tonight, for example, riding beside the general along the dark road from Hard Times to De Shroon's, he saw Grant's horse stumble. "Now he will swear," he thought, half expecting to see the rider go tumbling over the animal's head; "For an instant his moral status was on trial." But Grant lost neither his balance nor his temper. "Pulling up his horse, he rode on, and, to my utter amazement, without a word or sign of impatience."

Nor did the night march across the point of land, from Hard Times to De Shroon's, put an end to the need for sudden improvisation. Having bypassed Grand Gulf—which he could not allow to remain alive for long, so close in his rear—Grant still was faced with the problem of where to effect a landing on the Mississippi bank, in order to return for a strike at the fortified bluff from its vulnerable landward flank. A look at the map suggested Rodney, another twelve miles downstream. But that would not only give the troops a considerable distance to march, and the defenders time to improve their position and call in reinforcements, it would also place the bluecoats on the far side of Bayou Pierre, which would have to be crossed when they turned back north. Yet to make a landing short of the point where the bayou flowed westward into the river, five miles below, might be to founder the army in some unmapped and unsuspected swamp.

What was needed was a guide, a sympathetic native of the region, and Grant sent a detachment of soldiers across the river in a skiff, with instructions to bring back what he wanted. They returned before midnight with an east-bank slave who filled the bill. At first he had been unwilling to come, and in fact had had to be taken by force, but now that he found himself in the lamp-lighted headquarters tent, facing the Union commander across an unrolled chart, he turned cooperative. "Look here," Grant said. "Tell me where this road leads to—starting where you see my finger here on the map and running down that way." The Negro studied the problem, then shook his head. "That road fetches up at Bayou Pierre," he said. "But you can't go that way, 'cause it's plum full of backwater."

The thing to do, he replied to further questions, was to go ashore at Bruinsburg, six miles below De Shroon's. This would still be south of Bayou Pierre, but at least it was only half as far as Rodney. Moreover, there was a good road leading from there to Grand Gulf by way of Port Gibson, which lay ten miles inland, well back from the trackless swamps and canebrakes of the river bottoms. At Bruinsburg, the captive slave explained, "you can leave the boats and the men can walk on high ground all the way. The best houses and plantations in all the country are there, sir, all along that road."

So Bruinsburg it was. By midmorning of this last day of April—while Sherman was launching his demonstration against Haines Bluff, fifty air-line miles to the north, and Grierson was pressing southward along the railroad below Brookhaven, the same distance to the east—all four of McClernand's divisions and one of McPherson's, some 23,000 men in all, had completed their debarkation and were slogging inland toward Port Gibson.

"When this was effected," Grant declared years later, "I felt a degree of relief scarcely ever equaled since." Then he told why. "I was now in the enemy's country, with a vast river and the stronghold of Vicksburg between me and my base of supplies. But I was on dry ground on the same side of the river with the enemy. All the campaigns, labors, hardships, and exposures from the month of December previous to this time that had been made and endured were for the accomplishment of this one object."

$$\star\ 4\ \star$$

For all his northern birth and starchy manner, which some continued to find personally distasteful, Pemberton by now had either sustained or won the confidence not only of his military superiors but also of the people of Mississippi, who came within his charge. His four-month sequence of successes in the face of threats from all points of the compass far outweighed their original prejudice against him. On May Day, for example—unaware that Sherman was knocking at Vicksburg's upper gate or that Grant, with half his army over the river, already was marching inland from below—an editor in the capital, where the department commander had his headquarters, was taking a sanguine view of the situation.

"It would be idle to say that our state and country was not in a position of great peril," he declared. "Yet, strange as it may seem to our readers, we have never felt more secure since the fall of Donelson. The enemy will never reach Jackson; we are satisfied of that. . . . General Pemberton, assisted by vigilant and accomplished officers, is watching the movements of the enemy, and at the proper time will pounce upon him. Let us give the authorities all the assistance we can, and trust their superior and more experienced judgment as to the management of the armies. We know we have a force sufficient, if properly handled, not only to defeat but to rout and annihilate Grant if he ventures far from his river base." As for doubts as to the proper handling of this sufficient force: "Let any man who questions the ability of General Pemberton only think for a moment of the condition the department was in when he was first sent here. No general has evinced a more sleepless vigilance in the discharge of his duty, or accomplished more solid and gratifying results."

Nor was this merely the opinion of one uninformed civilian. With reservations, Joseph E. Johnston shared his view. Despite the gloom into which his inspection of the Vicksburg defenses had thrown him, back in December when he was placed in charge of the central theater to coordinate the efforts of Bragg in Tennessee and Pemberton in Mississippi, the Virginian since had warmed to the Pennsylvanian as a result of his apparent skill in fending off the combinations designed for his destruction. In mid-March, reviewing the situation from three hundred miles away in Tennessee, he congratulated him handsomely. "Your activity and vigor in the defense of Mississippi must have secured for you the confidence of the people of Mississippi," he wrote, and added: "I have no apprehension for Port Hudson from Banks. The only fear is that the canal may enable Grant to unite their forces. I believe your arrangements at Vicksburg make it perfectly safe, unless that union should be effected."

Applause was one thing, assistance quite another: as

Pemberton soon found out. Despite the denial of help from the vast department across the river, and despite the January transfer of three quarters of his cavalry to Middle Tennessee, he was so encouraged by the flooding of Grant's canal in March that he mistook the subsequent withdrawal of the diggers to Milliken's Bend for an abandonment by the Federals of their entire campaign. On April 11 he notified Johnston that the canal was no longer a danger, that Grant appeared to be pulling back to Memphis, and that he was therefore sending, as requested, a brigade to reinforce Bragg at Tullahoma. Five days later, however, with the blue army still in evidence on the opposite bank and Porter's gunboats preparing for their run past the batteries that night, he recalled the detached brigade, which by then was in northern Mississippi. "[Grant's] movement up the river was a ruse," he wired Johnston. "Certainly no more troops should leave this department." In fact, he said, it was he who stood in gravest need of help.

Nothing came of that. Then on April 20, with Porter's ironclads riding at anchor near New Carthage, McClernand moving farther down the Louisiana bank, and Grierson on the rampage east of Grenada—"part and parcel of the formidable invasion preparing before my eyes"—Pemberton stepped up his plea for reinforcements: especially for the return of his 6000 troopers under Van Dorn, the loss of whom had left him three-fourths blind. "Heavy raids are making from Tennessee deep into this state," he warned. "Cavalry is indispensable to meet these expeditions. The little I have is . . . totally inadequate. Could you not make a demonstration with a cavalry force on their rear?" He protested that he had "literally no cavalry from Grand Gulf to Yazoo City, while the enemy is threatening to [cross] the river between Vicksburg and Grand Gulf, having now twelve vessels below the former place."

Johnston, obliged as he presently was to send Forrest to Alabama after Streight, not only would not agree to make a demonstration against West Tennessee; he also declined to lessen the strength of Bragg's mounted arm, which included Joe Wheeler and John Hunt Morgan as well as Forrest and Van Dorn, despite the fact that Van Dorn was nominally on loan from Pemberton. It turned out, moreover, that the Pennsylvanian's previous successes worked against him now. Matters had seemed as dark several times before, in the course of the past four months, and he had managed to survive without assistance; apparently Johnston believed he would do as well again. At any rate he was still of his former opinion: "Van Dorn's cavalry is absolutely necessary to enable General Bragg to hold the best part of the country from which he draws supplies."

In effect this amounted to signing Van Dorn's death warrant, since it kept him within range of a Tennessee doctor's wife and her husband's pistol, which wound up his career in early May. Pemberton was inclined to think that in the end it might amount to much the same thing for Vicksburg, referred to by Jefferson Davis as "the nailhead that held the South's two halves together." For suddenly now the news grew more alarming. Two nights later, April 22, five unarmored steamboats ran the batteries, obviously to provide the means for a crossing, somewhere below, by the bluecoats slogging down the western bank. Throughout the week that followed, Pemberton sent what little cavalry he had in pursuit of Grierson, whose raiders were disrupting the interior of the state and playing havoc with his lines of supply and communication.

Then on April 29 word came from John S. Bowen, commanding at Grand Gulf, that the place was under heavy attack by gunboats attempting to soften him up for an assault by infantry waiting in transports across the river at Hard Times. Scarcely had the news arrived next morning that the ironclads had retired, severely battered, than Pemberton was notified that Haines Bluff was under similar pressure to the north. By the time he learned that this too had been beaten off, a follow-up message from Bowen informed him that the Union fleet had slipped past Grand Gulf in the darkness, transports and all, and was unloading soldiers in large numbers at east-bank Bruinsburg, ten miles below. Then came word that the Federals had resumed their pounding of Haines Bluff. Deciding that the downriver threat was the graver of the two, Pemberton resolved to reinforce Bowen, whom he instructed to contest the blue advance on Port Gibson.

On May Day, with the issue still in doubt below — so he thought, though it could scarcely be in doubt for long; the enemy strength was reported at 20,000 men, while Bowen had considerably less than half that many — he appealed once more to Johnston for assistance, bolstering his plea with a wire directly to the President. Davis replied that, in addition to urging Johnston to send help from Tennessee, he was doing all he could to forward troops from southern Alabama. Army Secretary James A. Seddon, alerted to the danger, informed Pemberton that "heavy reinforcements" would start at once by rail from Beauregard in Charleston.

Both messages were gratifying, communicating assurance of assistance from above. But all the harassed Vicksburg commander got from Johnston was advice. "If Grant's army lands on this side of the river," the Virginian replied from Tullahoma, "the safety of Mississippi depends on beating it. For that object you should unite your whole force."

A Georgia-born West Pointer, John Bowen had left the old army after a single hitch as a lieutenant and had prospered as a St Louis architect before he was thirty, at which age he offered his sword to the newly formed Confederacy. Promoted to brigadier within ten months, he now was thirty-two and eager for further advancement, having spent more than a year in grade because of a long convalescence from a wound taken at Shiloh, where he led his brigade of Missourians with distinction. On the afternoon of April 30, marching his 5500 soldiers out of Grand Gulf and across Bayou Pierre to meet Grant's 23,000 moving inland from Bruinsburg after their downriver creep past his blufftop guns in the darkness, he carried proudly in his pocket a dispatch received last night from Pemberton, congratulating him on the repulse of Porter's ironclads: "In the name of the army, I desire to thank you and your troops for your gallant conduct today. Keep up the good work. . . . Yesterday I warmly recommended you for a major-generalcy. I shall renew it."

Bowen had it very much in mind to keep up the good work. Despite the looming four-to-one odds and the changed nature of his task now that he and the blue invaders were on the same bank of the river, he welcomed this opportunity to deal with them ashore today as he had dealt with them afloat the day before. Four miles west of Port Gibson before nightfall, he put his men in a good defensive position astride a wooded ridge just short of a fork in the road leading east from Bruinsburg. Presently the Federals came up and his pickets took

them under fire in the moonlight. Artillery deepened
the tone of the argument, North and South, but soon
after midnight, as if by mutual consent, both sides quieted down to wait for daylight.

McClernand opened the May Day fight soon after
sunrise, advancing all four of his divisions under Peter
Osterhaus, A. J. Smith, Alvin Hovey, and Eugene Carr.
The road fork just ahead placed him in something of a
quandary, lacking as he did an adequate map, but this
was soon resolved by a local Negro who informed him
that the two roads came together again on the near side
of Port Gibson, his objective. He sent Osterhaus to the
left as a diversion in favor of the other three commanders, who were charged with launching the main effort
on the right.

Grant came up at midmorning to find the battle in
full swing and McClernand in some confusion, his heavily engaged columns being out of touch with each other
because the two roads that wound along parallel ridges
—"This part of Mississippi stands on edge" was how
Grant put it—were divided by a timber-choked ravine
that made lateral communication impossible. The result
was that McClernand's right hand quite literally did not
know what his left was doing, though the fact was neither was doing well at all.

In his perplexity he called for help from McPherson,
who supplied it by sending one brigade of John A.
Logan's division to the left and another to the right.
"Push right along. Close up fast," the men heard Grant
say as they went past the dust-covered general sitting a
dust-covered horse beside the road fork. They did as he
said, and arrived on the left in time to stall a rebel
counterattack that had already thrown Osterhaus off
balance, while on the right they added the weight

needed for a resumption of the advance. Outflanked and heavily outnumbered on the road to the south, Bowen at last had to pull back to the outskirts of Port Gibson, where he rallied his men along a hastily improvised line and held off the blue attackers until nightfall ended the fighting.

Casualties were about equal on both sides; 832 Confederates and 875 Federals had fallen or were missing. Bowen had done well and he knew it, considering the disparity of numbers, but he also knew that to fight here tomorrow, against lengthened odds and without the advantage of this morning's densely wooded terrain, would be to invite disaster. At sundown he notified Pemberton that he would "have to retire under cover of night to the other side of Bayou Pierre and await reinforcements."

Pemberton, who had arrived in Vicksburg from Jackson by now, had already sent word that he was "hurrying reinforcements; also ammunition. Endeavor to hold your own until they arrive, though it may be some time, as the distance is great." At 7.30, having received Bowen's sundown message, he rather wistfully inquired: "Is it not probable that the enemy will himself retire tonight? It is very important, as you know, to retain your present position, if possible. . . . You must, however, of course, be guided by your own judgment. You and your men have done nobly." But Bowen by then had followed up his first dispatch with a second: "I am pulling back across Bayou Pierre. I will endeavor to hold that position until reinforcements arrive."

He withdrew skillfully by moonlight, unpursued and unobserved, destroying the three bridges over the bayou and its south fork, northwest and northeast of Port Gibson, and took up a strong position on the opposite bank, covering the wrecked crossing of the railroad to Grand Gulf, which he believed would be Grant's next objective.

But Grant did not come that way, at least not yet. Finding Port Gibson empty at dawn, he pressed on through and gave James Wilson a brigade-sized detail with which to construct a bridge across the south fork of Bayou Pierre, just beyond the town. Wilson was experienced in such work, having built no less than seven such spans in the course of the march from Milliken's Bend, and besides he had plenty of materials at hand, in the form of nearby houses which he tore down and cannibalized. By midafternoon the job was finished, "a continuous raft 166 feet long, 12 feet wide, with three rows of large mill-beams lying across the current, and the intervals between them closely filled with buoyant timber; the whole firmly tied together by a cross-floor or deck of 2-inch stuff." So Wilson later described it, not without pride, adding that he had also provided side rails, corduroy approaches over quicksand, and abutments "formed by building a slight crib-work, and filling in with rails covered by sand."

Grant was impressed, but he did not linger to admire the young staff colonel's handiwork. The second of McPherson's three divisions having arrived that morning, he was given the lead today, with orders to march eight miles northeast to Grindstone Ford, which he reached soon after dark. He was prevented from crossing at once because the fine suspension bridge had been destroyed at that point, but Wilson was again at hand and had it repaired by daylight of May 3, when McPherson pressed on over. Near Willow Springs, two miles beyond the stream, he encountered and dislodged a small hostile force which retreated toward Hankinson's

Ferry, six miles north, where the main road to Vicksburg crossed the Big Black River. Instructing McPherson to keep up the march northward in pursuit, Grant detached a single brigade to accompany him westward in the direction of Grand Gulf.

McClernand, coming along behind McPherson, whom he was ordered to follow north, was alarmed to learn what Grant had done, striking off on his own like that, and sent a courier galloping after him with a warning: "Had you not better be careful lest you may personally fall in with the enemy on your way to Grand Gulf?" But Grant was not only anxious to reach that place as soon as possible, and thus reestablish contact with the navy and with Sherman, who was on the march down the Louisiana bank; he also believed that Bowen, chastened by yesterday's encounter, would fall back beyond the Big Black as soon as he discovered that his position on Bayou Pierre had been turned upstream.

In this the northern commander was quite right. Reinforcements had reached Bowen from Jackson and Vicksburg by now, but they only increased his force to about 9000, whereas he reckoned the present enemy strength at 30,000, augmented as it was by a full division put ashore at Bruinsburg the night before. When he learned, moreover, that this host had bridged both forks of Bayou Pierre to the east of Port Gibson and was headed for the crossings of the Big Black, deep in his rear, he lost no time in reaching the decision Grant expected. At midnight, finding that his staff advisers "concurred in my belief that I was compelled to abandon the post at Grand Gulf," he "then ordered the evacuation, the time for each command to move being so fixed as to avoid any delay or confusion."

The retrograde movement went smoothly despite

the need for haste. Bringing off all their baggage—
which Pemberton, when informed of their predica-
ment, had authorized them to abandon lest it slow their
march, but which Bowen declared he was "determined
to and did save"—the weary veterans and the newly arrived reinforcements set off northward, leaving the
blufftop intrenchments, which they had defended so
ably against the ironclad assault four days ago, yawning
empty behind them in the early morning sunlight.

Soon after they disappeared over the northern horizon Porter arrived with four gunboats, intending to
launch a new attack. He approached with caution, remembering his previous woes and fearing a rebel trick,
but when he found the Grand Gulf works abandoned he
did not let that diminish his claim for credit for their
reduction. "We had a hard fight for these forts," he
wrote Secretary Welles, "and it is with great pleasure
that I report that the Navy holds the door to Vicksburg." He announced that his fire had torn the place to
pieces, leaving it so covered with earth and debris that
no one could tell at a glance what had been there before
the bombardment. "Had the enemy succeeded in finishing these fortifications no fleet could have taken
them," he declared, quite as if he had subdued the batteries in the nick of time, and added: "I hear nothing of
our army as yet; was expecting to hear their guns as we
advanced on the forts."

He heard from "our army" presently with the arrival
of its commander, who had got word of the evacuation
while en route from Grindstone Ford and had ridden
ahead of the infantry with an escort of twenty troopers.
Grant was glad to see the admiral, but most of all—after
seven days on a borrowed horse, with "no change of un-
derclothing, no meal except such as I could pick up

sometimes at other headquarters, and no tent to cover me"—he was glad to avail himself of the admiral's facilities. After a hot bath, a change of underwear borrowed from one of the naval officers, and a square meal aboard the flagship, he got off a full report to Halleck on the events of the past four days.

"Our victory has been most complete, and the enemy thoroughly demoralized," he wrote. Bowen's defense of Port Gibson had been "a very bold one and well carried out. My force, however, was too heavy for his, and composed of well-disciplined and hardy men who know no defeat and are not willing to learn what it is." After this unaccustomed flourish he got down to the matter at hand. "This army is in the finest health and spirits," he declared. "Since leaving Milliken's Bend they have marched as much by night as by day, through mud and rain, without tents or much other baggage, and on irregular rations, without a complaint and with less straggling than I have ever before witnessed. . . . I shall not bring my troops into this place, but immediately follow the enemy, and, if all promises as favorable hereafter as it does now, not stop until Vicksburg is in our possession."

He was on his own, however, in a way he had neither intended nor foreseen. His plan had been to use Grand Gulf as a base, accumulating a reserve of supplies and marking time with Sherman and McPherson, so to speak, while McClernand took his corps downriver to cooperate with Banks in the reduction of Port Hudson, after which the two would join him for a combined assault on Vicksburg. But he found waiting for him today at Grand Gulf a three-week-old letter from Banks, dated April 10 and headed Brashear City—75 miles west of New Orleans and equally far south of Port Hudson—informing him of a change in procedure made necessary, according to the Massachusetts general, by unexpected developments in western Louisiana which would threaten his flank and rear, including New Orleans itself, if he moved due north from the Crescent City as originally planned. Instead, he intended to abolish this danger with an advance up the Teche and the Atchafalaya, clearing out the rebels around Opelousas before returning east to Baton Rouge for the operation against Port Hudson with 15,000 men. He hoped to open this new phase of the campaign next day, he wrote, and if all went as planned he would return to the Mississippi within a month—that is, by May 10—at which time he would be ready to co-operate with Grant in their double venture.

Reading the letter, Grant experienced a considerable shock. He had expected Banks to have twice as many troops already in position for a quick slash at Port Hudson, to be followed by an equally rapid boat ride north to assist in giving Vicksburg the same treatment. Now all that went glimmering. Some 30,000 men poorer than he had counted on being, he was on his own: which on second thought had its advantages, since the Massachusetts general outranked him and by virtue of his seniority would get the credit, from the public as well as the government, for the reduction of both Confederate strongholds and the resultant clearing of the Mississippi all the way to the Gulf. Grant absorbed the shock and quickly made up his mind that he was better off without him. Banks having left him on his own, he would do the same for Banks.

"To wait for his cooperation would have detained me at least a month," he subsequently wrote in explanation of his decision. "The reinforcements would not have reached 10,000 men after deducting casualties and necessary river guards at all high points close to the river for over 300 miles. The enemy would have strengthened his position and been reinforced by more men than Banks could have brought. I therefore determined to move independently of Banks, cut loose from my base, destroy the rebel force in rear of Vicksburg, and invest or capture the city."

So much he intended, though he had not yet decided exactly how he would go about it. One thing he knew, however, was that the change of plans called for an immediate speed-up of the accumulation of supplies, preliminary to launching his all-out drive on the rebel citadel two dozen air-line miles to the north. A look at the Central Mississippi interior, with its lush fields, its many grazing cattle, and its well-stocked plantation houses—"of a character equal to some of the finest villas on the Hudson," a provincial New York journalist called these last—had convinced him that the problem was less acute than he had formerly supposed. "This country will supply all the forage required for anything like an active campaign, and the necessary fresh beef," he informed Halleck. "Other supplies will have to be drawn from Milliken's Bend. This is a long and precarious route, but I have every confidence in succeeding in doing it." Accordingly, he ordered this supply line shortened, as soon as the river had fallen a bit, by the construction of a new road from Young's Point to a west-bank landing just below Warrenton. "Everything depends upon the promptitude with which our supplies are forwarded," he warned. He had already directed that two towboats make a third run past the Vicksburg guns with heavy-laden barges. "Do this with all expedition," he told the quartermaster at Milliken's Bend, "in

48 hours from receipt of orders if possible. Time is of immense importance."

Hurlbut was ordered to forward substantial reinforcements from Memphis without delay, as well as to lay in a sixty-day surplus of rations, to be kept on hand for shipment downriver at short notice. To Sherman, hurrying south across the way, went instructions to collect 120 wagons en route, load them with 100,000 pounds of bacon, then pile on all the coffee, sugar, salt, and crackers they would hold. "It is unnecessary for me to remind you of the overwhelming importance of celerity in your movements," Grant told him, outlining the situation as he saw it now on this side of the river: "The enemy is badly beaten, greatly demoralized, and exhausted of ammunition. The road to Vicksburg is open. All we want now are men, ammunition, and hard bread. We can subsist our horses on the country, and obtain considerable supplies for our troops."

With all this paper work behind him, he left Grand Gulf at midnight and rode eastward under a full moon to rejoin McPherson, who had reached Hankinson's Ferry that afternoon and had already dispatched cavalry details to probe the opposite bank of the Big Black River. From his new headquarters Grant kept stressing the need for haste. "Every day's delay is worth 2000 men to the enemy," he warned a supply officer, and kept goading him with questions that called for specific answers: "How many teams have been loaded with rations and sent forward? I want to know as near as possible how we stand in every particular for supplies. How many wagons have you ferried over the river? How many are still to bring over? What teams have gone back for rations?"

His impatience was such that he had no time for

head-shaking or regrets. Learning on May 5 that one of the two towboats and all the barges had been lost the night before in attempting the moonlight run he had ordered, he dismissed the loss with the remark: "We will risk no more rations to run the Vicksburg batteries," and turned his attention elsewhere. This touch of bad luck was more than offset the following day by news that Sherman had reached Hard Times, freeing McPherson's third division from guard duty along the supply route, and was already in the process of crossing the river to Grand Gulf. The red-haired general was in excellent spirits, having learned that four newspaper reporters had been aboard the towboat that was lost. "They were so deeply laden with weighty matter that they must have sunk," he remarked happily, and added: "In our affliction we can console ourselves with the pious reflection that there are plenty more of the same sort."

One thing Grant did find time for, though, amid all his exertions at Hankinson's Ferry. On the 7th he issued a general order congratulating his soldiers for their May Day victory near Port Gibson, which he said extended "the long list of those previously won by your valor and endurance." He was proud of what they had accomplished so far in the campaign, he assured them, and proudest of all that they had endured their necessary privations without complaint. Then he closed on a note of exhortation. "A few days' continuance of the same zeal and constancy will secure to this army the crowning victory over the rebellion. More difficulties and privations are before us. Let us endure them manfully. Other battles are to be fought. Let us fight them bravely. A grateful country will rejoice at our success, and history will record it with immortal honor."

★　★　★

Pemberton at this stage was by no means "badly
beaten." Neither was he "greatly demoralized," any
more than Vicksburg's defenders were "exhausted of
ammunition." Nor was the road to the city "open," despite Grant's suppositions in his May 3 note urging
Sherman to hurry down to get in on the kill. It was true,
on the other hand, that the southern commander had
been acutely distressed by the news that the blue invaders were landing in force on the east bank of the river
below Grand Gulf, for he saw only too clearly the dangers this involved. "Enemy movement threatens Jackson, and, if successful, cuts off Vicksburg and Port
Hudson from the east," he wired Davis on May Day,
before he knew the outcome of the battle for Port Gibson, and he followed this up next morning, when he
learned that Bowen had withdrawn across Bayou Pierre,
with advice to Governor John J. Pettus that the state ar-
chives be removed from the capital for safekeeping;
Grant most likely would be coming this way soon. Another appeal to Johnston for "large reinforcements" to
meet the "completely changed character of defense,"
now that the Federals were established in strength on
this side of the river, brought a repetition of yesterday's advice: "If Grant crosses, unite all your troops to
beat him. Success will give back what was abandoned to
win it."

If this proposed abandonment included Vicksburg,
and presumably it did, Pemberton was not in agreement. He already had ordered all movable ordnance and
ammunition sent to that place from all parts of the state,
in preparation for a last-ditch fight if necessary, and he

arrived in person the following day, about the same time
Grant rode into Grand Gulf with a twenty-trooper escort. For all his original alarm, Pemberton felt considerably better now. Davis and Seddon had promised
reinforcements from Alabama and South Carolina—
5000 were coming from Charleston by rail at once, the
Secretary wired, with another 4000 to follow—and
Sherman had withdrawn from in front of Haines Bluff,
reducing by half the problem of the city's peripheral defense. Johnston moreover had agreed at last, now that
Streight had been disposed of, to send some cavalry
under Forrest to guard against future raids across the
Tennessee line. Much encouraged, Pemberton telegraphed Davis: "With reinforcements and cavalry
promised in North Mississippi, think we will be all
right."

His new confidence was based on a reappraisal of the
situation confronting him now that Bowen, with his approval, had fallen back across the Big Black River, which
curved across his entire right front and center. Not only
did this withdrawal make a larger number of troops
available for the protection of a much smaller area; it
also afforded him the interior lines, so that a direct attack from beyond the arc could be met with maximum
strength by defenders fighting from prepared positions.
Presumably Grant would avoid that, but Pemberton
saw an even greater advantage proceeding from the
concentration behind the curved shield of the Big Black.
It greatly facilitated what he later called "my great object," which was "to prevent Grant from establishing a
base on the Mississippi River, above Vicksburg." Until
the invaders accomplished this they would be depen-
dent for supplies on what could be run directly past the
gun-bristled bluff, a risky business at best, or freighted

down the opposite bank, along a single jerry-built road that was subject to all the ravages of nature.

As Pemberton saw it, his opponent's logical course would be to extend his march up the left bank of the Big Black, avoiding the bloodshed that would be involved in attempting a crossing until he was well upstream, in position for an advance on Haines Bluff from the rear and the establishment there of a new base of supplies, assisted and protected by Porter's upper flotilla, which would have returned up the Yazoo to meet him. But the southern commander did not intend to stand idly by, particularly while the latter stages of the movement were in progress. "The farther north [Grant] advanced, toward my left, from his then base below, the weaker he became; the more exposed became his rear and flanks; the more difficult it became to subsist his army and obtain reinforcements." At the moment of greatest Union extension and exposure, the defenders—reinforced by then, their commander hoped, from all quarters of the Confederacy—would strike with all their strength at the enemy's flanks and rear, administering a sudden and stunning defeat to a foe for whom, given the time and place, defeat would mean disaster, perhaps annihilation.

Such was the plan. And though there were obvious drawbacks—the region beyond the Big Black, for example, would be exposed to unhindered depredations; critics would doubtless object, moreover, that Grant might adopt a different method of accomplishing his goal—Pemberton considered the possible consummation of his design well worth the risk. Having weighed the odds and assessed his opponent's probable intentions from his actions in the past, he was content to let the outcome test the validity of his insight into the mind of his adversary. "I am a northern man; I know my people," he was to say. Besides, he believed that the Federals, obliged to hold on to one base to the south while reaching out for another to the north, had little choice except to act as he predicted. It was true that in the interim they "might destroy Jackson and ravage the country," he admitted, "but that was a comparatively small matter. To take Vicksburg, to control the valley of the Mississippi, to sever the Confederacy, to ruin our cause, a base upon the eastern bank immediately above was absolutely necessary."

Whatever else was desirable in the conflict now about to be resumed, he knew he would need all the soldiers he could get for the close-up defense of the line on the Big Black. In this connection, at the same time he informed Richmond of the pending evacuation of Grand Gulf he requested permission to bring the so-far unthreatened garrison of Port Hudson north for a share in the coming struggle. "I think Port Hudson and Grand Gulf should be evacuated," he wired Davis on May 2, "and the whole force concentrated for defense of Vicksburg and Jackson." Accordingly, in conformity with Johnston's advice to "unite all your troops," he ordered Franklin Gardner, his ranking subordinate commanding the lower fortress, to strip the garrison to an absolute minimum and move with all the rest of the men to Jackson; those remaining behind would follow as soon as Richmond confirmed his request for total evacuation. On May 7, however, Davis replied that he approved of the withdrawal from Grand Gulf, but that "to hold both Vicksburg and Port Hudson is necessary to a connection with the Trans-Mississippi." So Pemberton countermanded the order to Gardner. He was to return at once to Port Hudson "and hold it to the last. President says both places must be held."

Such discouragement as this occasioned had been offset in advance, at least in part, by the defeat three nights ago of Grant's third attempt to run supplies downriver past the Vicksburg batteries. The sunken towboat and the flaming barges—not to mention the four Yankee journalists, who had not drowned, as Sherman had so fervently hoped, but had been fished out of the muddy water as prisoners of war—were evidence of improvement in the marksmanship of the gunners on the bluff, although it had to be conceded that the brilliant moonlight gave them an advantage they had lacked before. Another encouragement came soon afterwards from Johnston, who replied on May 8 to a report in which Pemberton explained his preparations for defense: "Disposition of troops, as far as understood, judicious; can be readily concentrated against Grant's army."

If this was guarded, it was also approving, which was something altogether new from that direction. Then next day came the best news of all: Johnston himself would be coming soon to Vicksburg to inspirit the men and lend the weight of his genius to the defense of the Gibraltar of the West. Acting under instructions from Davis, Seddon had ordered the general to proceed from Tullahoma "at once to Mississippi and take chief command of the forces, giving to those in the field, as far as practicable, the encouragement and benefit of your personal direction." Johnston was suffering at the time from a flare-up of his Seven Pines wound, but he replied without apparent hesitation: "I shall go immediately, although unfit for service."

He left Tennessee next morning, May 10, having complied with the Secretary's further instructions to have "3000 good troops" follow him from Bragg's army as reinforcements.

Pemberton took new hope at the prospect of first-hand assistance from on high; now he could say, with a good deal more assurance than he had felt when he used the words the week before, "Think we will be all right." But there were flaws in the logic of his approach to the central problem, or at any rate errors in the conclusion to which that logic had led him. His assessment of Grant's intention was partly right, but it was also partly wrong: right, that is, in the conviction that what his opponent wanted and needed was a supply base above Vicksburg, but wrong as to how he would go about getting what he wanted. By now Grant had nine of his ten divisions across the Mississippi and had reached the final stage of his week-long build-up for an advance, though not in the direction Pemberton had supposed and planned for.

McPherson had been shifted eight miles east to Rocky Springs, leaving Hankinson's Ferry to be occupied by Sherman, two of whose three divisions were with him, while McClernand was in position along the road between those two points. In connection with the problem of supply, Grant had been collecting all the transportation he could lay hands on, horses, mules, oxen, and whatever rolled on wheels, ever since the Bruinsburg crossing. The result was a weird conglomeration of vehicles, ranging from the finest plantation carriages to ramshackle farm wagons, with surreys and buckboards thrown in for good measure, all piled to the dashboards and tailgates with supplies—mainly crates of ammunition and hardtack, the two great necessities

for an army on the move—constantly shuttling back
and forth between the Grand Gulf steamboat landing
and Rocky Springs, where Grant had established headquarters near McPherson.

Sherman, being farthest in the rear, had a close-up
view of vehicular confusion that seemed to him to be
building up to the greatest traffic snarl in history, despite the fact that there was still not transportation
enough to supply more than a fraction of the army's
needs. It was his conclusion that Grant's headlong impatience to be up and off was plunging him toward a
logistic disaster. By May 9 he could put up with it no
longer. "Stop all troops till your army is partially supplied with wagons, and then act as quickly as possible,"
he advised his chief, "for this road will be jammed as
sure as life if you attempt to supply 50,000 men by one
single road."

The prompt reply from Rocky Springs gave the red-
head the shock of his military life. Previously he had
known scarcely more of Grant's future plans than Pemberton knew from beyond the Big Black River, but suddenly the veil of secrecy was lifted enough to give him
considerably more than a glimmer of what he had never
suspected until now. "I do not calculate upon the possibility of supplying the army with full rations from
Grand Gulf," Grant told him. "I know it will be impossible without constructing additional roads. What I do
expect, however, is to get up what rations of hard bread,
coffee, and salt we can, and make the country furnish
the balance."

This clearly implied, if it did not actually state, that
he intended to launch an invasion, much as Cortez and
Scott had done in Mexico, without a base from which to
draw supplies. And so he did. Back in December, re-

turning through North Mississippi to Memphis after the destruction of his forward depot at Holly Springs, he had discovered that his troops could live quite easily off the country by the simple expedient of taking what they wanted from the farmers in their path. "This taught me a lesson," he later remarked, and now the lesson was about to be applied. Moreover, the success of Grierson, whose troopers had lacked for nothing in the course of a 600-mile ride that had "knocked the heart out of the state"—so Grant himself declared in passing along to Washington the news of the raid—was a nearer and more recent example of what might be accomplished along those lines. For his own part, in the course of his march from Bruinsburg through Port Gibson to Rocky Springs, he had observed that "beef, mutton, poultry, and forage were found in abundance," along with "quite a quantity of bacon and molasses." What was more, every rural commissary "had a run of stone, propelled by mule power, to grind corn for the owners and their slaves. All these [could be] kept running . . . day and night . . . at all plantations covered by the troops." He felt sure there would be enough food and forage of one sort or another for all his men and animals, leaving room in the makeshift train for ammunition and such hard-to-get items as salt and coffee, provided there were no long halts during which the local supplies would be exhausted. All that was required was that he keep his army moving, and that was precisely what he intended to do, from start to finish, for tactical as well as logistic reasons.

His 45,000 effectives were roughly twice as many as Pemberton had behind the curved shield of the Big Black River; he was convinced that he could whip him in short order with a frontal attack. "If Blair were up

now," he told Sherman, who was still awaiting the arrival of the division that had feinted at Haines Bluff, "I
believe we could be in Vicksburg in seven days." But
that would leave some 10,000 rebels alive in his rear at
Jackson, which was connected by rail not only to Vicksburg but also to the rest of the Confederacy, so that
reinforcements could be hurried there from Bragg and
the East until they outnumbered him as severely as he
had outnumbered Pemberton, thus turning the tables
on him.

His solution was to strike both north and east, severing the rail connection between Jackson and Vicksburg
near the Big Black crossing, while simultaneously closing in on the capital. He would capture the inferior
force at that place, if possible, but at any rate he would
knock it out of commission as a transportation hub or a
rallying point; after which he would be free to turn on
Vicksburg unmolested, approaching it from the east
and north, and thus either take the citadel by storm or
else establish a base on the Yazoo from which to draw
supplies while starving the cut-off defenders into surrender.

Sherman had much of this explained to him when he
rode over to Rocky Springs that afternoon, in considerable perturbation, for what he called "a full conversation" with the army commander. But his doubts persisted, much as they had done after he had agreed to
stage the Haines Bluff demonstration. "He is satisfied
that he will succeed in his plan," he said of Grant in a
letter urging Blair to hasten his crossing from Hard
Times, "and, of course, we must do our full share."
Though he would "of course" co-operate fully in carrying out his chief's design, he wanted it understood from
the start—and placed indelibly on the record—that he

was doing so with something less than enthusiasm and against his better judgment.

Grant by now was accustomed to his lieutenant's mercurial ups and downs, and he did not let them discourage him or influence his thinking. The following day, May 10—the Sunday Joe Johnston left Tullahoma for Jackson—he heard again from Banks, who informed him, in a letter written four days ago at Opelousas, that he was making steady progress up the Teche, clearing out the rebels on his flank, and expected to turn east presently for Port Hudson. "By the 25th, probably, and by the 1st certainly, we will be there," he promised. Convinced more than ever that he had done right not to wait for Banks, Grant replied that he was going ahead on his own. Previously he had told him nothing of his plans, not even that he would not be meeting him; but now he did, on the off-chance that Banks might be of assistance. "Many days cannot elapse before the battle will begin which is to decide the fate of Vicksburg," he wrote, "but it is impossible to predict how long it may last. I would urgently request, therefore, that you join me or send all the force you can spare to co-operate in the great struggle for opening the Mississippi River."

Similarly, at this near-final moment, he got off a dispatch to the general-in-chief, announcing that he was leaving Banks to fend for himself against Port Hudson while the Army of the Tennessee cut loose from its base at Grand Gulf and plunged inland in order to come upon Vicksburg from the rear. "I knew well that Halleck's caution would lead him to disapprove of this course," he subsequently explained; "but it was the only one that gave any chance of success." Besides, such messages were necessarily slow in transmission, having to be taken overland from Hard Times to Milliken's Bend, then north by steamboat all the way to Cairo before they could be put on the wire, and Grant saw a certain advantage in this arrangement. "The time it would take to communicate with Washington and get a reply would be so great that I could not be interfered with until it was demonstrated whether my plan was practicable."

This done, he turned to putting the final touches to the plan he had evolved. McClernand would move up the left bank of the Big Black, guarding the crossings as he went, and strike beyond Fourteen Mile Creek at Edwards Station, on the railroad sixteen miles east of Vicksburg. McPherson would move simultaneously against Jackson, and Sherman would be on call to assist either column, depending on which ran into the stiffest resistance. On the 11th, Grant advanced all three to

their jump-off positions: McClernand on the left, as near Fourteen Mile Creek as possible "without bringing on a general engagement," Sherman in the center, beyond Cayuga, and McPherson on the right, near Utica. "Move your command tonight to the next crossroads if there is water," Grant told McPherson, "and tomorrow with all activity into Raymond. . . . We must fight the enemy before our rations fail, and we are equally bound to make our rations last as long as possible."

Before dawn the following morning, May 12, they were off. The second phase of the campaign designed for the capture of Vicksburg was under way.

Advancing through a rugged and parched region, McClernand's troops found that the only way they could quench their thirst, aggravated by the heat of the day and the dust of the country roads, was to drive the opposing cavalry beyond Fourteen Mile Creek, which was held by a rebel force covering Edwards Station, some four miles to the north. By midafternoon they had done just that. "Our men enjoyed both the skirmish and the water," the commander of the lead division reported. Sherman, coming up on the right, accomplished this same purpose by throwing "a few quick rounds of cannister" at the gray vedettes, who promptly scampered out of range. Pioneers rebuilt a bridge the Confederates had burned as they fell back, and several regiments crossed the creek at dusk, establishing a bridgehead while the two corps went into bivouac on the south bank, prepared to advance on Edwards in the morning.

But that was not to be. McPherson, when within two miles of Raymond at 11 o'clock that morning, had encountered an enemy force of undetermined strength, "judiciously posted, with two batteries of artillery so placed as to sweep the road and a bridge over which it was necessary to pass." This was in fact a single brigade of about 4000 men, recently arrived from Port Hudson under John Gregg, who had come out from Jackson the day before, under orders from Pemberton to cover the southwest approaches to the capital. Informed that the Federals were moving on Edwards, over near the Big Black River, he assumed that the blue column marching toward him from Utica was only "a brigade on a marauding excursion," and he was determined not only to resist but also, if possible, to slaughter the marauders. The result was a sharp and—considering the odds—surprisingly hot contest, in which seven butternut regiments took on a whole Union corps.

McPherson threw Logan's division against the wooded enemy position, only to have it bloodily repulsed. While the other two were coming forward, Logan rallied in time to frustrate a determined counterattack and follow it up with one of his own. By now, however, having learned what it was he had challenged —and having suffered 514 casualties, as compared to McPherson's 442—Gregg had managed to disengage and was withdrawing through Raymond. Five miles to the east, one third of the distance to Jackson, he met W. H. T. Walker, who had marched out to join him with a thousand men just arrived from South Carolina. Gregg halted and faced about, ready to try his hand again; but there was no further action that day. Entering Raymond at 5 o'clock, McPherson decided to stop for the night. "The rough and impracticable nature of the country, filled with ravines and dense undergrowth, prevented anything like an effective use of artillery or a very rapid pursuit," he explained in a sundown dispatch to the army commander.

Grant was seven miles away, at the Dillon plantation on Fourteen Mile Creek with Sherman, and when he learned the outcome of the battle whose guns he had heard booming, five miles off at first, then fading eastward into silence, he revised his over-all plan completely. Edwards could wait. If Jackson was where the enemy was—and the determined resistance at Raymond seemed to indicate as much—he would go after him in strength; he would risk no halfway job in snuffing out a segment of the rebel army concentrated near a rail hub that gave it access to reinforcements from all quarters of the South.

Accordingly, at 9.15 he sent orders assigning all three of his corps commanders new objectives for tomorrow and prescribing that each would begin his march "at daylight in the morning." McPherson would move against Clinton, on the railroad nine miles north, then eastward that same distance along the right-of-way to Jackson. Sherman would turn due east from his present bivouac at Dillon, swinging through Raymond so as to come upon the objective from the south. McClernand, after detaching one division to serve as a rear guard in the event that the Confederates at Vicksburg attempted to interfere by crossing the Big Black, would come along behind Sherman and McPherson, prepared to move in support of either or both as they closed in on the Mississippi capital.

Such were Grant's instructions, and presently he had cause to believe that he had improvised aright. Two days ago McPherson had passed along a rumor that "some of the citizens in the vicinity of Utica say Beauregard is at or near Jackson." If the Charleston hero was there it was practically certain he had not come alone. And now there arrived a second dispatch from McPherson, headed 11 P.M. and relaying another rumor that heavy Confederate reinforcements were moving against him out of Jackson, intending to fight again at Raymond soon after sunup. He did not know how much fact there was in this, he added, but he would "try to be prepared for them." Grant had confidence in McPherson, especially when he was forewarned as he was now, and did not bother to reply. Besides, whether it was true or false that the rebels were marching in force to meet him west of their capital, he already had made provisions to counter such a threat by ordering all but one of his ten divisions, some 40,000 men in all, to move toward a convergence on that very objective "at daylight in the morning."

All three columns moved on schedule. By early afternoon McPherson was in Clinton, nine miles from Jackson, and Sherman was six miles beyond Raymond, about the same distance from the Mississippi capital. A lack of determined resistance seemed to indicate that last night's rumor of heavy reinforcements was in error, and this, plus reports from scouts that Pemberton had advanced in force to the vicinity of Edwards, caused Grant to modify his strategy again. McPherson was instructed to spend the rest of the day wrecking the railroad west of Clinton, then resume his eastward march at first light tomorrow, May 14, tearing up more track as he went. Sherman, half a dozen miles to the south, would regulate his progress so that both corps would approach the Jackson defenses simultaneously.

McClernand, instead of following along to furnish unneeded support, would turn north at Raymond and march on Bolton Depot, eight miles west of Clinton,

occupying a strong position in case Pemberton attempted a farther advance along the railroad toward his
threatened capital. There was of course the possibility
that the Confederate commander might lunge southward, across Fourteen Mile Creek, with the intention of
attacking the Federal army's rear and severing its connection with Grand Gulf: in which case he would be re-
moving himself from the campaign entirely, at least for
the period of time required for him to discover that he
had plunged into a vacuum. For Grant not only had no
supply line; he had no rear, either, in the sense that
Pemberton might suppose. Such rear as Grant had he
had brought with him, embodied in McClernand, who
now had orders to take up a position at Bolton, astride
the railroad about midway between Vicksburg and Jackson, facing west. Moreover, once the capital had fallen
and the blue army turned its attention back to its prime
objective, the blufftop citadel forty-five miles away,
what was now its rear would automatically become its
front; McClernand, already in position for an advance,
once more would take the lead, with Sherman and
McPherson in support. For all the improvisatorial nature of his tactics, Grant, like any good chess player, was
keeping a move or two ahead of the game.

By midmorning of May 14, slogging eastward under
a torrential rain that quickly turned the dusty roads into
troughs of mud, Sherman was within three miles of
Jackson. At 10 o'clock, while peering through the steely
curtain of the downpour to examine the crude fortifications to his front, he heard the welcome boom of guns
off to the north; McPherson was on schedule and in
place. While Sherman reconnoitered toward Pearl
River for an opening on the flank, McPherson deployed
for a time-saving frontal attack, to be launched astride

the railroad. He waited an hour in the rain, lest the cartridge boxes of his troops be filled with water, like buck-
ets under a tap, when they lifted the flaps to remove
their paper-wrapped ammunition, and then at 11
o'clock, the rain having slacked to a drizzle at last, ordered his lead division forward across fields of shin-
deep mud.

The rebel pickets faded back to the shelter of their
intrenchments, laying down a heavy fire that stopped
the bluecoats in their tracks and flung them on their
faces in the mud. By now it was noon. McPherson impa-
tiently reformed his staggered line, having lost an even
300 men, and sent the survivors forward again. This
time they found the rebel infantry gone. Only a handful
of cannoneers had remained behind to serve the seven
guns left on line and be captured by McPherson's jubi-

lant soldiers. Sherman had the same experience, two miles to the south, except that he found ten guns in the abandoned works he had outflanked. Not only were his spoils thus greater than McPherson's; his casualties were fewer, numbering only 32. The Confederates, under Gregg and Walker, who had fallen back from east of Raymond the night before, had lost just over 200 men before pulling out of their trenches to make a hairbreadth getaway to the north.

The Battle of Jackson was over, such as it was, and Grant had taken the Mississippi capital at a bargain price of 48 killed, 273 wounded, and 11 missing.

He was there to enjoy in person the first fruits of today's sudden and inexpensive victory. Sherman, riding in from the south—and noting with disapproval some "acts of pillage" already being committed by early arrived bluecoats under the influence "of some bad rum found concealed in the stores of the town"—was summoned by a courier to the Bowman House, Jackson's best hotel, where he found Grant and McPherson celebrating the capture of Jeff Davis's home-state capital, the third the South had lost in the past two years. From the lobby they had a view, through a front window, of the State House where the rebel President had predicted, less than six months ago, that his fellow Mississippians would "meet and hurl back these worse than vandal hordes."

Quick as the two generals had been to reach the heart of town, riding in ahead of the main body, they were slower than the army commander's young son Fred. His mother and brother had gone back North after the second running of the Vicksburg batteries, but Fred had stayed on to enjoy the fun that followed, wearing his fa-

ther's dress sword and sash—which the general himself
had little use for, and almost never wore—as badges of
rank. Grant, an indulgent parent, later explained that
the boy "caused no trouble either to me or his mother,
who was at home. He looked out for himself and was in
every battle of the campaign. His age, then not quite
thirteen, enabled him to take in all he saw, and then to
retain a recollection of it that would not be possible in
more mature years." Fred's recollection of the capture
of Jackson was saddened, however, by his failure to get a
souvenir he badly wanted. He and a friendly journalist
had seen from the outskirts of town a large Confederate
flag waving from its staff atop the golden dome of the
capitol. Mounted, they hurried ahead of the leading infantry column, tethered their horses in front of the big
stone building, and raced upstairs—only to meet, on his
way down, "a ragged, muddy, begrimed cavalryman"
descending with the rebel banner tucked beneath his
arm. For Fred, a good measure of the glory of Jackson's
capture had departed, then and there.

Grant could sympathize with the boy's disappointment, but he had just been handed something considerably more valuable to him than the lost flag or even the
seventeen guns that had been taken in the engagement
that served as prelude to the occupation of the capital.
Charles Dana arrived in mid-celebration with a dispatch
just delivered by a courier from Grand Gulf. Signed by
the Secretary of War and dated May 5, it had been sent
in response to a letter in which Dana had given him a
summation of Grant's plan "to lose no time in pushing
his army toward the Big Black and Jackson, threatening
both and striking at either, as is most convenient. . . . He
will disregard his base and depend on the country for
meat and even for bread." Now Stanton replied:

General Grant has full and absolute authority to enforce his own commands, to remove any person who,
by ignorance, inaction, or any cause, interferes with or
delays his operations. He has the full confidence of the
Government, is expected to enforce his authority, and
will be firmly and heartily supported; but he will be
responsible for any failure to exert his powers. You
may communicate this to him.

There was more here than met the eye. Stanton of
course had authority over Halleck, so that if—or rather,
as Grant believed from past experience, *when*—the time
came for the general-in-chief to protest that Grant had
disobeyed orders by abandoning Banks and striking out
on his own, he would find—if indeed he had not found
already—that Stanton, and presumably Lincoln as well,
had approved in advance the course Grant had adopted.
Nor was that all. Dana, having long since taken a position alongside the army commander in his private war
against McClernand, had been keeping the Secretary
copiously posted on the former congressman's military
shortcomings, large and small, and feeling him out as to
what the administration's reaction would be when
Grant decided the time had come for him to swing the
ax. Now the answer was at hand. Grant not only had
"full and absolute authority" to sit in judgment; he
would in fact be held "responsible for any failure to
exert his powers" in all matters pertaining to what he
considered his army's welfare and the progress of what
Stanton called his "operations," whether against the
rebels or McClernand.

It was no wonder then—protected as he now was
from the wrath of his immediate superior, as well as
from the machinations of his ranking subordinate—

that he was in good spirits during the hotel-lobby victory celebration.

All around him, the town was in a turmoil. "Many citizens [had] fled at our approach," one Federal witness later recalled, "abandoning houses, stores, and all their personal property, without so much as locking their doors. The Negroes, poor whites, and it must be admitted some stragglers and bummers from the ranks of the Union army, carried off thousands of dollars worth of property from houses, homes, shops and stores, until some excuse was given for the charge of 'northern vandalism,' which was afterwards made by the South. The streets were filled with people, white and black, who were carrying away all the stolen goods they could stagger under, without the slightest attempt at concealment and without let or hindrance from citizens or soldiers.... In addition ... the convicts of the penitentiary, who had been released by their own authorities, set all the buildings connected with that prison on fire, and their lurid flames added to the holocaust elsewhere prevailing." He observed that "many calls were made upon [Grant] by citizens asking for guards to protect their private property, some of which perhaps were granted, but by far the greater number [of these petitioners] were left to the tender mercies of their Confederate friends."

After all, Grant had not brought his army here to protect the private property of men in rebellion against the government that army represented; nor, for that matter, had it ever been his custom to deny his soldiers a chance at relaxation they had earned, even though that relaxation sometimes took a rather violent form. His purpose, rather, was to destroy all public property such as might be of possible comfort to the Confederacy. This applied especially to the railroads, the wrecking of which would abolish the Mississippi capital as a transportation hub, at least through the critical period just ahead. But that other facilities were not neglected was observed by a witness who testified that "foundries, machine shops, warehouses, factories, arsenals, and public stores were fired as fast as flames could be kindled." Sherman was the man for this work, Grant decided, and he gave him instructions "to remain in Jackson until he destroyed that place as a railroad center and manufacturing city of military supplies."

Meanwhile there was the campaign to get on with; Pemberton was hovering to the west, already on the near side of the Big Black, and beyond him there was Vicksburg, the true object of all this roundabout marching and such bloodshed as had so far been involved. McPherson was told to get his corps in hand and be prepared to set out for Bolton Depot at first light tomorrow to support McClernand, whose corps was no longer the army's rear guard, but rather its advance.

Having attended to this, Grant joined Sherman for a little relaxation of his own; namely, a tour of inspection to determine which of the local business establishments would be spared or burned. In the course of the tour they came upon a cloth factory which, as Grant said later, "had not ceased work on account of the battle nor for the entrance of Yankee troops." Outside the building "an immense amount of cotton" was stacked in bales; inside, the looms were going full tilt, tended by girl operatives, weaving bolts of tent cloth plainly stamped C.S.A. No one seemed to notice the two generals, who watched for some time in amused admiration of such oblivious industry. "Finally," Grant said afterwards, "I told Sherman I thought they had done work enough. The operatives were told they could leave and take with them what cloth they could carry. In a few minutes cotton and factory were in a blaze."

This done, Grant returned to the Bowman House for his first night's sleep on a mattress in two weeks. Joe Johnston, he was told, had occupied the same room the night before.

★ 5 ★

Johnston—not Beauregard, as rumor had had it earlier—had arrived at dusk the day before, at the end of a grueling three-day train ride from Tennessee by way of Atlanta, Montgomery, Mobile, and Meridian, only to find the Mississippi capital seething with reports of heavy Union columns advancing from the west. As night closed in, a hard rain began to fall, shrouding the city and deepening the Virginian's gloom still further, as was shown in a wire he got off to Seddon after dark: "I arrived this evening finding the enemy's force between this place and General Pemberton, cutting off communication. I am too late."

To Pemberton, still on the far side of the Big Black, he sent a message advising quick action on that general's part. To insure delivery, three copies were forwarded by as many couriers. "I have lately arrived, and learn that Major General Sherman is between us, with four divisions, at Clinton," Johnston wrote. "It is important to

re-establish communications, that you may be reinforced. If practicable, come up in his rear at once. To
beat such a detachment would be of immense value.
The troops here could cooperate. All the strength you
can quickly assemble should be brought. Time is all important."

He had at Jackson, he presently discovered, only two
brigades of about 6000 men with which to oppose the
25,000 Federals who were knocking at the western gates
next morning. After a sharp, brief skirmish and the sacrifice of seventeen guns to cover a withdrawal, he retreated seven miles up the Canton road to Tugaloo,
where he halted at nightfall, unpursued, and sent another message to Pemberton, from whom he had heard
nothing since his arrival, informing him that the capital
had been evacuated. He was expecting another "12,000
or 13,000" troops from the East, he said, and "as soon as
[these] reinforcements are all up, they must be united to
the rest of the army. I am anxious to see a force assembled that may be able to inflict a heavy blow upon the
enemy. . . . If prisoners tell the truth, the force at Jackson must be half of Grant's army. It would decide the
campaign to beat it, which can only be done by concentrating, especially when the remainder of the eastern
troops arrive." He himself could do little or nothing
until these men reached him, reducing the odds to
something within reason, but he did not think that
Pemberton should neglect any opportunity Grant afforded meanwhile, particularly in regard to his lines of
supply and communication. "Can he supply himself
from the Mississippi?" Johnston asked. "Can you not
cut him off from it, and above all, should he be compelled to fall back for want of supplies, beat him?"

This last was in accord with Pemberton's own decision, already arrived at before the second message was received. The first, delivered by one of the three couriers that morning at Bovina Station, nine miles east of Vicksburg, had taken him greatly by surprise. He had expected Johnston to come to his assistance in defense of the line along or just in front of the Big Black; yet here that general was, requesting him "if practicable" to come to *his* assistance by marching against the enemy's rear at Clinton, some twenty miles away. Pemberton replied that he would "move at once with the whole available force," explaining however that this included only 17,500 troops at best, since the remaining 9000 under his command were required to man the Warrenton-Vicksburg-Haines Bluff defenses, as well as the principal crossings of the Big Black, which otherwise would remain open in his rear, exposing the Gibraltar of the West to sudden capture by whatever roving segment of the rampant blue host happened to lunge in that direction. "In directing this move," he felt obliged to add, by way of protest, "I do not think you fully comprehend the position Vicksburg will be left in; but I comply at once with your request."

So he said. However, when he rode forward to Edwards, where his mobile force of three divisions under Loring, Carter Stevenson, and Bowen was posted four miles east of the Big Black, he learned that a Union column, reportedly five divisions strong—it was in fact McClernand's corps, with Blair attached as guard for the wagon train—was at Raymond, in position for a northward advance on Bolton. If Pemberton marched on Clinton, as Johnston suggested, ignoring this threat to his right flank as he moved eastward along the railroad, he would not only be leaving Vicksburg and the remaining two divisions under M. L. Smith and John H.

Forney in grave danger of being gobbled up while his back was turned; he would also be exposing his east-bound force to destruction at the hands of the other half of the Northern army. Perplexed by this dilemma, and mindful of some advice received two days ago from Richmond that he "add conciliation to the discharge of duty"—"Patience in listening to suggestions . . . is sometimes rewarded," Davis had added—he decided the time had come for him to call a council of war, something he had never done before in all his thirty years of military service.

Assembling the general officers of the three divisions at Edwards Station shortly after noon, he laid John-ston's message before them and outlined the tactical problems it posed. Basically, what he had to deal with was a contradiction of orders from above. As he under-stood the President's wishes, he was not to risk losing Vicksburg by getting too far from it, whereas Johnston was suggesting a junction of their forces near Jackson, forty miles away, in order to engage what he called a "detachment" of four—in fact, five—divisions, with-out reference to or apparent knowledge of the five-division column now at Raymond, both of which out-numbered the Confederates at Edwards. Pemberton, on the other hand, did not strictly agree with either of his two superiors, preferring to await attack in a prepared position near or behind the Big Black River, with a chance of following up a repulse with a counterattack designed to cut off and annihilate the foe.

These three views could not be reconciled, but nei-ther did he consider that any one of them could be ig-nored; so that, like the nation at large, this Northerner who sided with the South was torn and divided against himself. That was his particular nightmare in this nightmare interlude of his country's history. According to an officer on his staff, the Pennsylvanian's trouble now and in the future was that he made "the capital mistake of trying to harmonize instructions from his superiors diametrically opposed to each other, and at the same time to bring them into accord with his own judgment, which was averse to the plans of both."

Nor was the council of much assistance to him in finding a way around the impasse. Though a majority of the participants favored complying with Johnston's suggestion that the two forces be united, they were obliged to admit that it could not be accomplished by a direct march on Clinton, which was plainly an invitation to disaster. Meanwhile Pemberton's own views, as he told Johnston later, "were strongly expressed as unfavorable to any advance which would remove me from my base, which was and is Vicksburg." Apparently he limited himself to this negative contention. But finally Loring —known as "Old Blizzards" since his and Tilghman's spirited repulse of the Yankee gunboats above Greenwood—suggested an alternate movement, southeast nine miles to Dillon, which he believed would sever Grant's connection with Grand Gulf and thus force him either to withdraw, for lack of supplies, or else to turn and fight at a disadvantage in a position of Pemberton's choice. Stevenson agreed, along with others, and Pemberton, though he disliked the notion of moving even that much farther from Vicksburg, "did not, however, see fit to put my own judgment and opinions so far in opposition as to prevent a movement altogether."

He approved the suggestion, apparently for lack of having anything better to offer, and adjourned the council after giving the generals instructions to be ready to march at dawn. At 5.40, on the heels of the adjournment, he got off a message informing Johnston of his intentions. "I shall move as early tomorrow morning as practicable with a column of 17,000 men," he wrote, explaining the exact location of Dillon so that Johnston would have no trouble finding it on a map which was enclosed. "The object is to cut the enemy's communications and to force him to attack me, as I do not consider my force sufficient to justify an attack on the enemy in position or to attempt to cut my way to Jackson."

Johnston received this at 8.30 next morning, May 15, by which time he had withdrawn another three miles up the Canton road, still farther from the intended point of concentration at Clinton. Though the message showed that Pemberton had anticipated the Virginian's still unreceived suggestion that he attempt to "cut [Grant] off from [the Mississippi]," Johnston no longer favored such a movement. "Our being compelled to leave Jackson makes your plan impracticable," he replied, and repeated—despite Pemberton's objection to being drawn still farther from his base—his preference for an eastward march by the mobile force from Vicksburg: "The only mode by which we can unite is by your moving directly to Clinton, informing me, that [I] may move to that point with about 6000 troops. I have no means of estimating the enemy's force at Jackson. The principal officers here differ very widely, and I fear he will fortify if time is left him. Let me hear from you immediately."

Evidently Johnston believed that Grant was going to hole up in the Mississippi capital and thus allow him time to effect a junction between the Vicksburg troops and his own, including the "12,000 or 13,000" reinforcements expected any day now from the East. If so, he was presently disabused. A reply from Pemberton, written early the following morning but not delivered until after dark, informed him that the advance on Dillon—badly delayed anyhow by the need for building a bridge across a swollen creek—had been abandoned, in accordance with his wishes, and the direction of march reversed. It was Pemberton's intention, as explained in the message, to move north of the railroad, swing wide through Brownsville to avoid the mass of Federals reported to be near Bolton, and converge on Clinton as instructed. "The order of countermarch has been issued," he wrote, and followed a description of his proposed route with the words: "I am thus particular, so that you may be able to make a junction with this army."

The Vicksburg commander at last had abandoned his objections to what Johnston had called "the only mode by which we can unite." He was, or soon would be, moving east toward his appointed destination. But there was an ominous postscript to the message, written in evident haste and perhaps alarm: "Heavy skirmishing is now going on to my front."

★   ★   ★

What that portended Johnston did not know; but Grant did. Before he retired to the hotel room his adversary had occupied the night before the fall of Jackson, he received from McPherson one of the three copies of Johnston's message urging Pemberton to "come up in [Sherman's] rear at once." This windfall was the result of a ruse devised some months ago by Hurlbut, who banished from Memphis, with considerable fanfare, a citizen found guilty of "uttering disloyal and threatening sentiments," though he was in secret, as Hurlbut knew, a thoroughly loyal Union man. The expulsion, along with his continued expression of secessionist views after his removal to the Mississippi capital, won him the sympathy and admiration of the people there: so much so, indeed, that he was one of the three couriers entrusted with copies of Johnston's urgent message. He delivered it, however, not to Pemberton but to McPherson, who passed it promptly along to Grant.

"Time is all important," the Virginian had written. Grant agreed. By first light next morning, May 15, McPherson was marching west from the capital, leaving Sherman to accomplish its destruction while he himself moved toward a junction with McClernand, who had been instructed simultaneously by Grant: "Turn all your forces toward Bolton Station, and make all dispatch in getting there. Move troops by the most direct road from wherever they may be on the receipt of this order."

McPherson's three divisions had seventeen miles to go, and McClernand's four—five, including Blair—were variously scattered, from Raymond back to Fourteen Mile Creek. Each corps got one division to Bolton by late afternoon—Hovey and Logan, in that order—while the others camped along the roads at sundown. Carr and Osterhaus were three miles south, with A. J. Smith between them and Raymond, where Blair was. John McArthur and Marcellus Crocker, commanding McPherson's other two divisions, were bivouacked beside the railroad leading back to Clinton. Riding out from Jackson to that point before nightfall, Grant ordered McClernand to move on Edwards in the morning, supported by McPherson, but warned him "to watch for the enemy and not bring on an engagement unless he felt very certain of success."

The fog of war, gathering again to obscure the Confederate purpose, had provoked this note of caution; but it was dispersed once more at 5 o'clock next morning, when two Union-sympathizing employees of the Vicksburg-Jackson Railroad were brought to Grant at Clinton. They had passed through Pemberton's army in the night, they said, and could report that it was moving east of Edwards with a strength of about 25,000 men.

Though this was in fact some 7500 high, it was still some 10,000 fewer than Grant had on hand. But he was taking no unavoidable chances. Deciding to ignore Johnston, who by now was a day's march north of Jackson at Calhoun Station, he ordered Sherman to "put one division with an ammunition train on the road at once, with directions to its commander to march with all possible speed until he comes upon our rear." The remaining division was to hurry its demolition work and follow along as soon as might be. The orders to McClernand and McPherson were unaltered; all that was changed by this second dispersal of the war fog was the weight of the blow about to be delivered. Now that he knew Pemberton's strength and had him spotted, Grant intended to hit him with everything he had.

At about the time the railroad men were telling all they knew, McClernand started forward in high spirits. "My corps, again, led the advance," he was to say proudly in a letter giving his friend Lincoln an account of the campaign. Such was indeed the case. Three roads led west from the vicinity of Bolton to a junction east of Edwards, and McClernand used all three: Hovey on the one to the north, Osterhaus and Carr on the one in the middle, and Smith on the one to the south. Blair followed Smith, and McPherson's three divisions followed Hovey. Rebel cavalry was soon encountered, gray phantoms who fired and scampered out of range while the blue skirmishers flailed the woods with bullets. Then at

7.30, five miles short of Edwards, Smith came upon a screen of butternut pickets and dislodged them, exposing a four-gun battery, which he silenced. He wanted to plunge on, despite the signs that the high ground ahead was occupied in strength, but McClernand told him to hold what he had till Blair came up to keep his exposed left flank from being turned.

Immediately on the heels of this, a rattle of gunfire from the north signified that Osterhaus and Hovey had also come upon johnnies to their front. McClernand inspected the rebel position as best he could from a distance and, finding it formidable, decided to hang on where he was until the situation could be developed. Having obeyed Grant's instructions "to watch for the enemy," he was also mindful of the injunction "not [to] bring on an engagement unless he felt very certain of success." At this point, with his various columns a mile or two apart and facing a wooded ridge a-swarm with graybacks, he was not feeling very certain about anything at all. What he mainly felt was lonely.

Countermarching in obedience to the message received early that morning from Johnston, Pemberton had been warned by his outriders of the Union host advancing westward along the three roads from Bolton and Raymond. When this danger was emphasized by the "heavy skirmishing" mentioned in the postscript to his reply that he was moving north and east toward a junction at Clinton, he knew he had a fight on his hands, wanted or not, and to avoid the risk of being caught in motion, strung out on the road to Brownsville, he hastily put his troops in position for receiving the attack he knew was coming.

Whether his choice of ground was "by accident or design," as Grant ungenerously remarked, there could be no doubt that Pemberton chose well. Just south of the railroad and within a broad northward loop of rain-swollen Baker's Creek, a seventy-foot eminence known as Champion Hill—so called because it was on a plantation belonging to a family of that name—caused the due-west road from Bolton to veer south around its flank, joining the middle road in order to cross a timbered ridge that extended southward for three miles, past the lower of the three roads along which the enemy was advancing. Pemberton placed Stevenson's division on the hill itself, overlooking the direct approach from Bolton, and Bowen's and Loring's divisions along the ridge, blocking the other two approaches. Here, in an opportune position of great natural strength, he faced as best he could the consequences of his reluctant and belated compliance with his superior's repeated suggestion that he abandon the security of his prepared lines, along and just in front of the Big Black, for an attack on the Federal "detachment" supposed to be at Clinton.

Now, however, as the thing turned out, it was Pemberton who was about to be attacked, a dozen miles short of his assigned objective. And here, precisely midway between Vicksburg and Jackson, both of which were twenty-two miles away, was fought what at least one prominent western-minded historian was to call "the most decisive battle of the Civil War."

Grant did not much like the look of things when he came riding out from Bolton and reached the front, where the road veered south beyond the Champion house, to find Hovey exchanging long-range shots with the enemy on the tall hill just ahead. It seemed to him, as he said later, that the rebels "commanded all the ground in range." However, unlike McClernand on the two roads to the south, he was not content to hold his own while waiting for the situation to develop more or less of its own accord. Logan's division having arrived, he sent it to the right, to prolong the line and feel for an opening in that direction. This was about 10 o'clock; he preferred to wait for Crocker to come up and lend the weight of McPherson's second division to the attack. But Hovey by now was hotly engaged, taking punishment from the batteries on the height and protesting that he must either go forward or fall back. Grant unleashed him.

A former Indiana lawyer, of whom it was said that he had taken to the army "just as if he expected to spend his life in it," Hovey drove straight up the steep acclivity to his front, flinging back successive Confederate lines, until he reached and seized the eleven guns that had been pounding him from near the crest. His men were whooping with delight, proud but winded, when they were struck in turn by a powerful counterattack launched from a fringe of woods along the crest. "We ran, and ran manfully," one among them declared, explaining how he and his fellows had been swept back from the captured guns and down the slope they had climbed. Reinforced by Crocker's lead brigade, which had just arrived under George Boomer, they managed to hang on at the foot of the hill; but only by the hardest. One officer called the fighting there "unequal, terrible, and most sanguinary." For half an hour, he said, the troops "on each side took their turn in driving and being driven."

It was obvious that Hovey, who had left about one third of his division lying dead or wounded on the hillside, could not hold out much longer unassisted. Then one of the survivors looked over his shoulder and saw the army commander speaking to the colonel in charge of Crocker's second brigade, which was coming forward along the road behind them. "I was close enough to see his features," the man was to recall. "Earnest they were, but sign of inward movement there was none." This was the Grant of Belmont, Donelson, and Shiloh, reacting to adversity here as he had reacted there. If the face was "cool and calculating," the soldier observed, it was also "careful and half-cynical." He could not catch the spoken words across the distance, but they were as characteristic as the calm, enigmatic mask or the habitual cigar stump that was wedged between its teeth.

"Hovey's division and Boomer's brigade are good troops," Grant was saying. "If the enemy has driven them he is not in good plight himself. If we can go in again here and make a little showing, I think he will give way."

But it developed that a good deal more than this one additional brigade would have to join the melee at the base of Champion Hill if Grant was to make what he called "a little showing." With McPherson's third divi-

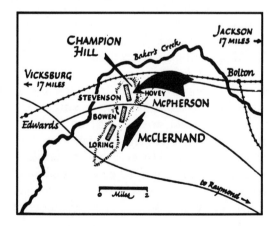

sion still too far away to be of help in time, he had to call on Logan, who had been sent to probe the rebel left. And this, as Grant admitted later, was the salvation of Pemberton today.

Logan had ridden around the north end of the hill, where the terrain was more open and gently rolling. He was sitting on horseback, surveying the scene, when a private who had wandered on his own came up to him and remarked laconically, gesturing off to the right: "General, I've been over the rise yonder, and it's my idea that if you'll put a regiment or two over there you'll get on their flank and lick 'em easy." Logan took a look for himself and saw that the man was right; Pemberton's left was "in the air" and the way to his rear was practically unobstructed, including the single bridge over Baker's Creek by which he could fall back.

Just then, however, the order to return and support the hard-pressed Hovey was received; Logan had to defer pressing the advantage the amateur tactician had discovered. Learning of this when it was too late to take full advantage of the maneuver, Grant remarked with hindsight: "Had McClernand come up with reasonable promptness, or had I known the ground as I did afterwards, I cannot see how Pemberton could have escaped with any organized force."

The reference to McClernand was something more, this time, than merely another point scored in the private war Grant waged on paper against the former congressman from his home state. Pemberton, observing the lack of enemy aggressiveness to the south, had reinforced his staggered left by shifting troops northward from his center, which was disposed along the ridge. Bowen brought them to Stevenson's assistance on the

run, arriving just in time to launch the savage counterattack that drove Hovey's exultant soldiers back down
the hill. Like Grant, however, Pemberton was finding
that he would need more than this to keep up the
pressure or even hold what he had won; so he sent for
Loring.

That general—referred to as "a scared turkey" by a
member of Stonewall Jackson's staff during the Romney
controversy, two Christmases ago, which had almost resulted in Jackson's retirement from the army and which
had been settled only with Loring's transfer to the West
—was already in a state of agitation because Bowen's
departure had left him alone on the ridge, with four blue
divisions in plain sight. When the summons came for
him to follow Bowen he declined. It would be suicidal,
he protested. All this time, the pressure against Stevenson was mounting, and when Logan added the weight
of his division it became unsupportable. Old Blizzards
moved at last, in response to repeated calls from Pemberton; but too late. He was scarcely in motion northward, about 4 o'clock, when the whole Confederate left
flank gave way.

Stevenson's men fell back in a panic, and though
Pemberton managed to rally them with a personal appeal, the damage was done. The eleven retaken guns
were lost again, this time for good, and Bowen's division
—having, as one officer remarked, "sustained its reputation by making one of its grand old charges, in which
it bored a hole through the Federal army"—now found
itself unsupported and nearly surrounded; whereupon it
"turned around and bored its way back again," following Stevenson's pell-mell flight down to Baker's Creek,
where it formed a rear-guard line in an attempt to hold
off the bluecoats until Loring too could make his escape

across the stream. Darkness fell and there was still no sign of Loring. Bowen waited another two hours, still maintaining his position, then gave it up and crossed in good order, burning the bridge when his last man was safe on the west bank.

Casualties here, after three hours of skirmishing and four of actual battle, had been much the heaviest of the campaign. Grant had lost 2441 men, Pemberton 3624, including prisoners cut off in the retreat—plus 11 guns and, as it turned out, all of Loring's division. Finding his path along the ridge blocked by victorious Federals, he swung west, then back south, and after a brief skirmish in which Lloyd Tilghman was killed by a cannonball while covering the withdrawal, made a rapid getaway around McClernand's open flank. By the following evening he was in Crystal Springs, twenty-five miles south of Jackson, and two days later he was with Johnston at Canton, an equal distance north of the capital. Except for the loss of Tilghman, whose courage and ability had been proved at Fort Henry and Fort Pemberton, Loring's disappearance was more a source of mystery than regret for the army of which he had lately been a part, since he had contributed little to the battle except to assist in the show of strength that immobilized McClernand.

Grant felt much the same way about McClernand, whose 15,000-man command—including Blair but not Hovey, who fought beyond McClernand's control and suffered almost half the army's casualties—had lost a total of 17 dead and 141 wounded in the course of what a brigade commander with McPherson called "one of the most obstinate and murderous conflicts of the war." Despite the fact that not a single man had been killed in three of the four divisions to the south, elation over the

victory scored by the three divisions to the north was
tinged with sorrow at its cost. "I cannot think of this
bloody hill without sadness and pride," Hovey was to
say, and an Illinois soldier, roaming the field when the
fighting was over, was struck by the thought that no
moral solution had been arrived at as a result of all the
bloodshed. "There they lay," he said of the dead and
wounded all around him, "the blue and the gray inter-
mingled; the same rich, young American blood flowing
out in little rivulets of crimson; each thinking he was in
the right."

Grant was more interested just now in military solu-
tions, and he believed he had reached one. "We were
now assured of our position between Johnston and
Pemberton," he subsequently declared, "without a possibility of a junction of their forces."

Others in his army believed they saw an even more
profitable outcome of the struggle on Champion Hill.
"Vicksburg must fall now," a participant wrote home
that night; "I think a week may find us in possession. It
may take longer," he added on second thought, "but the
end will be the same."

While Pemberton's depleted army fell back through
the darkness to a position covering the Big Black crossing, eight miles to the west, Grant let his soldiers sleep
till dawn, by which time Wilson's engineers had the
bridge over Baker's Creek rebuilt, then took up the pursuit. McClernand once more had the lead, though Blair
was detached to rejoin Sherman, who by now was close
at hand with his other two divisions. "We have made
good progress today in the work of destruction," he had
written Grant the day before, as he prepared to leave the
Mississippi capital. "Jackson will no longer be a point of

danger. The land is devastated for thirty miles around."

Next morning—Sunday, May 17—while Grant was crossing Baker's Creek to come to grips with Pemberton again, Sherman passed through Bolton and encountered other signs of devastation. Seeing some soldiers drawing water from a well in front of "a small hewn-log house" beside the road, he turned his horse in at the gate to get a drink. The place had been rifled, its furnishings wrecked and strewn about the yard, and though such acts of vandalism were fairly common at this stage of the campaign—brought on, so to speak, by an excess of skylark energy and delight that things were going so well for the army of invasion—this one appeared to have been committed with an extra measure of glee and satisfaction. When Sherman had one of the men hand him a book he saw lying on the ground beside the well, he found out why. It was a copy of the United States Constitution, with the name *Jefferson Davis* written on the title page.

This was the property the Confederate President's brother had secured for him the year before, when Brierfield was occupied by Butler, and though in the course of his December visit Davis had expressed the hope that he would be spared further depredations, it had not turned out that way. For him, as for his septuagenarian brother, the blue pursuit had been unrelenting. "Joe Davis's plantation was not far off," Sherman later recalled. "One of my staff officers went there, with a few soldiers, and took a pair of carriage horses, without my knowledge at the time. He found Joe Davis at home, an old man, attended by a young and affectionate niece; but they were overwhelmed with grief to see their country overrun and swarming with Federal troops."

Grant meanwhile was pushing west. About 7 o'clock

he came upon Pemberton's new position—and found it
even stronger, in some respects, than the one the rebels
had occupied "by accident or design" the day before.
This time, however, it was clearly by design. Not only
had the position been prepared overnight for just such
an emergency as the Confederates now faced; it was
here, in fact, that Pemberton had wanted to do his fighting in the first place.

The railroad bridge, which had been floored to provide for passage of his artillery and wagons, was at the
apex of a horseshoe bend of the Big Black, whose high
west bank afforded the guns emplaced along it an excellent field of fire out over the low-lying eastern bank and
the mile-long line of rifle pits already dug across the
open end of the horseshoe. Parapeted with bales of cotton brought from surrounding plantations, the line was
a strong one, even without the concentric support of the
guns emplaced to its rear, its front being protected by a
shallow bayou that abutted north on the river and south
on an impenetrable cypress brake. Whatever came at
the men in these pits would have to come straight up
the narrow railroad embankment, a suicidal prospect in
the face of all that massed artillery, or across the
rain-swollen bayou, beyond which open fields stretched
for nearly half a mile, allowing the attackers little or
no cover except for a single copse of woods about
three hundred yards in front of the far left, where guns
were also grouped in expectation. Still unaware that
Loring had skedaddled, Pemberton held this intrenched
bridgehead in hopes that Old Blizzards would show up
in time for a share in the impending fight at the gates of
Vicksburg, which was less than a dozen miles down the
road.

What showed up instead was the Yankees. One look

at the position his opponent had selected—Pemberton, after all, was a trained engineer, with a reputation for skill in the old army—told Grant that he stood an excellent chance of suffering the bloodiest of repulses if he attempted a frontal attack. Fortunately, though, he had instructed Sherman to swing north of Edwards for a crossing at Bridgeport, five miles upstream; so that all Grant had to do here, for the present, was keep up a show of strength to hold Pemberton in place while Sherman got his three divisions over the river above and came down on his flank.

But McClernand had other ideas. Troubled perhaps by his poor showing yesterday—though he would not hesitate presently to claim a lion's share of the credit for the Champion Hill success, on grounds that Hovey's division was from his corps—he moved vigorously today, sending Carr and Osterhaus respectively north and south of the railroad to confront the rebels crouched behind their cotton parapets. An assault was a desperate thing to venture against the dug-in Confederates and all those high-sited batteries in their rear, he knew, but he was quite as determined as Grant to "make a little showing," if not a big one. So was Michael Lawler, commanding Carr's second brigade, which had worked its way into the copse on the far right.

A big man, over 250 pounds in weight and so large of girth that he had to wear his sword belt looped over one shoulder, Lawler was Irish, forty-nine years old, and lately an Illinois farmer. His favorite Tipperary maxim, "If you see a head, hit it," was much in his mind as he peered across the chocolate-colored bayou at the rebel intrenchments three hundred yards away. Many heads were visible there, inviting him to hit them, and at last he could bear it no longer. Stripped to his shirt sleeves because of the midday heat, he stood up, swinging his sword, and ordered his four regiments forward on the double. The bayou was shoulder-deep in places, but the Iowa and Wisconsin soldiers floundered straight across it in what a reporter called "the most perilous and ludicrous charge I witnessed during the war," and came mud-plastered up to the enemy line with a whoop, having suffered 199 casualties in the three minutes that had elapsed since they left the copse.

The loss was small compared to the gain, however, for the rebels broke rearward, avoiding contact, only to find that the bridge had been set afire in their rear to keep the close-following bluecoats from surging across in their wake. Lawler's reward was 1200 prisoners—more men, he said, than he himself had brought into action—out of a final total of 1751 Confederates killed and captured, along with 18 guns, when the other brigades took fire from his example and rushed forward, breaking the gray line all down its length. Grant's losses were 276 killed and wounded, plus 3 missing, presumably left at the bottom of the bayou now in his rear.

Across the way, Pemberton had watched the disintegration of his skillfully drawn line and the quick subtraction of a brigade from his dwindling army. Neither was truly catastrophic; he still held the high west bank of the river, and the bridge the Federals might have used for a crossing was burning fiercely in the noonday sunlight; but he was depressed by the failure of his men to hold a position of such strength. If they would not stand fast here, where would they stand fast? Years later, a member of his staff was to say: "The affair of Big Black bridge was one which an ex-Confederate participant naturally dislikes to record."

It was unpleasant to remember, and it had been even more unpleasant to observe. Presently, moreover, word came from upstream that Sherman had forced a crossing at Bridgeport, capturing the dozen pickets on duty at that point. There was nothing for it now but to continue the retreat or be outflanked. Pemberton gave the necessary orders and the westward march got under way, as it had done after yesterday's bloodier action, except that this time there would be no halt until Vicksburg itself was reached.

Then what? He did not know how well his troops would fight with their backs to the wall, but this most recent action was not an encouraging example of their mettle. Some thirty hours ago he had had 17,500 effectives in his mobile force, and now he was down to a good deal less than half that many. In fact it was nearer a third, 5375 having been killed, wounded, or captured, while as many more had wandered off with Loring. As he rode westward, accompanied by his chief engineer, a young major named Samuel Lockett, Pemberton's distress increased and his confidence touched bottom. "Just thirty years ago," he said at last, breaking a long and painful silence, "I began my military career by receiving my appointment to a cadetship at the U.S. Military Academy, and today—that same date—that career is ended in disaster and disgrace."

Lockett tried to reassure the general by reminding him that two fresh divisions stood in the Vicksburg intrenchments, which had been designed to withstand repeated assaults by almost any number of men. Besides, he said, Joe Johnston would be reinforced at Canton in the event of a siege, and would come to the beleaguered city's relief with all the skill for which he was famous, North and South. "To all of which," the major recalled afterwards, "General Pemberton replied that my youth and hopes were the parents of my judgment; he himself did not believe our troops would stand the first shock of an attack."

A dispatch had already gone to Johnston that morning, announcing the results of yesterday's battle and warning that Haines Bluff would have to be abandoned if the Big Black position was outflanked or overrun. Accordingly, as the retreat got under way, orders were sent for the garrison on the Yazoo to fall back, all but two companies, who were to forward all stores possible and destroy the rest, "making a show of force until the approach of the enemy by land should compel them to retire." Provisions were much on Pemberton's mind, despite his dejection, and he issued instructions that, from Bovina on, "all cattle, sheep, and hogs belonging to private parties, and likely to fall into the hands of the enemy, should be driven within our lines." Similarly, corn was pulled from the fields along the way, "and all disposable wagons applied to this end." If it was to be a siege, food was likely to be as vital a factor as ammunition, and he did all he could in that respect.

The march continued, accompanied by the lowing of cows, the bleating of sheep, and the squealing of pigs, steadily westward. For all the Confederates knew, Sherman might have moved fast around their flank and beaten them to the goal. Then up ahead, as Pemberton was to remember it years later, "the outlines of the hill city rose slowly through the heated dust—Vicksburg and security. Passing raddled fields turning colorless from the powdered earth that rose beneath their tramp, the gray soldiers slacked off the turnpikes along the high ground until they came inside the city's breastworks. As word carried down the crooked line of march that the race to Vicksburg had been won, the footsore remnants in the rear flooded down the pike."

Sunset made a red glory over the Louisiana bayous; "The sky faded to a cool green and it was dark." Pemberton and his aides worked through the night, seeing to the comfort of the troops who had fought today and yesterday, bivouacked now in rear of the intrenchments, and inspecting the front-line defenses manned by the two divisions which had remained in the city all this time. Dawn gave light by which to check the overlapping fields of fire commanded by the 102 guns, light and heavy, emplaced along the semicircular landward fortifications. Midmorning brought reports from scouts that the two companies left at Haines Bluff were on their way to Vicksburg, having complied with the order to hold out as long as possible. Heavy columns of Federals were close behind them, while other blue forces were hard on the march from Bovina.

Before they arrived—as they presently did, to begin the investment—a messenger came riding in with a reply to yesterday's dispatch to Johnston, who had moved southwest from Canton to a position northeast of Brownsville. Pemberton's spirits had risen considerably since his confession of despair as he fell back from the Big Black the day before, but what his superior had to say was scarcely of a nature to raise them further. For one thing, the Virginian said nothing whatsoever about relief, either now or in the future. As he saw it, the choice had been narrowed to evacuation or surrender.

May 17, 1863.

LIEUTENANT GENERAL PEMBERTON:

Your dispatch of today . . . was received. If Haines Bluff is untenable, Vicksburg is of no value and cannot be held. If, therefore, you are invested at Vicksburg, you must ultimately surrender. Under such circumstances, instead of losing both troops and place, we must, if possible, save the troops. If it is not too late, evacuate Vicksburg and its dependencies, and march them to the northeast.

> Most respectfully, your obedient servant,
> J. E. JOHNSTON, General.

★　★　★

Even if Pemberton had wanted to follow this advice—which he did not, considering it in violation of orders from the Commander in Chief that the place be held at all costs—compliance was altogether beyond his means. Before he had time for more than brief speculation as to what effect these words might have on his chances of survival, Union guns were shelling his outer works. The siege had begun, and Grant was jockeying for positions from which to launch an all-out assault, intending to bring the three-week-old campaign, which had opened on his birthday, to the shortest possible end.

Yesterday's rout on the Big Black had seemed to indicate what the result of one hard smash at the rebel lines would be, and Grant's spirits had risen more or less in ratio to the droop of his opponent's. If roads could be found, he said as he watched the enemy abandon the high western bank, he intended to advance in three columns of one corps each, "and have Vicksburg or Haines Bluff tomorrow night." While Wilson and his engineers were collecting materials for replacing the burned railroad bridge, he rode up to Bridgeport and found Sherman hard at work laying India-rubber pontoons for a crossing in force. Soon after dark the first of his three divisions started over, their way lighted by pitch pine bonfires on both banks. Grant and his red-haired lieutenant sat on a log and watched the troops move westward over the Big Black, faces pale in the firelight and gun barrels catching glints from the flames as "the bridge swayed to and fro under the passing feet." Sherman was to remember it so. A water-colorist of some skill back in the days when there had been time for such diversions, he thought the present scene "made a fine war picture."

By daybreak all three divisions were across. Riding south to see whether McClernand and McPherson had done as well, Grant left instructions for Sherman to march northwest in order to interpose between Vicksburg and the forts on the Yazoo. By 10 o'clock this had been done. A detachment sent northward found Haines Bluff unoccupied, its big guns spiked, and made contact with the Union gunboats on the river below, signaling them to steam in close and tie up under the frowning blufftop that had defied them for so long. Grant now had the supply base he wanted, north of the city.

Presently he came riding up, to find his friend Sherman gazing down at the Chickasaw Bayou region below, from which he had launched his bloody and fruitless assault against these heights five months ago. Up to now, the Ohioan had had his reservations about this eighth attempt to take or bypass Vicksburg, saying flatly, "I tremble for the result. I look upon the whole thing as one of the most hazardous and desperate moves of this or any other war." Now his doubts were gone, replaced by enthusiasm: as was shown when he turned to Grant, standing quietly by, and abruptly broke the silence.

"Until this moment I never thought your expedition a success," he said; "I never could see the end clearly until now. But this is a campaign. This is a success if we never take the town."

Grant shared his friend's enthusiasm, if not his verbal exuberance, with regard to a situation brought about by a combination of careful strategy, flawlessly improvised tactics, sudden marches, and hard blows delivered with such triphammer rapidity that the enemy had never been given a chance to recover the balance he lost when the blue army, feinting coincidentally at Haines Bluff, swarmed ashore at Bruinsburg, forty-five air-line miles away. At no time in the past three weeks, moreover, had the outlook been so bright as it was now.

All three corps had crossed the Big Black, the final natural barrier between them and their goal, and were converging swiftly upon the hilltop citadel by three main roads so appropriate to their purpose that they might have been surveyed with this in mind. Sherman advanced from the northeast on the Benton road, McPherson from due east, along the railroad and the Jackson turnpike, and McClernand from the southeast on the Baldwin's Ferry road. By nightfall, after a few brief skirmishes along the ill-organized line of rebel outposts—invariably abandoned at the first suggestion of real pressure—the lead elements of all three columns were in lateral contact with each other and in jump-off positions for tomorrow's assault.

Next morning, May 19, while they completed their dispositions, the men were in high spirits. They were in fact, like Sherman, "a little giddy with pride" at the re-alization of all they had accomplished up to now. In the twenty days since they crossed the Mississippi, they had

marched 180 miles to fight and win five battles—Port
Gibson, Raymond, Jackson, Champion Hill, Big Black
River—occupy a Deep South capital, inflict over 7000
casualties at a cost of less than 4500 of their own, and
seize no less than fifty pieces of field artillery, not to
mention two dozen larger pieces they found spiked in
fortifications they outflanked. In all this time, they had
not lost a gun or a stand of colors, and they had never
failed to take an assigned objective, usually much more
quickly than their commanders expected them to do.
And now, just ahead, lay the last and largest of their objectives: Vicksburg itself, the ultimate prize for which
the capture of all those others had served as prelude.

Their belief that they would carry the place by storm,
here and now, was matched by Grant, who issued his
final orders before noon. "Corps commanders will push

forward carefully, and gain as close position as possible
to the enemy's works, until 2 P.M.; at [which] hour they
will fire three volleys of artillery from all the pieces in
position. This will be the signal for a general charge of
all the army corps along the whole line." A closing sentence, intended to forestall the lapse of discipline that
would attend a too-informal victory celebration, expressed the measure of his confidence that the assault
would be successful, bringing the campaign to a trium-
phant close today: "When the works are carried, guards
will be placed by all division commanders to prevent
their men from straggling from their companies."

At the appointed hour, the guns boomed and the blue
clots of troops rushed forward, shoulder to shoulder,
cheering as they vied for the honor of being first to scale
the ridge: whereupon, as if in response to the same signal, a long low cloud of smoke, torn along its bottom
edge by the pinkish yellow stabs of muzzle flashes,
boiled up with a great clatter from the rebel works
ahead. The racket was so tremendous that no man could
hear his own shouts or the sudden yelps of the wounded
alongside him.

What was immediately apparent, however, amid a
confusion of sound so uproarious that it was as if the
whole mad scene were being played in pantomime, was
that the assault had failed almost as soon as it got
started. Sherman, watching from a point of vantage near
the north end of the line, put it simplest in a letter he
wrote home that night: "The heads of the columns have
been swept away as chaff thrown from the hand on a
windy day." Others, closer up, had a more gritty sense
of what had happened. Emerging into the open, an Illinois captain saw "the very sticks and chips, scattered
over the ground, jumping under the hot shower of rebel

bullets." Startled, he and his company plunged forward, tumbled into a cane-choked ravine at the base of the enemy ridge, and hugged the earth for cover and concealment.

All up and down the line it was much the same for those who had not scattered rearward at the first burst of fire; once within point-blank musket range, there was little the attackers could do but try to stay out of sight until darkness gave them a chance to pull back without inviting a bullet between the shoulder blades. As they lay prone the fire continued, cutting the stalks of cane, one by one, so that "they lopped gently upon us," as if to assist in keeping them hidden. Through the remaining hours of daylight they stayed there, with bullets twittering just above the napes of their necks. Then they returned through the gathering dusk to the jump-off positions they had left five hours ago. Reaching safety after a hard run, the captain and other survivors of his company "stopped and took one long breath, bigger than a pound of wool."

Pemberton was perhaps as surprised as the bluecoats were at their abrupt repulse. In reporting to the President—the message would have to be smuggled out, of course, before it could be put on the wire for Richmond —that his army was "occupying the trenches around Vicksburg," he added proudly: "Our men have considerably recovered their morale."

Meanwhile he strengthened his defenses and improved the disposition of his 20,000 effectives. M. L. Smith's division had the left, Forney's the center, and Stevenson's the right, while Bowen's was held in immediate reserve, under orders to be prepared to rush at a moment's notice to whatever point needed bolstering. There was a crippling shortage of intrenching tools, only about five hundred being on hand. "They were entirely inadequate," an engineer officer later declared, but "the men soon improvised wooden shovels [and used] their bayonets as picks." They had indeed "considerably recovered," now that they had stopped running, and they were hungry for revenge for the humiliations they had been handed, particularly day before yesterday on the Big Black River. If the Yankees would keep coming at them the way they had come this afternoon, the Confederates hoped they would keep it up forever.

In point of fact, that was pretty much what Grant had in mind. He had suffered 942 casualties and inflicted less than 200, thus coming close to reversing the Big Black ratio, but he still thought the ridge could be carried by assault. Conferring next morning with his corps commanders he found them agreed that this first effort had failed, in Sherman's words, "by reason of the natural strength of the position, and because we were forced by the nature of the ground to limit our attacks to the strongest part of the enemy line, viz., where the three principal roads entered the city." Nothing could be done about the first of these two drawbacks, but the second could be corrected by careful reconnaissance. Better artillery preparations would also be of help, it was decided, in softening up the rebel works; moreover, the navy could add the weight of its metal from the opposite side of the ridge, Porter having returned from a two-week expedition up the Red River to Alexandria, where he had met Banks coming north from Opelousas on May 6. Grant told McClernand, Sherman, and McPherson to spend today and tomorrow preparing "for a renewed assault on the 22d, simultaneously, at 10 A.M."

Riding his line while the work was being pushed, he found the men undaunted by their repulse the day before, though they were prompt to let him know they were weary of the meat-and-vegetables diet on which they had been subsisting for the past three weeks. Turkey and sweet potatoes were fine as a special treat, it seemed, but such rich food had begun to pall as a regular thing. A private looked up from shoveling, recognized Grant riding by, and said in a pointed but conversational tone: "Hardtack." Others took up the call, on down the line, raising their voices with every repetition of the word, until finally they were shouting with all their might. "Hardtack! Hardtack!" they yelled as the army commander went past. "Hardtack! Hardtack!" Finally he reined in his horse and informed all those within earshot that the engineers were building a road from the Yazoo steamboat landing, "over which to supply them with everything they needed." At this, as he said later, "the cry was instantly changed to cheers." That night there was hardtack for everyone, along with beans, and coffee to wash it down. The soldiers woke next morning strengthened for the work that was now at hand.

For the first time in history, a major assault was launched by commanders whose eyes were fixed on the hands of watches synchronized the night before. This was necessary in the present case because the usual signal guns would not have been heard above the din of the preliminary bombardment, which included the naval weapons on both flanks, upstream and down, and six mortar boats already engaged for the past two days in what one defender contemptuously called "the grand but nearly harmless sport of pitching big shells into Vicksburg."

All night the 13-inch naval mortars kept heaving their 200-pound projectiles into the checkerboard pattern of the city's streets and houses, terrifying citizens huddled under their beds and dining-room tables. ("Vertical fire is never very destructive of life," the same witness remarked. "Yet the howling and bursting shells had a very demoralizing effect on those not accustomed to them.") Then at dawn the 200 guns on the landward side chimed in, raising geysers of dirt on the ridge where the Confederates were intrenched and waiting.

At 9.30, in compliance with Grant's request, Porter closed the range with four gunboats from below and took the lower water batteries under fire. He was supposed to keep this up until 10.30, half an hour past the scheduled time for the infantry assault to open, but since he could see no indication that the army had been successful in its storming attempt, he kept up the fire for an extra hour before dropping back downriver and out of range. One ironclad, the *Tuscumbia*, was severely battered and forced to retire before the others. Otherwise, though he reported that this was altogether the hottest fire his boats had yet endured, Porter suffered little damage in the bows-on fight, aside from a few men wounded. He could not see, however, that he had accomplished much in the way of punishing the defenders. Nor was there any evidence that the army had done any better.

As a matter of fact, the army had done a good deal worse, though not for lack of trying. At the appointed hour the men of all three corps rushed forward, the advance waves equipped with twenty-foot scaling ladders to be used against steep-walled strongpoints, of which there were many along the ridge ahead. "The rebel line, concealed by the parapet, showed no sign of unusual activity," Sherman observed from his point of vantage to the north, "but as our troops came in fair view, the enemy rose behind their parapet and poured a furious fire upon our lines. . . . For about two hours we had a severe and bloody battle, but at every point we were repulsed." It was much the same with McPherson and McClernand, to the south, who also lost heavily as a result of these white-of-their-eyes tactics employed by the Confederates. At several points, left and right and center, individual groups managed to effect shallow penetrations, despite what an Illinois colonel called "the most murderous fire I ever saw," but were quickly expelled or captured by superior forces the enemy promptly brought to bear from his mobile reserve. Those blue-coats who crouched in the ravines and ditches at the base of the ridge, taking shelter there as they had done three days ago, were dislodged by the explosion in their midst of 12-inch shells which the defenders rolled downhill after lighting the fuzes.

On McClernand's front a heavier lodgment was effected at one point, and the general, taking fire at the sight of his troops flaunting their banners on the rebel works, sent word to Grant that he had "part possession of two forts, and the stars and stripes are floating over them." If the other two corps "would make a diversion in my favor," he thought he could enlarge his gains and perhaps score an absolute breakthrough. At any rate, he earnestly declared, "a vigorous push ought to be made all along the line."

Grant was with Sherman when the message reached him. "I don't believe a word of it," he said. Sherman protested that the note was official and must be credited. Though he had just called off his own attack, admitting failure, he offered to renew it at once in the light

of this appeal from McClernand. Grant thought the
matter over, then told the redhead he "might try it
again" at 3 o'clock, if no contrary orders reached him
before that time. Riding south, he detached one of
McPherson's divisions to support McClernand and authorized a resumption of the attack on the center as
well.

Promptly at 3, Sherman launched his promised second assault, but found it "a repetition of the first,
equally unsuccessful and bloody." McPherson had the
same unpleasant experience. McClernand, still afire
with hope, threw the borrowed division into the fray—
though not in time to maintain, much less widen or
deepen, the penetration of which he had been so proud.
A whooping counterattack by T. N. Waul's Texas Le-
gion killed or captured all but a handful of Federals at
that point. By sundown the firing had died to a sputter,
and at nightfall the survivors crept back across the
corpse-pocked fields to the safety of the lines they had
left with such high hopes that morning.

Some measure of their determination and valor was
shown by a comparison of their losses today with those
of three days ago. The previous assault had ended with
two stands of colors left on the forward slope of the
enemy ridge; this time there were five. Moreover, the
casualties exceeded this five-two ratio. Less than a thousand men had fallen the time before, including 165
killed or missing, whereas this time the figures went
above three thousand—3199, to be exact—with 649 in
the killed-or-missing category. In other words, Grant
had lost in the past three days almost as many soldiers as
he had lost in the past three weeks of nearly continuous
battle and maneuver which had brought him within
sight of the ramparts of Vicksburg only to be repulsed.

He was furious. "This last attack only served to increase our casualties without giving any benefit whatever," he wrote some twenty years later, still chagrined. Quick as ever to shift the blame for any setback or evidence of shortcoming—at Belmont it had been overexcited "higher officers"; at Donelson it had been McClernand; at Shiloh it had been Prentiss and Lew Wallace, although the former most likely had saved him from defeat; at Iuka it had been Rosecrans and the wind —he notified Halleck, two days after the second Vicksburg repulse: "The whole loss for the day will probably reach 1500 killed and wounded. General McClernand's dispatches misled me as to the real state of facts, and caused much of this loss. He is entirely unfit for the position of corps commander, both on the march and on the battlefield. Looking after his corps gives me more labor and infinitely more uneasiness than all the remainder of my department." And yet, on the day of battle itself, he included that general's misleading claims in his own dispatch informing Halleck of the outcome. "Vicksburg is now completely invested," he declared. "I have possession of Haines Bluff and the Yazoo; consequently have supplies. Today an attempt was made to carry the city by assault, but was not entirely successful. We hold possession, however, of two of the enemy's forts, and have skirmishers close under all of them. Our loss was not severe." As he wrote, his optimism grew; for that was the reverse of the coin. He would no more admit discouragement than he would entertain self-blame. "The nature of the ground about Vicksburg is such that it can only be taken by a siege," he judged, but added: "It is entirely safe to us in time, I would say one week if the enemy do not send a large army upon my rear."

He did not regret having made the assaults; he only regretted that they had failed. Besides, he subsequently explained, his high-spirited troops had approached the gates of Vicksburg with a three-week cluster of victories to their credit; they would never have settled down willingly to the tedium of siege operations unless they had first been given the chance to prove that the place could not be taken by storm. Now that this had been demonstrated, though at the rather excessive price of 4141 casualties, they took to spadework with a will, constructing their own complex system of intrenchments roughly parallel to those of the rebels, which in a few places were not much more than fifty yards away.

As they delved in the sandy yellow clay of the hillsides or drew their beads on such heads as appeared above the enemy parapets, they were encouraged by news of tangential victories, particularly on the part of the navy, which was on a rampage now that the outlying Confederate defenses had been abandoned. An expedition made up of the *DeKalb* and three tinclads, all under John Walker, had been sent up the Yazoo on May 20, the day after the first assault, and returned on the 23d, the day after the second, to report that the rebels had set their Yazoo City navy yard afire at the approach of the Union vessels, the flames consuming three warships under construction on the stocks, for an estimated loss of $3,000,000. This meant that there would be no successor to the *Arkansas*, which was welcome news indeed. But Porter was unsatisfied; he sent the expedition back upriver the next morning.

This time Walker steamed to within a dozen miles of Fort Pemberton, beyond Greenwood, destroying steamboats and sawmills as he went, then came back downstream to push 180 miles up the winding Sunflower River, where he caught and burned still more fugitive rebel steamboats. Returning this second time, he could report that these streams were no longer arteries of supply for the Confederates below the confluence of the Tallahatchie and the Yalobusha, nearly one hundred air-line miles from the beleaguered Vicksburg bluff.

Pemberton took the news of this without undue distress. After all, the Yazoo and the Sunflower were no longer of much interest to him; the Father of Waters was now his sole concern, and only about a dozen miles of that. "I have decided to hold Vicksburg as long as possible," he had replied to Johnston's last-minute dispatch urging evacuation, "with the firm hope that the Government may yet be able to assist me in keeping this obstruction to the enemy's free navigation of the Mississippi River. I still conceive it to be the most important point in the Confederacy." His outlook improved with the repulse of the first Federal assault, and on the eve of the second he was asking: "Am I to expect reinforcements? From what direction, and how soon? . . . The men credit and are encouraged by a report that you are near with a large force. They are fighting in good spirits, and the reorganization is complete."

After the second repulse, however, the defenders were faced with an unpleasant problem. For three days —six, in the case of those who had fallen in the first assault—Grant's dead and injured lay in the fields and ditches at the base of the Confederate ridge, exposed to the fierce heat of the early Mississippi summer. The stench of the dead, whose bodies were swollen grotesquely, and the cries of the wounded, who suffered the added torment of thirst, were intolerable to the men who had shot them down; yet Grant would not ask for a truce for burial or treatment of these unfortunates, evidently thinking that such a request would be an admission of weakness on his part.

Finally Pemberton could bear it no longer. On the morning of May 25 he sent a message through the lines to the Union commander: "Two days having elapsed since your dead and wounded have been lying in our front, and as yet no disposition on your part of a desire to remove them being exhibited, in the name of humanity I have the honor to propose a cessation of hostilities for two hours and a half, that you may be enabled to remove your dead and dying men." To Pemberton's relief, Grant at last "acceded" to this proposal. At 6 P.M. all firing was suspended while the Federals came forward to bury the dead where they lay and bring comfort to such few men as had survived the three-day torture. This done, they returned through the darkness to their lines and the firing was resumed with as much fury as before.

In nothing was Grant more "unpronounceable" than in this. He would berate, and in at least one case attack with his fists, any man he saw abusing a dumb animal; he had, it was said to his credit, no stomach for suffering; he disliked above all to ride over a field where there had been recent heavy fighting; he would not eat a piece of meat until it had been cooked to a char, past any sign of blood or even pinkness. Yet this he could do to his own men, this abomination perhaps beyond all others of the war, without expressed regret or apparent concern.

However, this too was the reverse of a coin, the other side of which was his singleness of purpose, his quality of intense preoccupation with what he called "the business," meaning combat. He took his losses as they came —they had, in fact, about been made up already with the arrival that week of a division of reinforcements from Memphis, and would be more than made up with the arrival, early the following week, of a second such division, while four more were being alerted even now for the trip downriver from Tennessee, Missouri, and Kentucky to bring his mid-June total to 71,000 effectives—for the sake of getting on with the job to which he had set his hand. Long ago in Mexico, during a lull in the war, he had written home to the girl he was to marry: "If we have to fight, I would like to do it all at once and then make friends." He felt that way about it still, and now that he was calling the turn, he wanted no interludes or delays; he wanted it finished, and he believed the finish was in sight. "The enemy are now undoubtedly in our grasp," he told Halleck the day before the burial truce. "The fall of Vicksburg and the capture of most of the garrison can only be a question of time."

This was not to say there would be no more setbacks and frustrations. There would indeed, war being the chancy thing it was, and Grant knew it: which perhaps was why he had dropped his prediction, made two days before, that the fall of the city would be accomplished within "I would say one week."

And in fact there was one such mishap three days later, two days after the burial truce, this time involving the navy. In the course of drawing his lines for the siege, Sherman had begun to suspect, from the amount of artillery fire he drew, that the Confederates were shifting guns from their upper water batteries to cover the landward approaches, particularly on their far left. Requested by Grant to test the facts of the case, Porter on May 27 sent the *Cincinnati* to draw the fire of the guns "if still there," covering her movements with four other ironclads at long range. She started downriver at 7 o'clock in the morning, commanded by G. M. Bache, and by 10 the matter had been settled beyond doubt. Not only were the guns still there, but they sank the *Cincinnati*.

Rounding to in order to open fire, she took a pair of solids in her shell room and a third in her magazine. As she tried to make an upstream escape, a heavy shot drove through her pilot house and her starboard tiller was carried away, along with all three flagstaffs. Hulled repeatedly by plunging fire, she began filling rapidly. Bache, with five of his guns disabled in short order, tried to get beyond range and tie the vessel up to the east bank before she sank, but could not make it. She went down in three fathoms of water, still within range of the enemy guns, and what remained of her crew had to swim for their lives. The total loss, aside from the *Cincinnati* herself, was 5 killed, 14 wounded, and 15 missing, presumed drowned.

Convinced that Bache and his crew had done their best under disadvantageous circumstances, Porter accepted the loss of the ironclad—the third since his arrival in early December—as one of the accidents of war, and did not relax on that account his pressure against the rebels beleaguered on their bluff.

He already had the approval of Grant for his conduct of naval affairs. Replying to a message in which the admiral informed him that Banks, although he had wound up his West Louisiana campaign at last, would "not [be] coming here with his men. He is going to occupy the attention of Port Hudson, and has landed at Bayou Sara, using your transports for the purpose," Grant told Porter: "I am satisfied that you are doing all that can be done in aid of the reduction of Vicksburg. There is no doubt of the fall of the place ultimately, but how long it will be is a matter of doubt. I intend to lose no more men, but to force the enemy from one position to another without exposing my troops."

★ 6 ★

Banks had done a good deal more by now than merely "occupy the attention of Port Hudson." Crossing the Mississippi on the day after Grant's second repulse at Vicksburg, he completed his investment of the Louisiana stronghold on May 26, and next morning —simultaneous with the sinking of the *Cincinnati*, 240 winding miles upriver—launched his own all-out assault, designed to bring to a sudden and victorious end a campaign even more circuitous than Grant's. That general had covered some 180 miles by land and water before returning to his approximate starting point and placing his objective under siege, whereas Banks had marched or ridden about three times that far, as the thing turned out, to accomplish the same result.

However, not only was the distance greater; the numerical odds had been tougher, at least at the start. Back in mid-March, when Farragut ran two ships past the fuming hundred-foot bluff, Banks had maneuvered on the landward side, only to discover that the defenders had more men inside the works than he had on the outside. This gave him pause, as well it might, and while he pondered the problem he learned that Grant, whom he had expected to join him in reducing Port Hudson as a prelude to their combined movement against Vicksburg, was stymied north of the latter place, involved in a series of canal and bayou experiments which seemed likely to delay him for some time. Thinking it over, Banks decided to accomplish his assignment on his own. If he could not take Port Hudson, he would do as Grant was trying to do upriver. He would go around it.

It was not only that he was disinclined to wait and share the glory, politically ambitious though he was. He also believed he could not, and with cause. Nearly half of the 35,000 troops in his department were nine-month volunteers whose enlistments would be expiring between May and August; they would have to be used before summer or not at all. However, there was about as much need for caution as there was for haste, since more than half of this total, long- and short-term men alike, were required to garrison Baton Rouge, New Orleans, and various other points along the Mississippi and the Gulf. As a result of these necessary smaller detachments, his five divisions were reduced to about 5000 men each. Three of the five were with him near Port Hudson, under C. C. Augur, William Emory, and Cuvier Grover, while the fourth was at New Orleans under Thomas W. Sherman. Leaving Augur to hold Baton Rouge, Banks set out downriver with the other two on March 25 to join Godfrey Weitzel, commanding his fifth division at Brashear City, near Grand Lake and the junction of the Atchafalaya River and Bayou Teche.

Previously, in January, Weitzel had ascended the former stream for a few miles, intending to establish an alternate route, well removed from the guns of Port Hudson, from the mouth of Red River to the Gulf. In this he had failed, not so much because of interference from Richard Taylor's scratch command of swamp-bound rebels, which he had thrown into precipitate retreat, but mainly because he had found the Atchafalaya choked with brush at that season of the year. Banks believed that this time he would succeed, and he hoped to abolish Taylor as a continuing threat. He intended in fact to capture him, bag and baggage, having worked out his plans with that in mind.

Taylor had about 4000 troops between the Teche and the Atchafalaya, his flanks protected right and left by two captured Union warships, the gunboat *Diana* and the armed ram *Queen of the West*, the former having been ambushed and seized that week near Pattersonville, when she imprudently ventured up the bayou, and the latter having been brought down from the Red River the week before to prevent her destruction or recapture by Farragut after his run past Port Hudson. Banks had four Gulf Squadron gunboats with which he planned to neutralize these two turncoat vessels, and he intended to bag Taylor's entire land force by sending one division from his 15,000-man command across Grand Lake to land in the rear of the rebels while he engaged them in front with his other two divisions. Hemmed in and outnumbered nearly four to one, Taylor would have to choose between surrender and annihilation.

On April 11, in accordance with his design, Banks moved Emory and Weitzel from Brashear across the Atchafalaya to Berwick, and while they were advancing up the left bank of the Teche next day, skirmishing as they went, Grover put his troops aboard transports, escorted by the quartet of gunboats, and set out across the lake for a landing on the western shore within a mile of Irish Bend, an eastward loop of the Teche, control of

which would place him squarely athwart the only Confederate line of retreat. Despite some irritating delays,
the maneuver seemed to be going as planned; the skirmishing continued in front and Grover got his division
ashore six miles in the enemy rear; Banks anticipated a
Cannae. But Taylor got wind of what was up and reacted fast. Leaving a handful of men to put up a show of
resistance to the two blue divisions in his front, he
swung rearward with the rest to attack Grover and if
possible drive him into the lake.

On the 13th heavy fighting ensued. The shoestring
force managed to delude and delay Emory and Weitzel
while the main body fell on Grover. Though the latter
was not driven into the lake, he was held in check while
Taylor withdrew up the Teche in the darkness, foiling
the plans so carefully laid for his destruction. In three
days of intermittent action the Federals had lost 577
killed and wounded, the Confederates somewhat less,
although there was considerable disagreement between
the two commanders, then and later, as to the number
of prisoners taken on each side, Taylor afterwards protesting that Banks had claimed the capture of more men
than had actually opposed him.

Whatever the truth of his claims in this regard, and
despite his failure to bring off the Cannae he intended,
there could be no doubt that Banks, after a season of
rather spectacular defeats in Virginia at the hands of
Stonewall Jackson, had won his first clear-cut victory in
the field. And next day, when he received word that the
Diana and the *Queen* had been destroyed—the former
burned by the rebels, who could not take her with them
up the narrow Teche, and the latter sunk by the four
Union gunboats, who blew her almost literally out of
the water as soon as she entered Grand Lake and came

within their range—his elation knew no bounds. More-over, two of the gunboats steamed forthwith up the Atchafalaya and found it open to navigation all the way to the mouth of the Red, fifty miles above Port Hudson. This meant that Banks had the bypass he had been seek-ing, though of course it would be of small practical use until Vicksburg had likewise been bypassed or reduced.

Since there was no news that Grant had succeeded in any of his experimental projects in that direction, the Massachusetts general decided to explore some vistas he saw opening before him as a result of Taylor's defeat and withdrawal. Within two weeks New Orleans would have been returned to Federal control a solid year, and yet this principal seaport of the South had even less commerce with the outside world today than she had enjoyed in the days of the blockade runners, mainly be-cause the rebel land forces had her cut off from those regions that normally supplied her with goods for ship-ment. One of the richest of these lay before him now: the Teche. Return of the Teche country to Union con-trol, along with its vast supplies of cotton, salt, lumber, and foodstuffs, would restore New Orleans to her right-ful place among the world's great ports and would dem-onstrate effectively, as one observer pointed out, "that the conquests of the national armies instead of destroy-ing trade were calculated to instill new life into it."

There was one drawback. Such a movement up the long riverlike bayou stretching north almost to Alexan-dria, even though unopposed, might throw him off his previously announced schedule, which called for a meeting with Grant at Baton Rouge on May 10 for a combined attack, first on Port Hudson and then on Vicksburg. But Banks decided the probable gains were worth the risk. Besides, May 10 was nearly a month away, and he hoped to have completed his conquest of the region before then. If not, then Grant could wait, just as he had kept Banks waiting all this time.

Eager for more victories now that he had caught the flavor, the former Bay State governor put his three divisions on the march up the right bank of the Teche without delay. Two days later—April 16: Porter's blue-jackets were steeling themselves for their run past the Vicksburg batteries that night, and Grierson's troopers would ride out of La Grange the following morning—

he entered New Iberia and pushed on next day to the Vermilion River, which branched southward from the Teche near Vermilionville. Finding Taylor's rear guard drawn up on the opposite bank to contest a crossing, the bluecoats forced it with a brief skirmish, rebuilt the wrecked bridge, and on April 20 marched into Opelousas, evacuated two days earlier by the Louisiana government which had moved there a year ago when Farragut steamed upriver from New Orleans and trained his guns on Baton Rouge.

Taylor did not challenge the occupation of this alternate capital, but continued to fall back toward Alexandria, having received from Kirby Smith at Shreveport, his Transmississippi headquarters, a message expressing "gratification at the conduct of the troops under your command" and congratulating Taylor for the skill he had shown "in extricating them from a position of great peril."

Banks called a halt in order to rest his men for a few days and consolidate his gains, which were considerable. Conquest of the Teche had brought within his grasp large quantities of lumber, 5000 bales of cotton, many hogsheads of sugar, an inexhaustible supply of salt, and an estimated 20,000 head of cattle, mules, and horses. He later calculated the value of these spoils to have been perhaps as high as $5,000,000 and pointed out that even this liberal figure should be doubled, since the goods it represented had not only come into Federal hands but had also been kept from the Confederates beyond the Mississippi, for whom they had been in a large part intended. Nor was that all. There were human spoils as well.

Back in New Orleans the year before, Ben Butler had begun to enlist freedmen and fugitive slaves in what he called his Corps d'Afrique; now Banks continued this recruitment in the Teche. Two such regiments were organized at Opelousas, with about 500 men in each. Styled the 1st and 3d Louisiana Native Guards, the former was composed of "free Negroes of means and intelligence," with colored line officers and a white lieutenant colonel in command, while the latter was made up largely of ex-slaves whose officers were all white. There was considerable speculation, in the army of which they were now a part, as to how they would behave in combat—when and if they were exposed to it, which many of their fellow soldiers thought inadvisable —but Banks was willing to abide the issue until it had been settled incontrovertibly under fire.

Taylor by now had reached the Red at Gordon's Landing, where the *Queen of the West* had been blasted and captured back in February, thirty miles below Alexandria. Renamed Fort De Russy, the triple-casemated battery had held the low bluff against all comers, and on May 4 its staunchness was proved again when it was attacked by the two gunboats that had come up the Atchafalaya from Grand Lake after sinking the *Queen*. Leading the way, however, was the *Albatross*, which had got past Port Hudson with Farragut in mid-March. She closed the range to five hundred yards and kept up a forty-minute bombardment, supported by the other two ships at longer range, before dropping back with eleven holes punched in her hull and most of her spars and rigging shot away.

Fifty miles downriver next morning, having given up hope of reducing the fort on their own, the three ships met Porter—who, after completing the ferrying of Grant's two lead divisions across the Mississippi, had taken possession of Grand Gulf three days ago—coming up the Red with three of his ironclads, a steam ram, and a tug. This seemed quite enough for the task of reduction, but when he reached Fort De Russy late that afternoon, prepared to throw all he had at the place, he found it abandoned, its casemates yawning empty. Threatened from the rear by Banks, who had ended his Opelousas rest halt and resumed his northward march beyond the headwaters of the Teche, the garrison had retreated to avoid capture. Porter continued on to Alexandria next day, May 6, to find that Taylor had also fallen back from there.

A couple of hours later, Banks marched in at the head of his three-division column. He was in fine spirits, still wearing his three-week-old aura of victory, and Porter was impressed—particularly by the outward contrast between this new general and the one he had been working alongside for the past four months around Vicksburg. "A handsome, soldierly-looking man," the admiral called the former Speaker of the House, "though rather theatrical in his style of dress." The impression was one of nattiness and sartorial elegance; Banks in fact was something of a military dude. "He wore yellow gauntlets high upon his wrists, looking as clean as if they had just come from the glove-maker; his hat was picturesque, his long boots and spurs were faultless, and his air was that of one used to command. In short, I never saw a more faultless-looking soldier."

Banks was about as proud as he was dapper, and with cause. His Negro recruits more than made up—in numbers at any rate, though it was true their combat value was untested—for the casualties he had suffered in the course of his profitable campaign up the Teche, and his present position at Alexandria gave him access to the entire Red River Valley, a region quite as rich as the one he had just traversed, and far more extensive. With elements already on the march for Natchitoches, fifty air-line miles upriver, and Taylor still fading back from contact, he saw more vistas opening out before him. He also realized, however, that they were unattainable just yet.

"The decisive battle of the West must soon be fought near Vicksburg," Kirby Smith was telling a subordinate even now. "The fate of the Trans-Mississippi Department depends on it, and Banks, by operating here, is thrown out of the campaign on the Mississippi."

Banks agreed, although unwillingly, that he must first turn back east to resume his collaboration with Grant for the reduction of Vicksburg and Port Hudson. Then perhaps, with the Mississippi unshackled throughout its length, he would return up the Red to explore those new vistas stretching all the way to Texas. Grant meanwhile, having won the Battle of Port Gibson, crossed Bayou Pierre, and put his three divisions into jump-off positions for the advance on Jackson, was calling urgently for the Massachusetts general to join him at once in front of Vicksburg; "But I must say, without qualifications," the latter replied on May 12, "that the means at my disposal do not leave me a shadow of a chance to accomplish it." Though he was "dying with a kind of vanishing hope to see [our] two armies acting together against the strong places of the enemy," he had "neither water nor land transportation to make the movement by the river or by land. The utmost I can accomplish," he told Grant, "is to cross for the purpose of operating with you against Port Hudson."

Once more having reached a decision he wasted no time. Two days later, ending a week's occupation in the course of which he sent no less than 2000 spoils-laden

The Beleaguered City 239

wagons groaning south, he began his withdrawal from Alexandria. The march prescribed was via Simmesport for a crossing at Bayou Sara, a dozen miles above Port Hudson, but Banks himself did not accompany the three divisions on their overland trek; he went instead by boat, first down the Red, then down the Atchafalaya to Brashear City, where he caught a train for New Orleans. With him rode the fifty-two-year-old Emory, whose health had failed in the field and who had been succeeded by Halbert Paine, fifteen years his junior and the only non–West Pointer in Banks's army with so much rank—aside from Banks himself, of course—though he could claim the distinction of having shared a law office with Lincoln's friend Carl Schurz before the war. In New Orleans, Banks gave Emory the task of defending the city with a stripped-down garrison left behind by Thomas Sherman, who was instructed to put most of his men aboard transports bound for Baton Rouge to join Augur for an advance on Port Hudson.

As Banks planned it, the two divisions marching north from Baton Rouge would converge on the objective at the same time as the three marching south from Bayou Sara. For all the omnivorous reading he had done since his days as a bobbin boy in his home-state spinning mills, he may or may not have known that in thus intending to unite two widely divided columns on the field of battle he was attempting what Napoleon had called the most difficult maneuver in the book. If so, nonprofessional though he was, he showed no qualms beyond those normally involved in getting some 20,000 troops from one place—or in this case two places—to another.

What was more, he brought it off. Advancing simultaneously north and south, the two bodies converged on schedule, May 25. Next day they completed their investment, and the following morning they launched an all-out assault on the 7000 rebels penned up inside Port Hudson.

★   ★   ★

Like Pemberton, who was nine years his senior, Franklin Gardner was a northern-born professional who married South—his father-in-law was ex-Governor Alexander Mouton, who presided over the legislative body that voted Louisiana out of the Union—then went with his wife's people when the national crisis forced a choice. New York born and Iowa raised, the son of a regular army colonel who had been Adjutant General during the War of 1812, he had graduated from West Point in the class of '43, four places above Ulysses Grant and one below Christopher Augur, whose division was part of the blue cordon now drawn around the bastion Gardner was defending. A brigadier at Shiloh and with Bragg in Kentucky, he had been promoted to major general in December, shortly before his fortieth birthday, and sent to command the stronghold John C. Breckinridge had established at Port Hudson after being repulsed at Baton Rouge in August. By early April his strength had risen beyond 15,000 men, but it had since been whittled down to less than half that as a result of levies by the department commander, reacting to upriver pressure from Grant while Banks was off in the Teche.

On May 4, in response to what turned out to be Pemberton's final call, Gardner set out for Jackson with all but a single brigade, only to receive on May 9 at Osyka, just north of the Mississippi line, a dispatch instructing him to return at once to Port Hudson and hold it "to the last," this being Pemberton's interpretation of the President's warning that "both Vicksburg and Port Hudson [are] necessary to a connection with Trans-Mississippi."

Gardner did as he was told, and got back there barely ahead of Banks. His strength report of May 19—the date of Grant's first assault on the Vicksburg intrenchments, 120 air-line miles upriver—showed an "aggregate present" of 5715 in his three brigades, plus about one thousand artillerists in the permanent garrison. That was also the date on a message Joe Johnston addressed to Gardner from north of the Mississippi capital, which had fallen on the day after his arrival the week before: "Evacuate Port Hudson forthwith, and move with your troops toward Jackson to join other troops which I am uniting. Bring all the fieldpieces that you have, with their ammunition and the means of transportation. Heavy guns and their ammunition had better be destroyed, as well as the other property you may be unable to remove."

By the time the courier got there, however, he found a ring of Federal steel drawn tightly around the blufftop fortress. He could only report back to Johnston that Port Hudson, like Vicksburg 240 roundabout miles upriver, was besieged.

The Union navy had reappeared ahead of the Union army. On May 4, meeting Porter at the mouth of the Red, Farragut gave over his blockade duties from that point north and steamed back down the Mississippi to Port Hudson. For three days, May 8–10, he bombarded the bluff from above and below, doing all he could to soften it up for Banks, who was still at Alexandria. Upstream were the *Hartford* and the *Albatross*, patched up since her recent misfortune at Fort De Russy, while the downstream batteries were engaged by the screw sloops *Monongahela* and *Richmond*, the gunboat *Genesee*, and the orphaned ironclad *Essex*, which had been downriver ever since her run past Vicksburg the summer before.

Coming overland down the western bank, Farragut conferred with Banks on his arrival from New Orleans, May 22. The rebels had given him shell for shell, he said, and shown no sign of weakening under fire, but he assured the general that the navy would continue to do its share until the place had been reduced. Banks thanked him and proceeded to invest the bluff on its landward side, north and east and south, depending on the fleet to see that the beleaguered garrison made no westward escape across the river and received no reinforcements or supplies from that direction.

Assisted meanwhile by Grierson's well-rested troopers, who had ridden up from Baton Rouge with the column from the south, he drew his lines closer about the rebel fortifications. On May 26, with ninety guns in position opposing Gardner's thirty-one, he issued orders for a full-scale assault designed to take the place by storm next morning. Weitzel, Grover, and Paine were north of the Clinton railroad, which entered the works about midway, Augur and Sherman to the south. The artillery preparation would begin at daybreak, he explained, augmented by high-angle fire from the navy, and the five division commanders would "dispose their troops so as to annoy the enemy as much as possible during the cannonade by advancing skirmishers to kill the enemy's cannoneers and to cover the advance of the assaulting column."

This was somewhat hasty and Banks knew it, but he had reasons for not wanting to delay the attempt for the sake of more extensive preparations. First, like Grant eight days ago at Vicksburg, he believed the rebels were demoralized and unlikely to stand up under a determined blow if it was delivered before they had time to recover their balance. Second, and more important still, he was anxious to wind up the campaign and return to New Orleans; Emory was already complaining that he was in danger of being swamped by an attack from Mobile, where the Confederates had some 5000 men— twice as many as he himself had for the defense of the South's first city—or from Brashear, to which Taylor was free to return now that Banks had left the Teche. This was indeed a two-pronged danger; in fact, despite the cited lack of transportation, it had been the real basis for the Massachusetts general's refusal to join Grant in front of Vicksburg. However, for all his haste, the special orders he distributed on the 26th for the guidance of his subordinates in next day's operation were meticulous and full. Attempting to forestall confusion by assigning particular duties, he included no less than eleven numbered paragraphs in the order, all of them fairly long except the last, which contained a scant half-dozen words: "Port Hudson must be taken tomorrow."

At first it appeared that the order would be carried out, final paragraph and all; but around midmorning, when the thunder of the preliminary bombardment subsided and Weitzel went forward according to plan, driving the rebel skirmishers handsomely before him, he found that this unmasked their artillery, which opened point-blank on his troops with murderous effect. The bluecoats promptly hit the dirt and hugged it while their own batteries came up just behind them and unlimbered, returning the deluge of grape and canister at a range of two hundred and fifty yards. Crouched under all that hurtling iron and lead from front and rear, the men were badly confused and lost what little sense of direction they had retained during their advance through a maze of obstructions, both natural and man-made. "The whole fight took place in a dense forest of magnolias, mostly amid a thick undergrowth, and among ravines choked with felled and fallen timber, so that it was difficult not only to move but even to see," a participant was to recall, adding that what he had been involved in was not so much a battle or a charge as it was "a gigantic bush-whack."

Paine and Grover, moving out in support of Weitzel, ran into the same maelstrom of resistance, with the same result. So did Augur, somewhat later, when his turn came to strike the Confederate center just south of the railroad. But all was strangely quiet all this while on the far left. At noon Banks rode over to look into the cause of this inaction, and found to his amazement that Tom Sherman had "failed utterly and criminally to bring his men into the field." The fifty-two-year-old Rhode Islander was at lunch, surrounded by "staff officers all with their horses unsaddled." As usual, despite the multiparagraphed directive, someone—in this case about 3500 someones, from the division commander down to the youngest drummer—had not got the word.

Nettled by the dressing-down Banks gave him along with peremptory orders to "carry the works at all hazards," Sherman got his two brigades aligned at last and took them forward shortly after 2 o'clock. He rode at their head, old army style; but not for long. A conspicuous target, he soon tumbled off his horse, and the surgeons had to remove what was left of the leg he had been shot in.

Command of the division passed to William Dwight,

who had resigned as a West Point cadet ten years ago to go into manufacturing in his native Massachusetts at the age of twenty-one, but had returned to military life on the outbreak of the war. However, for all the youth and vigor which had enabled him to survive three wounds and a period of captivity after being left for dead on the field of Williamsburg a year ago next month, Dwight could do no more than Sherman had done already. His pinned-down men knew only too well that to attempt to rise, with all those guns and rifles trained on them from behind the red clay parapets ahead, would mean at best a trip back to the surgery where the doctors by now were sawing off their former commander's leg.

To attempt a farther advance, either here or on the east, was clearly hopeless; yet Banks was unwilling to call it a day until he had made at least one more effort. Weitzel's division, which had opened the action that morning around to the north, had gained more ground than any of the other four, causing one observer to remark that if he had "continued to press his attack a few minutes longer he would probably have broken through the Confederate defense and taken their whole line in reverse." Now that the defenders were alert and had the attackers zeroed in, that extra pressure would be a good deal harder to exert, but Banks at any rate thought it worth a try.

Orders were sent to the far right for a resumption of the assault, and were passed along to the colonel commanding the two regiments lately recruited in the Teche, the 1st and 3d Louisiana Native Guards. Held in reserve till now, they were about to receive their baptism of fire: a baptism which, as it turned out, amounted to total immersion. A Union staff officer who watched them form for the attack described what happened.

"They had hardly done so," he said, "when the extreme left of the Confederate line opened on them, in an exposed position, with artillery and musketry and forced them to abandon the attempt with great loss."

But that was only part of the story. Of the 1080 men in ranks, 271 were hit, or one out of every four. They had accomplished little except to prove, with a series of disjointed rushes and repulses over broken ground and through a tangle of obstructions, that the rebel position could not be carried in this fashion. Yet they had settled one other matter effectively: the question of whether Negroes would stand up under fire and take their losses as well as white men. "It gives me pleasure to report that they answered every expectation," Banks wrote Halleck. "In many respects their conduct was heroic. No troops could be more determined or more daring."

This was but a fraction of the day-long butcher's bill, which was especially high by contrast; 1995 Federals had fallen, and only 235 Confederates. In reaction, Banks told Farragut next day that Port Hudson was "the strongest position there is in the United States." Though he frankly admitted, "No man on either side can show himself without being shot," he was no less determined than he had been before the assault was launched. "We shall hold on today," he said, "and make careful examinations with reference to future operations."

That morning—unlike Grant after his second repulse, five days earlier at Vicksburg—he had requested "a suspension of hostilities until 2 o'clock this afternoon, in order that the dead and wounded may be brought off the field." Gardner consented, not only to this but also to a five-hour extension of the truce when it was found that the grisly harvest required a longer time for gleaning.

Meanwhile Banks was writing to Grant, bringing him up to date on events and outlining the problem as he saw it now. "The garrison of the enemy is 5000 or 6000 men," he wrote. "The works are what would ordinarily be styled 'impregnable.' They are surrounded by ravines, woods, valleys, and bayous of the most intricate and labyrinthic character, that make the works themselves almost inaccessible. It requires time even to understand the geography of the position. [The rebels] fight with determination, and our men, after a march of some 500 or 600 miles, have done all that could be expected or required of any similar force." A postscript added an urgent request: "If it be possible, I beg you to send me at least one brigade of 4000 or 5000 men. This will be of vital importance to us. We may have to abandon these operations without it."

No such reinforcements would be coming either now or later from Grant, who had his hands quite full upriver; but Banks had no real intention of abandoning the siege. "We mean to harass the enemy night and day, and to give him no rest," he declared in a message to Farragut that same day, and he followed this up with another next morning: "Everything looks well for us. The rebels attempted a sortie upon our right last evening upon the cessation of the armistice, but were smartly and quickly repulsed." Two days later, May 31, when the admiral informed him that three Confederate deserters had stated that "unless reinforcements arrive they cannot hold out three days longer," Banks replied: "Thanks for your note and the cheering report of the deserters. We are closing in upon the enemy, and will have him in a day or two."

So he said. But presently a dispatch arrived from Halleck, dated June 3, which threatened to cut the ground from under the besieging army's feet. Like Grant, and perhaps for the same reasons, Banks had kept the general-in-chief in the dark as to his intentions until it was too late for interference, and Old Brains expressed incredulity at the secondhand reports of what had happened. "The newspapers state that your forces are moving on Port Hudson instead of co-operating with General Grant, leaving the latter to fight both Johnston and Pemberton. As this is so contrary to all your instructions, and so opposed to military principles, I can hardly believe it true." That it was true, however, was shown by a bundle of letters he received that same day from Banks, announcing his intention to move southeast from Alexandria. "These fully account for your movement on Port Hudson, which before seemed so unaccountable," Halleck wrote next morning. But he still did not approve, and he said so in a message advising Banks to get his army back on what the general-in-chief considered the right track. "I hope that you have ere this given up your attempt on Port Hudson and sent all your spare forces to Grant. . . . If I have been over-urgent in this matter, it has arisen from my extreme anxiety lest the enemy should concentrate all his strength on one of your armies before you could unite, whereas if you act together you certainly will be able to defeat him."

Banks bristled at being thus lectured to. It irked him, moreover, that the authorities did not seem to take into account the fact that he was the senior general on the river. If any reproach for noncooperation was called for, it seemed to him that it should have been aimed at Grant. "Since I have been in the army," he replied in mid-June, when the second message reached him, "I have done all in my power to comply with my orders. It is so in the position I now occupy. I came here not only for the purpose of cooperating with General Grant, but by his own suggestion and appointment." In time Halleck came round. "The reasons given by you for moving against Port Hudson are satisfactory," he conceded in late June. "It was presumed that you had good and sufficient reasons for the course pursued, although at this distance it seemed contrary to principles and likely to prove unfortunate."

If this was not altogether gracious, Banks did not mind too much. He considered that he had already disposed of Halleck's bookish June 4 argument with a logical rebuttal, written by coincidence on the same day: "If I defend New Orleans and its adjacent territory, the enemy will go against Grant. If I go with a force sufficient to aid him, [bypassing Port Hudson,] my rear will be seriously threatened. My force is not large enough to do both. Under these circumstances, my only course seems to be to carry this post as soon as possible, and then to join General Grant. . . . I have now my heavy artillery in position, and am confident of success in the course of a week."

Here again he underestimated the rebel garrison's powers of resistance; Port Hudson was not going to fall within a month, much less a week. Gardner had drawn his semicircular lines with care, anchoring both extremities to the lip of the hundred-foot bluff overlooking the river, and had posted his troops for maximum effect, whatever the odds.

North of the railroad there were two main forts, one square, the other pentagonal, with a small redoubt be-

tween them, all three surrounded and tied together by a
network of trenches, occupied by two brigades under
I. G. W. Steedman and W. R. Miles. William Beall, a
Kentucky-born West Pointer, had his brigade, which
was as big as the other two combined, disposed to the
south along a double line of bastions, the largest of
which surmounted the crest of a ridge and was called the
Citadel because it dominated all the ground in that direction. These various major works, together with their
redans, parapets, ditches, and gun emplacements, were
mutually supporting, so that an advance on one invited
fire from those adjoining it.

Banks had discovered this first, to his regret, while
launching the May 27 assault. Since then, he had limited
his activities mainly to long-range bombardments and
the digging of lines of contravallation, designed to prevent a breakout and to protect his troops from sorties.
After two weeks of this, in the course of which a considerable number of his men were dropped by snipers, he
grew impatient and ordered a probing night action
which he characterized as an endeavor "to get within
attacking distance of the works in order to avoid the terrible losses incurred in moving over the ground in
front." Informed that the sudden lunge was to be preceded by a twenty-hour bombardment, Farragut, whose
ships by now were getting low on ammunition, protested mildly that he did not think the constant shelling
did much good. "After people have been harassed to a
certain extent, they become indifferent to danger, I
think," he said. But he added: "We will do all in our
power to aid you."

That power was not enough, as it turned out. At 3
o'clock in the morning, June 11, the blue infantry crept
quietly forward under cover of darkness—and found

the defenders very much on the alert. Though some men got through the abatis and up to the hostile lines, once the alarm was sounded they were quickly driven back, while those who chose not to run the gauntlet to regain their jump-off positions were taken captive. Except for lengthening the Federal casualty lists and increasing Confederate vigilance in the future, the action had no effect on anything whatever, so far as Banks and his shovel-weary, sniper-harassed men could discern: least of all on the siege, which continued as before.

His spirits were revived, however, by a message received two days later from Dwight, who reported that he had interrogated a quartet of Confederate deserters and had learned from them that the garrison, reduced by sickness to 3200 infantry and 800 artillerymen, was down to "about five days' beef." There were "plenty of peas, plenty of corn," but "no more meal." Starvation was staring the rebels in the face. In fact, a Mississippi regiment was said to be in such low spirits that it "drove about 50 head of cattle out of the works about a week ago," intending thereby to hasten the inevitable end. In short, Dwight wrote, "The troops generally wish to surrender, and despair of relief."

Next morning, June 13, Banks decided to test the validity of this report. His plan, as he explained it to Farragut, whose cooperation was requested, was to "open a vigorous bombardment at exactly a quarter past eleven this morning, and continue it for exactly one hour. . . . The bombardment will be immediately followed by a summons to surrender. If that is not listened to, I shall probably attack tomorrow." The guns roared on schedule, then stopped at the appointed time, and Banks sent forward under a white flag his demand for instant capitulation.

"Respect for the usages of war, and a desire to avoid unnecessary sacrifice of life, impose on me the necessity of formally demanding the surrender of the garrison of Port Hudson." That was the opening sentence of the page-long "summons," and it was balanced by another very like it at the close: "I desire to avoid unnecessary slaughter, and I therefore demand the immediate surrender of the garrison, subject to such conditions only as are imposed by the usages of civilized warfare. I have the honor to be, sir, very respectfully, your most obedient servant, *N. P. Banks*, Major General, Commanding."

The Confederate reply was prompt and a good deal briefer. "Your note of this date has just been handed to me, and in reply I have to state that my duty requires me to defend this position, and therefore I decline to surrender. I have the honor to be, sir, very respectfully, your most obedient servant, *Frank. Gardner*, Major General, Commanding C. S. Forces."

Banks had said that if his demands were not "listened to" he probably would launch a second full-scale assault next morning, all along the line. At daybreak, following a vigorous one-hour cannonade which apparently served little purpose except to warn the Confederates he was coming, he did just that. When the smoke cleared it was found that he had suffered the worst drubbing of the war, so far at least as a comparison of the casualties was concerned. On the far left, Dwight was misdirected by his guides, with the result that he was blasted into retreat before he even knew he was exposed. In the center, Augur and Paine attacked with vigor and were bloodily repulsed when they struck what turned out to be the strongest point of the enemy line, the priest-cap near the Jackson road; Paine himself fell, badly wounded, and was carried off the field. On the right, Grover and Weitzel were stopped in midcareer when it was demonstrated that no man could clear the fireswept ridge along their front and live. "In examining the position afterward," a Union officer declared, "I found [one] grass-covered knoll shaved bald, every blade cut down to the roots as by a hoe."

By noon it was apparent that the assault had failed in every sector. All that had been accomplished was a reduction of the range for the deadly snipers across the way, and the price exacted was far beyond the worth of a few yards of shell-torn earth. There was hollow mockery, too, in the respective losses, North and South. The Federals had 1792 killed, wounded, and missing subtracted from their ranks, while the Confederates had lost an over-all total of 47.

Four weeks of siege, highlighted by two full-scale assaults and one abortive night attack, had cost Banks more than 4000 casualties along his seven concave miles of front. His men, suspecting that they had inflicted scarcely more than one tenth as many casualties on the enemy, were so discouraged that the best he could say of them, in a note to Farragut that evening, was that they were "in tolerable good spirits." Presently, though, even this was more than he could claim. "The heat, especially in the trenches, became almost insupportable, the stenches quite so," a staff major later recalled. "The brooks dried up, the creek lost itself in the pestilential swamp, the springs gave out, and the river fell, exposing to the tropical sun a wide margin of festering ooze. The illness and mortality were enormous."

Counting noses four days after the second decisive repulse, Banks reported that he was down to 14,000 effectives, including the nine-month volunteers whose enlistments were expiring. This too was a source of discontent, which reached the stage of outright mutiny in at least one Bay State regiment, and the reaction was corrosive. Men whose time was nearly up did not "feel like desperate service," Banks told Halleck, while those who had signed on for the duration did not "like to lead where the rest will not follow."

Old Brains had a prescription for that, however. "When a column of attack is formed of doubtful troops," he answered, "the proper mode of curing their defection is to place artillery in their rear, loaded with grape and canister, in the hands of reliable men, with orders to fire at the first moment of disaffection. A knowledge of such orders will probably prevent any wavering, and, if not, one such punishment will prevent any repetition of it in your army."

This was perhaps reassuring, though in an unpleasant sort of way, since it showed the general-in-chief to be considerably more savage where blue rebels were concerned than he had ever been when his opponents wore butternut or gray. However, Banks had even larger problems than mutiny on his hands by then. Emory was crying havoc in New Orleans, which he protested was in grave danger of being retaken by the rebels any day now. "The railroad track at Terre Bonne is torn up. Communication with Brashear cut off," he notified Banks on June 20, adding: "I have but 400 men in the city, and I consider the city and the public property very unsafe. The secessionists here profess to have certain information that their forces are to make an attempt on the city."

Five days later—by which date Port Hudson had been under siege a month—he declared that the rebels bearing down on him were "known and ascertained to

be at least 9000, and may be more. . . . The city is quiet
on the surface, but the undercurrent is in a ferment."
"Something must be done for this city, and that
quickly," he insisted four days later. His anxiety continued to mount in ratio to his estimate of the number
of graybacks moving against him, until finally he said
flatly: "It is a choice between Port Hudson and New
Orleans. . . . My information is as nearly positive as
human testimony can make it that the enemy are 13,000
strong, and they are fortifying the whole country as they
march from Brashear to this place, and are steadily advancing. I respectfully suggest that, unless Port Hudson
is already taken, you can only save this city by sending
me reinforcements immediately and at any cost." What
was more, he said, the danger was not only from outside
New Orleans. "There are at least 10,000 fighting men
in this city (citizens) and I do not doubt, from what I see,
that these men will, at the first appearance of the enemy
within view of the city, be against us to a man. I have the
honor to be &c. *W. H. Emory*, Brigadier General, Commanding."

But Banks had no intention of loosening his grip on
the upriver fortress, which he believed—despite the
nonfulfillment of all his earlier predictions—could not
hold out much longer. Emory would have to take his
chances. If it came to the worst and New Orleans fell,
Farragut would steam down and retake it with the fleet
that would be freed for action on the day Port Hudson
ran up the white flag.

Meanwhile the signs were good. On June 29, no less
than thirty deserters stole out of the rebel intrenchments and into the Union lines, and though by now
Banks knew better than to judge the temper of the garrison by that of such defectors, he was pleased to learn

from those who arrived in the afternoon that their dinner had been meatless. In the future, they had been told,
the only meat they would get would be that of mules.
Judging by the adverse reaction of his own troops to a
far more palatable diet, Banks did not think the johnnies
would be likely to sustain their morale for long on that.
However, one of the butternut scarecrows brought with
him a copy of yesterday's *Port Hudson Herald*, which featured a general order issued the day before by Gardner,
"assuring the garrison that General Johnston will soon
relieve Vicksburg, and then send reinforcements here."
The southern commander declared as well, Banks
pointed out in passing the news along to Halleck, "his
purpose to defend the place to the last extremity."

Confident none the less "of a speedy and favorable
result"—so at least he assured the general-in-chief—
Banks kept his long-range batteries at work around the
clock, determined to give the Confederates no rest. The
fire at night was necessarily blind, but that by day was
skillfully directed by an observer perched on a lofty
yardarm of the *Richmond*, tied up across the river from
the bluff. He communicated by wigwag with a battery
ashore, which also had a signalman, and the two kept up
a running colloquy, not only to improve the marksmanship, but also to relieve the tedium of the siege.

"Your fifth gun has hit the breastwork of the big rifle
four times. Its fire is splendid. Can dismount it soon."

"You say our fifth gun?"

"Yes, from the left." But the next salvo brought a
shift of attention. "Your sixth gun just made a glorious
shot. . . . Let the sixth gun fire 10 feet more to the left."

"How now about the fifth and sixth guns?"

"The sixth gun is the bully boy."

"Can you give it any directions to make it more bully?"

"Last shot was little to the right."

Just then, however, the cannoneers were forced to call a halt. "Fearfully hot here," the battery signalman explained. "Several men sunstruck. Bullets whiz like fun. Have ceased firing for a while, the guns are so hot. Will profit by your directions afterward." Presently they resumed firing, though with much less satisfactory results, according to the observer high in the rigging of the *Richmond*.

"Howitzer shell goes 6 feet over the guns every shot. Last was too low, little too high again." Exasperated, he added: "Can't they, or won't they, depress that gun?"

"Won't, I guess. . . . Was that shot any better, and that?"

"Both and forever too high."

"We will vamose now. Come again tomorrow."

"Nine A.M. will do, will it not?"

"Yes; cease signaling."

★ 7 ★

The forces threatening New Orleans were no such host as Emory envisioned, but they were under the determined and resourceful Richard Taylor, who earlier, though much against his will, had struck at Grant's supposedly vital supply line opposite Vicksburg. "To break this would render a most important service," Pemberton had told Kirby Smith in early May, in one of his several urgent appeals for help across the way.

Returning to Alexandria as soon as Banks pulled out, Taylor prepared to move at once back down the Teche, threaten New Orleans, and thereby "raise such a storm as to bring General Banks from Port Hudson, the garrison of which could then unite with General Joseph Johnston in the rear of General Grant." On May 20, however, before he could translate his plan into action, he received instructions from Smith directing him to march in the opposite direction. "Grant's army is now supplied from Milliken's Bend by Richmond, down the Roundaway and Bayou Vidal to New Carthage," the department commander explained, and if Taylor could interrupt the flow of supplies along this route, the Federal drive on Vicksburg would be "checked, if not frustrated." He sympathized with Taylor's desire "to recover what you have lost in Lower Louisiana and to push on toward New Orleans," Smith added, "but the stake contended for near Vicksburg is the Valley of the Mississippi and the Trans-Mississippi Department; the defeat of General Grant is the *terminus ad quem* of all operations in the West this summer; to its attainment all minor advantages should be sacrificed."

Taylor agreed as to the object, but not as to the method, much preferring his own. However, as he said later, "remonstrances were of no avail." He turned his back on New Orleans, at least for the present, and set out up the Tensas, where he was joined by a division of about 4000 men under John G. Walker, a Missourian lately returned from Virginia, where he had commanded a division in Lee's army and was one of the many who could fairly be said to have saved the day at Sharpsburg.

Debarking June 5 on the east bank of the Tensas, some twenty-five miles west of Grant's former Young's Point headquarters, Taylor sent his unarmed transports back downstream to avoid losing them in his absence. Next day he surprised and captured a small party of Federals at Richmond, midway between the Tensas and the Mississippi, only to learn that Grant had established a new base up the Yazoo, well beyond the reach of any west-bank forces, and was no longer dependent on the one at Milliken's Bend. "Our movement resulted, and could result, in nothing," Taylor later admitted. All the same, he carried out his instructions by attacking, at dawn of the 7th, both Young's Point and Milliken's Bend, sending a full brigade against each.

Like Banks, Grant had been recruiting Negroes, but since he intended to use them as laborers rather than as soldiers, he had given them little if any military training apart from the rudiments of drill. Surprised in their camps by the dawn attacks, they panicked and fled eastward over the levee to the protection of Porter's upstream flotilla. The gunboats promptly took up the quarrel, blasting away at the exultant rebels, and Taylor, observing that the panic was now on the side of the pursuers, ordered Walker to retire on Monroe, terminus of the railroad west of Vicksburg, while he himself went back down the Tensas and up the Red to Alexandria. Once there, he returned his attention to Banks and New Orleans, glad to have done with what he called "these absurd movements" against a supposedly vital supply line which in fact had been abandoned for nearly a month before he struck it.

Though the losses had been unequal—652 Federals had fallen or were missing, as compared to 185 Confederates—Grant was not disposed to be critical of the outcome. Agreeing with Porter that the rebels had got "nothing but hard knocks," he was more laconic than reproachful in his mid-June report of the affair: "In this battle most of the troops engaged were Africans, who had little experience in the use of firearms. Their conduct is said, however, to have been most gallant, and I doubt not but with good officers they will make good troops."

Anyhow, this was beyond the circle of his immediate attention, which was fixed on the close-up siege of Vicksburg itself. Six divisions had been added by now to his original ten, giving him a total of 71,000 effectives disposed along two lines, back to back, one snuggled up to the semicircular defenses and the other facing rearward in case Joe Johnston got up enough strength and nerve to risk an attack from the east. Three divisions arrived in late May and early June from Memphis, the first of which, commanded by Jacob Lauman, was used to extend the investment southward, while the other two, under Nathan Kimball and William Sooy Smith, made up a fourth corps under Washburn, now a major general, and were sent to join Osterhaus, who had been left behind to guard the Big Black crossings while the two assaults were being launched. Frank Herron, who at twenty-five had won his two stars at Prairie Grove to become the Union's youngest major general, arrived from Missouri with his division on June 11 and extended the line still farther southward to the river, completing Grant's nine-division bear hug on Pemberton's beleaguered garrison. The final two were sent by Burnside from his Department of the Ohio. Commanded by

Thomas Welsh and Robert Potter, they constituted a
fifth corps under John G. Parke and raised the strength
of the rearward-facing force to seven divisions.

"Our situation is for the first time in the entire western campaign what it should be," Grant had written
Banks in the course of the build-up. And now that it was
complete, so was his confidence as to the outcome of the
siege, which he expressed not only in official correspondence but also in informal talks with his officers and
men. "Gen. Grant came along the line last night," an
Illinois private wrote home. "He had on his old clothes
and was alone. He sat on the ground and talked with the
boys with less reserve than many a little puppy of a lieutenant. He told us that he had got as good a thing as he
wanted here."

One item he would have liked more of was trained
engineers. Only two such officers were serving in that
capacity now in his whole army. However, as one of
them afterwards declared, this problem was solved by
the "native good sense and ingenuity" of the troops,
Middle Western farm boys for the most part, who
showed as much aptitude for such complicated work as
they had shown for throwing bridges over creeks and
bayous during the march that brought them here. According to the same officer, "Whether a battery was to
be constructed by men who had never built one before,
[or] a sap-roller made by those who had never heard the
name . . . it was done, and after a few trials well done."
Before long, a later observer remarked, "those who had
cut wood only for stoves would be speaking fluently of
gabions and fascines; men who had patiently smoothed
earth so that radishes might grow better would be talking affectionately of terrepleins for guns."

In all of this they were inspired by the same bustling

energy and quick adaptability on the part of the generals who led them; for one thing that characterized Grant's army was the youth of its commanders. McClernand, who was fifty-one, was the only general officer past fifty. Of the twenty-one corps and division commanders assigned to the Army of the Tennessee in the course of the campaign, the average age was under forty. And that promotion had been based on merit was indicated by the fact that the average age of the nine major generals was as low as that of the dozen brigadiers; indeed, excepting McClernand, it was better than one year lower. Moreover, nine of these twenty-one men were older than Grant himself, and this too was part of the reason for his confidence in himself and in the army which had come of age, so to speak, under his care and tutelage.

He considered it more than a match for anything the Confederates could bring against him—even under Joe Johnston, whose abilities he respected highly. One day a staff officer expressed the fear that Johnston was planning to fight his way into Vicksburg in order to help Pemberton stage a breakout; but Grant did not agree. "No," he said. "We are the only fellows who want to get in there. The rebels who are in now want to get out, and those who are out want to stay out. If Johnston tries to cut his way in we will let him do it, and then see that he don't get out. You say he has 30,000 men with him? That will give us 30,000 more prisoners than we now have."

This was not to say that the two repulsed assaults had taught him nothing. They had indeed, if only by way of confirming a first impression that the rebel works were formidable. One officer, riding west on the Jackson road, had found himself confronted by "a long line of high, rugged, irregular bluffs, clearly cut against the sky, crowned with cannon which peered ominously from embrasures to the right and left as far as the eye could see." Beyond an almost impenetrable tangle of timber felled on the forward slopes, "lines of heavy rifle pits, surmounted with head-logs, ran along the bluffs, connecting fort with fort, and filled with veteran infantry." The approaches, he said, "were frightful enough to appall the stoutest heart." Sherman agreed, especially after the two assaults which had cost the army more than four thousand casualties. "I have since seen the position at Sevastopol," he wrote years later, "and without hesitation I declare that at Vicksburg to have been the more difficult of the two."

Skillfully constructed, well sited, and prepared for a year against the day of investment, the fortifications extended for seven miles along commanding ridges and were anchored at both extremities to the lip of the sheer 200-foot bluff, north and south of the beleaguered city. Forts, redoubts, salients, redans, lunets, and bastions had been erected or dug at irregular intervals along the line, protected by overlapping fields of fire and connected by a complex of trenches, which in turn were mutually supporting. There simply was no easy way to get at the defenders. Moreover, Grant's three-to-one numerical advantage was considerably offset, not only by the necessity for protecting his rear from possible attacks by the army Johnston was assembling to the east, but also by the fact that, because of the vagaries of the up-ended terrain, his line of contravallation had to be more than twice the length of the line he was attempting to confront. "There is only one way to account for the hills of Vicksburg," a Confederate soldier had said a year ago, while helping to survey the present works. "After the Lord of Creation had made all the big moun-

tains and ranges of hills, He had left on His hands a
large lot of scraps. These were all dumped at Vicksburg
in a waste heap." One of Grant's two professional engineers was altogether in agreement, pronouncing the
Confederate position "rather an intrenched camp than
a fortified place, owing much of its strength to the difficult ground, obstructed by fallen trees to its front,
which rendered rapidity of movement and *ensemble* in
an assault impossible."

Yet even this ruggedness had its compensations. Although the hillsides, as one who climbed them said,
"were often so steep that their ascent was difficult to a
footman unless he aided himself with his hands," the
many ravines provided excellent cover for the besiegers,
and Grant had specified in his investment order: "Every
advantage will be taken of the natural inequalities of the
ground to gain positions from which to start mines,
trenches, or advance batteries." With the memory of
slaughter fresh in their minds as a result of their two
repulses, the men dug with a will. Knowing little or
nothing at the outset of the five formal stages of a siege
—the investment, the artillery attack, the construction
of parallels and approaches, the breaching by artillery or
mines, and the final assault—they told one another that
Grant, having failed to go over the rebel works, had decided to go under them instead.

Fortunately the enemy used his artillery sparingly,
apparently conserving ammunition for use in repelling
major assaults, but snipers were quick to shoot at targets
of opportunity: in which connection a Federal major
was to recall that "a favorite amusement of the soldiers
was to place a cap on the end of a ramrod and raise it just
above the head-logs, betting on the number of bullets
which would pass through it within a given time." Few

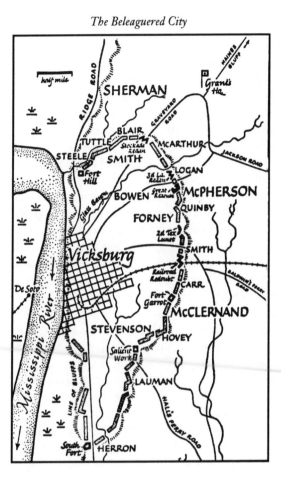

things on earth appealed to them more, as humor, than the notion of some butternut marksman flaunting his skill when the target was something less than flesh and blood. Mostly, though, they dug and took what rest they could, sweating in their wool uniforms and cursing the heat even more than they did the snipers. Soon they were old hands at siege warfare. "The excitement . . .

has worn away," a lieutenant wrote home from the trenches in early June, "and we have settled down to our work as quietly and as regularly as if we were hoeing corn or drawing bills in chancery."

Life in the trenches across the way—though the occupants did not call them that; they called them "ditches"—was at once more sedentary and more active. With their own 102 guns mostly silent and Grant's opposing 220 roaring practically all the time, they did nearly as much digging as the bluecoats, the difference being that they did it mainly in the same place, time after time, repairing damages inflicted by the steady rain of shells. Nor were they any less inventive. "Thunder barrels," for example—powder-filled hogsheads, fuzed at the bung—were found to be quite effective when rolled downhill into the enemy parallels and approaches. Similarly, such large naval projectiles as failed to detonate, either in the air or on contact with the ground, could be dug up, re-fuzed, and used in the same fashion to discourage the blue diggers on the slopes. However, despite such violent distractions, after a couple of weeks of spadework the two lines were within clod-tossing distance of each other at several points, and this resulted in an edgy sort of existence for the soldiers of both sides, as if they were spending their days and nights at the wrong end of a shooting gallery or in a testing chamber for explosives. "Fighting by hand grenades was all that was possible at such close quarters," a Confederate was to recall. "As the Federals had the hand grenades and we had none, we obtained our supply by using such of theirs as failed to explode, or by catching them as they came over the parapet and hurling them back."

Resistance under these circumstances implied a high

state of morale, and such was indeed the case. Grant's heavy losses in his two assaults—inflicted at so little cost to the defenders that, until they looked out through the lifting smoke and saw the opposite hillsides strewn with the rag-doll shapes of the Union dead, they could scarcely believe a major effort had been made—convinced them that the Yankees could never take the place by storm. What was more, they had faith in "Old Joe" Johnston, believing that he would raise the siege as soon as he got his troops assembled off beyond the blue horizon, whereupon the two gray forces would combine and turn the tables on the besiegers. Until then, as they saw it, all that was needed was firmness against the odds, and they stood firm.

Thanks to Pemberton's foresight, which included pulling corn along the roadside and driving livestock ahead of the army during its march from the Big Black, food so far was more plentiful inside the Confederate lines than it was in the noncombatant region beyond them. The people there were the first to feel the pinch of hunger; for the Federals, coming along behind the retreating graybacks, had consumed what little remained while waiting for roads to be opened to their new base on the Yazoo. "The soldiers ate up everything the folks had for ten miles around," a Union private wrote home. "They are now of necessity compelled to come here and ask for something to live upon, and they have discovered that they have the best success when the youngest and best-looking one in the family comes to plead their case, and they have some very handsome women here." This humbling of their pride did not displease him; it seemed to him no more than they deserved. "They were well educated and rich before their niggers ran away," he added, but adversity had brought

them down in the world. "If I was to meet them in Illinois I should think they were born and brought up
there."

Whether this last was meant as a compliment, and if
so to whom, he did not say. But at least these people
beyond the city's bristling limits were not being shot at;
which was a great deal more than could be said of those
within the gun-studded belt that girdled the bluff Vicksburg had been founded on, forty-odd years ago, by provision of the last will and testament of the pioneer
farmer and Methodist parson Newitt Vick. In a sense,
however, the bluff was returning to an earlier destiny.
All that had been here when Vick arrived were the
weed-choked ruins of a Spanish fort, around which the
settlement had grown in less than two generations into a
bustling town of some 4500 souls, mostly devoted to
trade with planters in the lower Yazoo delta but also
plagued by flatboat men on the way downriver from
Memphis, who found it a convenient place for letting
off what they called "a load of steam" that would not
wait for New Orleans. As it turned out, though, the
ham-fisted boatmen with knives in their boots and the
gamblers with aces and derringers up their sleeves were
mild indeed compared to what was visited upon them by
the blue-clad host sent against them by what had lately
been their government.

Now the bluff was a fort again, on a scale beyond the
most flamboyant dreams of the long-departed Span-
iards, and the residents spent much of their time, as one
of them said, watching the incoming shells "rising
steadily and shiningly in great parabolic curves, descending with ever-increasing swiftness, and falling
with deafening shrieks and explosions." The "ponder-

ous fragments" flew everywhere, he added, thickening the atmosphere of terror until "even the dogs seemed to share the general fear. On hearing the descent of a shell, they would dart aside [and] then, as it exploded, sit down and howl in a pitiful manner." Children, on the other hand, observed the uproar with wide-eyed evident pleasure, accepting it as a natural phenomenon, like rain or lightning, unable to comprehend—as the dogs, for example, so obviously did—that men could do such things to one another and to them.

"How is it possible you live here?" a woman who had arrived to visit her soldier husband just before the siege lines tightened asked a citizen, and was told: "After one is accustomed to the change, we do not mind it. But becoming accustomed: that is the trial."

Some took it better than others, in or out of uniform. There was for instance a Frenchman, "a gallant officer who had distinguished himself in several severe engagements," who was "almost unmanned" whenever one of the huge mortar projectiles fell anywhere near him. Chided by friends for this reaction, he would reply: "I no like ze bomb: I cannot fight him back!" Neither could anyone else "fight him back," least of all the civilians, many of whom took refuge in caves dug into the hillsides. Some of these were quite commodious, with several rooms, and the occupants brought in chairs and beds and even carpets to add to the comfort, sleeping soundly or taking dinner unperturbed while the world outside seemed turned to flame and thunder. "Prairie Dog Village," the blue cannoneers renamed the city on the bluff, while from the decks of ironclads and mortar rafts on the great brown river, above and below, and from the semicircular curve of eighty-nine sand-bagged battery emplacements on the landward side, they continued to pump their steel-packaged explosives into the checkerboard pattern of its streets and houses.

Like the men in the trenches, civilians of both sexes and all ages were convinced that their tormentors could never take Vicksburg by storm, and whatever their fright they had no intention of knuckling under to what they called the bombs. For them, too, Johnston was the one bright hope of deliverance. Old Joe would be coming soon, they assured each other; all that was needed was to hold on till he completed his arrangements; then, with all the resources of the Confederacy at his command, he would come swooping over the eastern horizon and down on the Yankee rear.

But presently, as time wore on and Johnston did not come, they were made aware of a new enemy. Hunger. By mid-June, though the garrison had been put first on half and then on quarter rations of meat, the livestock driven into the works ahead of the army back in May had been consumed, and Pemberton had his foragers impress all the cattle in the city. This struck nearer home than even the Union shells had done, for it was no easy thing for a family with milk-thirsty children to watch its one cow being led away to slaughter by a squad of ragged strangers. Moreover, the army's supply of bread was running low by now, and the commissary was directed to issue instead equal portions of rice and flour, four ounces of each per man per day, supplementing a quarter-pound of meat that was generally stringy or rancid or both. When these grains ran low, as they soon did, the experiment was tried of baking bread from dough composed of equal parts of corn and dried peas, ground up together until they achieved a gritty consistency not unlike cannon powder. "It made a nauseous composition," one who survived the diet was to recall with a shudder, "as the corn meal cooked in half the time the peas meal did, so the stuff was half raw. . . . It had the properties of india-rubber, and was worse than leather to digest."

Soon afterwards came the crowning indignity. With the last cow and hog gone lowing and squealing under the sledge and cleaver, still another experiment was tried: the substitution of mule meat for beef and bacon. Though it was issued, out of respect for religious and folk prejudices, "only to those who desired it," Pemberton was gratified to report that both officers and men considered it "not only nutritious, but very palatable, and in every way preferable to poor beef." So he said; but soldiers and civilians alike found something humiliating, not to say degrading, about the practice. "The rebels don't starve with success," a Federal infantryman observed jokingly from beyond the lines about this time. "I think that if I had nothing to eat I'd starve better than they do." Vicksburg's residents and defenders might well have agreed, especially when mule meat was concerned. Even if a man refused to eat such stuff himself, he found it disturbing to live among companions who did not. It was enough to diminish even their faith in Joe Johnston, who seemed in point of fact a long time coming.

Though at the outset the Virginian had sounded vigorous and purposeful in his assurance of assistance, Pemberton himself by now had begun to doubt the outcome of the race between starvation and delivery. "I am trying to gather a force which may attempt to relieve you. Hold out," Johnston wrote on May 19, and six days later he made this more specific: "Bragg is sending a division. When it comes, I will move to you. Which do you think is the best route? How and where is the enemy encamped? What is your force?"

Receiving this last on May 29—the delay was not extreme, considering that couriers to and from the city had to creep by darkness through the Federal lines, risking capture every foot of the way—the Vicksburg commander replied as best he could to his superior's questions as to Grant's dispositions and strength. "My men are in good spirits, awaiting your arrival," he added. "You may depend on my holding the place as long as possible." After waiting nine days and receiving no answer, he asked: "When may I expect you to move, and in what direction?" Three more days he waited, and still there was no reply. "I am waiting most anxiously to know your intentions," he repeated. "I have heard nothing from you since [your dispatch of] May 25. I shall endeavor to hold out as long as we have anything to eat." Three days more went by, and then on June 13 —two weeks and a day since any word had reached him from the world outside—he received a message dated May 29. "I am too weak to save Vicksburg," Johnston told him. "Can do no more than attempt to save you and your garrison. It will be impossible to extricate you unless you co-operate and we make mutually supporting movements. Communicate your plans and suggestions, if possible."

This was not only considerably less than had been expected in the way of help; it also seemed to indicate that Johnston did not realize how tightly the Union cordon was drawn about Vicksburg's bluff. In effect, the meager trickle of dispatches left Pemberton in a position not unlike that of a man who calls on a friend to make a strangler turn loose of his throat, only to have the friend inquire as to the strangler's strength, the position of his thumbs, the condition of the sufferer's windpipe, and just what kind of help he had in mind. So instead of "plans and suggestions," Vicksburg's defender tried to communicate some measure of the desperation he and his soldiers were feeling. "The enemy has placed several heavy guns in position against our works," he replied on June 15, "and is approaching them very nearly by sap. His fire is almost continuous. Our men have no relief; are becoming much fatigued, but are still in pretty good spirits. I think your movement should be made as soon as possible. The enemy is receiving reinforcements. We are living on greatly reduced rations, but I think sufficient for twenty days yet."

Having thus placed the limit of Vicksburg's endurance only one day beyond the Fourth of July—now strictly a Yankee holiday—Pemberton followed this up, lest Johnston fail to sense the desperation implied, with a more outspoken message four days later: "I hope you will advance with the least possible delay. My men have been thirty-four days and nights in the trenches, without relief, and the enemy within conversation distance. We are living on very reduced rations, and, as you know, are entirely isolated." He closed by asking bluntly, "What aid am I to expect from you?" This time the answer, if vague, was prompt. On June 23 a courier arrived with a dispatch written only the day before. "Scouts report the enemy fortifying toward us and the roads blocked," Johnston declared. "If I can do nothing to relieve you, rather than surrender the garrison, endeavor to cross the river at the last moment if you and General Taylor communicate."

To Pemberton this seemed little short of madness. Taylor had made his gesture against Young's Point and

Milliken's Bend more than two weeks ago; by now he was all the way down the Teche, intent on menacing New Orleans. But that was by no means the worst of Johnston's oversights, which was to ignore the presence of the Union navy. The bluejacket gun crews would have liked nothing better than a chance to try their marksmanship on a makeshift flotilla of skiffs, canoes, and rowboats manned by the half-starved tatterdemalions they had been probing for at long range all these weeks. Besides, even if the boats required had been available, which they were not, there was the question of whether the men in the trenches were in any condition for such a strenuous effort. They looked well enough to a casual eye, for all their rags and hollow-eyed gauntness, but it was observed that they tired easily under the mildest exertion and could serve only brief shifts when shovel work was called for.

The meager diet was beginning to tell. A Texas colonel reported that many of his men had "swollen ankles and symptoms of incipient scurvy." By late June, nearly half the garrison was on the sick list or in hospital. If Pemberton could not see what this meant, a letter he received at this time—June 28: exactly one week short of the date he had set, two weeks ago, as the limit of Vicksburg's endurance—presumed to define it for him in unmistakable terms. Signed "Many Soldiers," the letter called attention to the fact that the ration now had been reduced to "one biscuit and a small bit of bacon per day," and continued:

> The emergency of the case demands prompt and decided action on your part. If you can't feed us, you had better surrender us, horrible as the idea is, than suffer this noble army to disgrace themselves by desertion. I

tell you plainly, men are not going to lie here and per-
ish, if they do love their country dearly. Self-preserva-
tion is the first law of nature, and hunger will compel a
man to do almost anything. . . . This army is now ripe
for mutiny, unless it can be fed. Just think of one small
biscuit and one or two mouthfuls of bacon per day.
General, please direct your inquiries in the proper
channel, and see if I have not stated the stubborn facts,
which had better be heeded before we are disgraced.

★　　★　　★

"Grant is now deservedly the hero," Sherman wrote
home in early June, adding characteristically—for his
dislike of reporters was not tempered by any evidence of
affection on their part, either for himself or for Grant,
with whom, as he presently said, "I am a second self"—
that his friend was being "belabored with praise by
those who a month ago accused him of all the sins in the
calendar, and who next will turn against him if so blows
the popular breeze. Vox populi, vox humbug."
In point of fact, however, once the encompassing
lines had been drawn, the journalists could find little
else to write about that had not been covered during the
first week of the siege. And it was much the same for the
soldiers, whose only diversion was firing some fifty to
one hundred rounds of ammunition a day, as required
by orders. Across the way—though the Confederates
lacked even this distraction, being under instructions to
burn no powder needlessly—the main problem, or at
any rate the most constant one, was hunger; whereas for
the Federals it was boredom. "The history of a single
day was the history of all the others," an officer was to
recall.

Different men had different ways of trying to hasten the slow drag of time. Sherman, for instance, took horseback rides and paid off-duty visits to points of interest roundabout, at least one of which resulted in a scene he found discomforting, even painful. Learning that the mother of one of his former Louisiana Academy cadets was refugeeing in the neighborhood—she had come all the way from Plaquemine Parish to escape the attentions of Butler and Banks, only to run spang into Grant and Sherman—he rode over to tender his respects and found her sitting on her gallery with about a dozen women visitors. He introduced himself, inquired politely after her son, and was told that the young man was besieged in Vicksburg, a lieutenant of artillery. When the general went on to ask for news of her husband, whom he had known in the days before the war, the woman suddenly burst into tears and cried out in anguish: "You killed him at Bull Run, where he was fighting for his country!" Sherman hastily denied that he had "killed anybody at Bull Run," which was literally true, but by now all the other women had joined the chorus of abuse and lamentation. This, he said long afterwards, "made it most uncomfortable for me, and I rode away."

Other men had other spare-time diversions. Grant's, it was said, was whiskey. Some denied this vehemently, protesting that he was a teetotaler, while some asserted that this only appeared to be the case because of his low tolerance for the stuff; a single glass unsteadied him, and a second gave him the glassy-eyed look of a man with a heavy load on.

He himself had seemed to recognize the problem from the outset, if only by the appointment and retention of John A. Rawlins as his assistant adjutant general. A frail but vigorous young man, with a "marble pallor" to his face and "large, lustrous eyes of a deep black," Rawlins at first had wanted to be a preacher, but had become instead a lawyer in Galena, where Grant first knew him. His wife had died of tuberculosis soon after the start of the war, and he himself would die of the same disease before he was forty, but the death that seemed to have affected him most had been that of his father, an improvident charcoal burner who had died at last of the alcoholism that had kept him and his large family in poverty all his life. Rawlins, a staff captain at thirty and now a lieutenant colonel at thirty-two, was rabid on the subject of drink. He was in fact blunt in most things, including his relationship with Grant. "He bossed everything at Grant's headquarters," Charles Dana later wrote, adding: "I have heard him curse at Grant when, according to his judgment, the general was doing something that he thought he had better not do." Observing this, many wondered why Grant put up with it. Others believed they knew. "If you hit Rawlins on the head, you'll knock out Grant's brains," they said.

But they were wrong. Rawlins was not Grant's brain; he was his conscience, and a rough one, too, especially where whiskey was concerned. "I say to you frankly, and I pledge you my word for it," he had written eighteen months ago to Elihu Washburne, the general's congressional guardian angel, "that should General Grant at any time become an intemperate man or an habitual drunkard, I will notify you immediately, will ask to be removed from duty on his staff (kind as he has been to me) or resign my commission. For while there are times when I would gladly throw the mantle of charity over the faults of my friends, at this time and from a man of his position I would rather tear the mantle off and expose the deformity."

Grant had cause to believe that Rawlins meant it. And yet, despite the danger to his career and despite what a fellow staffer called Rawlins' "insubordination twenty times a day," he kept him on, both for his own good and the army's.

Since writing to Washburne, however, the adjutant had either changed his mind about disturbing the mantle or else he had been singularly forgetful. Despite periodic incidents thereafter, in which Grant was involved with alcohol, Rawlins limited his remarks to the general himself, apparently in the belief that he could handle him. And so he could, except for lapses. Anyhow, there was never any problem so long as Mrs Grant was around; "If she is with him all will be well and I can be spared," he later confided to a friend. The trouble seemed in part sexual, as in California nine years ago, and it was intensified by periods of boredom, such as now. Three weeks of slam-bang fighting and rapid maneuver had given way to the tedium of a siege, and Mrs Grant had been six weeks off the scene.

On June 5 Rawlins found a box of wine in front of the general's tent and had it removed, ignoring Grant's protest that he was saving it to toast the fall of Vicksburg. He learned, moreover, that the general had recently accepted a glass of wine from a convivial doctor. These were danger signs, and there were others that evening. Rawlins sat down after midnight and wrote Grant a letter. "The great solicitude I feel for the safety of this army leads me to mention, what I had hoped never again to do, the subject of your drinking. . . . Tonight when you should, because of the condition of your

health if nothing else, have been in bed, I find you
where the wine bottle has just been emptied, in company with those who drink and urge you to do likewise,
and the lack of your usual promptness and decision, and
clearness in expressing yourself in writing conduces to
confirm my suspicion." Rawlins himself had become
rather incoherent by now, whether from anger or from
sorrow; but the ending was clear enough. Unless Grant
would pledge himself "[not] to touch a single drop of
any kind of liquor, no matter by whom asked or under
what circumstances," Rawlins wanted to be relieved at
once from duty in the department.

Grant, however, left early next morning—apparently
before the letter reached him—on a tour of inspection
up the Yazoo River to Satartia, near which he had
posted a division in case Johnston came that way. The
two-day trip, beyond the sight and influence of Rawlins,
became a two-day bender.

Dana went with him, and on the way upriver from
Haines Bluff they met the steamboat *Diligent* coming
down. Grant hailed the vessel, whose captain was a
friend of his, transferred to her, and had her turned back
upstream for Satartia. Aboard was Sylvanus Cadwallader, a Chicago *Times* correspondent on the prowl for
news. It was he who had ridden into Jackson with Fred
Grant in mid-May, when they lost the race for the souvenir flag atop the capitol, and it was he who was to
leave the only detailed eyewitness account of Grant on a
wartime bender—specifically the two-day one which
already was under way up the Yazoo.

In some ways, for Cadwallader at least, it was more
like a two-day nightmare. "I was not long in perceiving
that Grant had been drinking," he wrote long afterwards, "and that he was still keeping it up. He made sev-

eral trips to the bar room of the boat in a short time, and became stupid in speech and staggering in gait." The reporter of course had heard rumors of Grant's predilection, but this was the first time he had seen him show it to the extent of intoxication. Alarmed by the general's "condition, which was fast becoming worse," he tried to get the captain and a lieutenant aide to intervene. Neither would; so Cadwallader undertook to do it himself. He got Grant into his stateroom, locked the door, "and commenced throwing bottles of whiskey which stood on the table, through the windows, over the guards, into the river." Grant protested, to no avail; the reporter "firmly, but good-naturedly declined to obey," and finally got him quieted. "As it was a very hot day and the stateroom almost suffocating, I insisted on his taking off his coat, vest and boots, and lying down on one of the berths. After much resistance I succeeded, and soon fanned him to sleep."

But that was only the beginning. Shortly before dark, when the *Diligent* neared Satartia, she met two gunboats steaming down, and a naval officer came aboard to warn that it was not safe for the unarmed vessel to proceed. Dana—who later reported tactfully in his *Recollections* that "Grant was ill and went to bed soon after we started"—knocked on the stateroom door to ask whether the boat should turn back. Grant, he said, was "too sick to decide," and told him: "I will leave it to you." Now that he was awake, however, though still not "recovered from his stupor," Cadwallader said, the general took it into his head "to dress and go ashore," despite the naval officer's warning. Once more the reporter prevailed, and got him back to bed. While he slept, the *Diligent* returned downstream in the darkness to Haines Bluff. Next morning, according to Dana,

Grant was "fresh as a rose, clean shirt and all, quite himself," when he came out to breakfast. "Well, Mr Dana," he observed, "I suppose we are at Satartia."

Cadwallader relaxed his guard, despite the 25-mile geographical error, presuming that "all necessity for extra vigilance on my part had passed," and was profoundly shocked to discover, an hour later, "that Grant had procured another supply of whiskey from on shore and was quite as much intoxicated as the day before." Again the reporter managed to separate the general from his bottle, only to have him insist on proceeding at once to Chickasaw Bayou. This would have brought them there "about the middle of the afternoon, when the landing would have been alive with officers, men, and trains from all parts of the army." Conferring with the captain as to the best means by which to avoid exposing Grant to "utter disgrace and ruin," Cadwallader managed to delay the departure so that they did not arrive until about sundown, when there was much less activity at the landing.

As luck would have it, they tied up alongside a sutler boat whose owner "kept open house to all officers and dispensed free liquors and cigars generously." Alarmed at the possibilities of disaster, the reporter slipped hastily over the rail, warned the sutler of what was afoot, and "received his promise that the general should not have a drop of anything intoxicating on his boat." Back aboard the *Diligent*, Cadwallader helped the escort to unload the horses for the five-mile ride to army headquarters northeast of Vicksburg; but when this was done he looked around and could find no sign of Grant. Fearing the worst, he hurried aboard the sutler boat "and soon heard a general hum of conversation and laughter proceeding from a room opening out of the ladies' cabin."

There he saw his worst fears realized. The sutler was seated at "a table covered with bottled whiskey and baskets of champagne," and Grant was beside him, "in the act of swallowing a glass of whiskey."

Cadwallader once more intervened, insisting that "the escort was waiting, and it would be long after dark before we could reach headquarters." Grant came along, though he plainly resented the interruption. His horse was a borrowed one called Kangaroo "from his habit of rearing on his hind feet and making a plunging start whenever mounted." That was his reaction now; for "Grant gave him the spur the moment he was in the saddle, and the horse darted away at full speed before anyone was ready to follow."

The road was crooked, winding among the many sloughs and bayous, but the general more or less straightened it out, "heading only for the bridges, and literally tore through and over everything in his way. The air was full of dust, ashes, and embers from campfires, and shouts and curses from those he rode down in his race." Cadwallader, whose horse was no match for Kangaroo, thought he had lost his charge for good. But he kept on anyhow, hoping against hope, and "after crossing the last bayou bridge three-fourths of a mile from the landing," caught up with him riding sedately at a walk.

Finding that Grant had become "unsteady in the saddle" as a result of the drink or drinks he had had from the sutler, and fearing "discovery of his rank and situation," the reporter seized Kangaroo's rein and led him off into a roadside thicket, where he helped the general to dismount and persuaded him to lie down on the grass and get some sleep. While Grant slept Cadwallader managed to hail a trooper from the escort, whom he instructed to go directly to headquarters "and report at once to Rawlins—and no one else—and say to him that I want an ambulance with a careful driver."

Waking before the ambulance got there, Grant wanted to resume his ride at once, but the reporter "took him by the arm, walked him back and forth, and kept up a lively rather one-sided conversation, till the ambulance arrived." Then there was the problem of getting the general into the curtained vehicle, which he refused to permit until, as Cadwallader said, "we compromised the question by my agreeing to ride in the ambulance also, and having our horses led by the orderly."

They reached headquarters about midnight to find the dark-eyed Rawlins and John Riggin, another staff officer, "waiting for us in the driveway." The reporter got out first, "followed promptly by Grant," who now gave him perhaps the greatest shock of the past two days. "He shrugged his shoulders, pulled down his vest, 'shook himself together,' as one just rising from a nap, and seeing Rawlins and Riggin, bid them good night in a natural tone and manner, and started to his tent as steadily as he ever walked in his life." Cadwallader turned to Rawlins, who was pale with rage—"The whole appearance of the man indicated a fierceness that would have torn me into a thousand pieces had he considered me to blame"—and said he was afraid, from what they had just seen, that the adjutant would think it was he, not Grant, who had been drinking.

"No, no," Rawlins said through clenched teeth. "I know him, I know him. I want you to tell me the exact facts, and all of them, without any concealment. I have a right to know them, and I will know them."

He heard them all, from start to finish, but he never reported the incident to Washburne, any more than

Dana did to the War Department, not only out of loyalty and friendship, but also perhaps on reflecting that if
anything brought about Grant's removal, or even his
suspension during an inquiry, command of the army
would pass automatically to McClernand, whom they
both despised. As for Cadwallader, despite assurances
from Rawlins—"He will not send you out of the department while I remain in it," the adjutant told him—
he spent an anxious night, "somewhat in doubt as to the
view of the matter Gen. Grant would take next day,"
and "purposely kept out of his way for twenty-four
hours to spare him the mortification I supposed he
might feel." As it turned out, he need not have worried.
"The second day afterward I passed in and out of his
presence as though nothing unusual had occurred. To
my surprise he never made the most distant allusion to
[the matter] then, or ever afterward."

From that time on, he said, it was "as if I had been
regularly gazetted a member of his staff." Passes from
Grant enabled the reporter to go anywhere he wanted;
he could requisition transportation and draw subsistence from quartermaster and commissary authorities;
his tent was always pitched near Grant's, and his dispatches often were sent in the official mail pouch; in
short, he "constantly received flattering personal and
professional favors and attentions shown to no one else
in my position." All this was in return for his respecting
a confidence which he kept for more than thirty years.
In 1896, a seventy-year-old sheep raiser out in California, he wrote his memoirs, including an account of
Grant's two-day trip up the Yazoo and back. For nearly
sixty years they remained in manuscript, and when at
last they were published, ninety years after the war was

over, they were attacked and the writer vilified by some
of the general's long-range admirers, who claimed that
what Cadwallader called "this Yazoo-Vicksburg adventure" never happened.

At any rate, no harm had resulted from the army
commander's two-day absence from headquarters, drunk
or sober. The repulse of Taylor at Milliken's Bend and
Young's Point by the gunboats, on the second day, increased Grant's confidence rather than his fretfulness,
which in fact seemed to be cured. "All is going on here
now just right," he wrote to a friend on June 15, and
added: "My position is so strong that I feel myself abun-
dantly able to leave it and go out twenty or thirty miles
with force enough to whip two such garrisons."

He had small use for Pemberton, characterizing him
as "a northern man [who] got into bad company." Nor
did he fear Joe Johnston. Though he respected his ability, he said he did not believe the Virginian could save
Vicksburg without "a larger army than the Confederates now have at any one place."

Next day, moreover, the watchful eye of former congressman Frank Blair enabled Grant to dispose of his
third opponent, John McClernand, and thus wind up
the private war he had been waging all this time. Scan-
ning the columns of the Memphis *Evening Bulletin*,
Blair spotted a congratulatory order McClernand had
issued to his corps, claiming the lion's share of the credit
for the victory he foresaw. Blair sent the clipping to
Sherman, who forwarded it to Grant next day, calling it
"a catalogue of nonsense" and "an effusion of vain-
glory and hypocrisy . . . addressed not to an army, but to
a constituency in Illinois." He also cited a War Department order, issued the year before, "which actually for-

bids the publication of all official letters and reports,
and requires the name of the writer to be laid before the
President of the United States for dismissal."

Grant had waited half a year for this, passing over
various lesser offenses in hopes that one would come
along which would justify charges that could not fail to
stick. But now that he had it he still moved with deftness
and precision, completing the adjustment of the noose.
That same day, June 17, he forwarded the clipping to
McClernand with a note: "Inclosed I send you what
purports to be your congratulatory address to the Thirteenth Army Corps. I would respectfully ask if it is a true
copy. If it is not a correct copy, furnish me one by
bearer, as required both by regulations and existing orders of the Department." Next day McClernand ac-
knowledged the validity of the clipping. "I am prepared
to maintain its statements," he declared. "I regret that
my adjutant did not send you a copy as he ought, and I
thought he had."

With the noose now snug, Grant sprang the trap:
"Major General John A. McClernand is hereby relieved
from command of the Thirteenth Army Corps. He will
proceed to any point he may select in the state of Illinois
and report by letter to Headquarters of the Army for
orders."

Grant signed the order after working hours, suppos-
ing that it would be delivered the following morning,
but when James Wilson came in at midnight and heard
what was afoot—there was bad blood between him and
McClernand; the two had nearly come to blows a couple of weeks ago—he urged Rawlins to let him deliver
the order in person, without delay, lest something come
up—a rebel sortie at dawn, for example, which might
enable McClernand to distinguish himself as he had

done at Shiloh—to cause its suspension or cancellation. Rawlins agreed, and Wilson put on his dress uniform, summoned the provost marshal and a squad of soldiers, and set out through the darkness for McClernand's headquarters. Arriving about 2 o'clock in the morning, he demanded that the general be roused. Presently he was admitted to McClernand's tent, where he found the former congressman seated at a table on which two candles burned. Apparently he knew what to expect, for he too was in full uniform and his sword lay before him on the table. Wilson handed him the order, remarking that he had been instructed to see that it was read and understood. McClernand took it, adjusted his glasses, and perused it.

"Well, sir, I am relieved," he said. Then, looking up at Wilson, whose expression did not mask his satisfaction, he added: "By God, sir, we are both relieved!"

He did not intend to take this lying down, but he soon found that Grant had played the old army game with such skill that his opponent was left without a leg to stand on. "I have been relieved for an omission of my adjutant. Hear me," McClernand wired Lincoln from Cairo on his way to Springfield, their common home. From there he protested likewise to Halleck, suggesting the possible disclosure of matters that were dark indeed: "How far General Grant is indebted to the forbearance of officers under his command for his retention in the public service, I will not undertake to state unless he should challenge it. None know better than himself how much he is indebted to that forbearance."

That might be, but it was no help to the general up in Illinois; Grant challenged nothing, except to state that he had "tolerat[ed] General McClernand long after I thought the good of the service demanded his removal."

In time, there came to Springfield a letter signed "Your friend as ever, A. Lincoln," in which the unhappy warrior was told: "I doubt whether your present position is more painful to you than to myself. Grateful for the patriotic stand so early taken by you in this life-and-death struggle of the nation, I have done whatever has appeared practicable to advance you and the public interest together." However: "For me to force you back upon Gen. Grant would be forcing him to resign. I cannot give you a new command, because we have no forces except such as already have commanders." In short, the President had nothing to offer his fellow-townsman in the way of balm, save his conviction that a general was best judged by those "who have been with him in the field. . . . Relying on these," Lincoln said in closing, "he who has the right needs not to fear."

This was perhaps the unkindest cut of all, since McClernand knew only too well what was likely to happen to his reputation if judgment was left to Sherman and McPherson and their various subordinate commanders, including the army's two remaining ex-congressmen Blair and Logan. Among all these, and on Grant's staff, there was general rejoicing at his departure. Edward O. C. Ord, who had fought under Grant at Iuka, had just arrived to take charge of a sixth corps intended to consist of the divisions under Herron and Lauman; instead, he replaced McClernand.

Three days later, on June 22, Sherman was given command of the rearward line, which was strengthened by shifting more troops from in front of Vicksburg. "We want to whip Johnston at least 15 miles off, if possible," Grant explained. Steele succeeded Sherman, temporarily, and the siege went on as before.

No less than nine approaches were being run, all with

appropriate parallels close up to the enemy trenches, so that the final assault could be launched with the lowest possible loss in lives. Mines were sunk under rebel strongpoints, and on June 25 two of these were exploded on McPherson's front, the largest just north of the Jackson road. It blew off the top of a hill there, leaving a big, dusty crater which the attackers occupied for a day and then abandoned, finding themselves under heavy plunging fire from both flanks and the rear.

The mine accomplished little, but contributed greatly to the legend of the siege by somehow lofting a Negro cook, Abraham by name, all the way from the Confederate hilltop and into the Federal lines. He landed more or less unhurt, though terribly frightened. An Iowa outfit claimed him, put him in a tent, and got rich charging five cents a look. Asked how high he had been blown, Abraham always gave the same answer, coached perhaps by some would-be Iowa Barnum. "Donno, massa," he would say, "but tink bout tree mile."

Mostly, though, the weeks passed in boredom and increasing heat, under whose influence the Confederates appeared to succumb to a strange apathy during the final days of June. A Federal engineer remarked that their defense "was far from being vigorous." It seemed to him that the rebel strategy was "to wait for another assault, losing in the meantime as few men as possible," and he complained that this had a bad effect on his own men, since "without the stimulus of danger . . . troops of the line will not work efficiently, especially at night, after the novelty has worn off." Another trouble was that they foresaw the end of the siege, and no man coveted the distinction of being the last to die.

Not that all was invariably quiet. Occasionally there

were flare-ups, particularly where the trenches approached conjunction, and the snipers continued to take their toll. Though the losses were small, the suffering was great. "It looked hard," a Wisconsin soldier wrote, "to see six or eight poor fellows piled into an ambulance about the size of Jones's meat wagon and hustled over the rough roads as fast as the mules could trot and to see the blood running out of the carts in streams almost."

Taunts were flung as handily as grenades, back and forth across the lines, the graybacks asking, "When are you folks going to come on into town?" and the bluecoats replying that they were in no hurry: "We are holding you fellows prisoner while you feed yourselves." There was much fraternization between pickets, who arranged informal truces for the exchange of coffee and tobacco, and the same Federal engineer reported that the enemy's "indifference to our approach became at some points almost ludicrous." Once, for example, when the blue sappers found that as a result of miscalculation a pair of approach trenches would converge just inside the rebel picket line, the two sides called a cease-fire and held a consultation at which it was decided that the Confederates would pull back a short distance in order to avoid an unnecessary fire fight. At one stage of the discussion a Federal suggested that the approaches could be redesigned to keep from disturbing the butternut sentries, but the latter seemed to think that it would be a shame if all that digging went to waste. Besides, one said, "it don't make any difference. You Yanks will soon have the place anyhow."

Grant thought so, too. By now, in fact—though he kept his soldiers burrowing, intending to launch his final assault from close-up positions in early July—he was giving less attention to Pemberton than he was to

Johnston, off in the opposite direction, where Sherman described him as "vibrating between Jackson and Canton" in apparent indecision. Blair had reported earlier, on returning from a scout, that "every man I picked up was going to Canton to join him. The negroes told me their masters had joined him there, and those who were too old to go, or who could escape on any other pretext, told me the same story."

This had a rather ominous sound, as if hosts were gathering to the east, but Grant was not disturbed. He had access, through the treacherous courier, to many of the messages that passed between his two opponents. He knew what they were thinking, what the men under them were thinking, and what the beleaguered citizens were thinking. He spoke of their expectations in a dispatch he sent Sherman on June 25, the day the slave Abraham came hurtling into the hands of the Iowans: "Strong faith is expressed by some in Johnston's coming to their relief. [They] cannot believe they have been so wicked as for Providence to allow the loss of their stronghold of Vicksburg. Their principal faith seems to be in Providence and Joe Johnston."

By then—the fortieth day of siege—it had been exactly a month since the man in whom Vicksburg's garrison placed its "principal faith" assured Pemberton: "Bragg is sending a division. When it joins I will come to you." The division reached him soon afterwards, under Breckinridge, and was combined with the three already at hand under Loring, Samuel French, and Walker; Johnston's present-for-duty strength now totaled 31,226 men, two thirds of whom had joined him since his arrival in mid-May. But he found them quite deficient in equipment, especially wagons, and deferred

action until such needs could be supplied. In the interim
he got into a dispute with the Richmond authorities,
protesting that he had only 23,000 troops, while Seddon
insisted that the correct figure was 34,000. Finally the
Secretary told him: "You must rely on what you have,"
and urged him to move at once to Pemberton's relief.
But Johnston would not be prodded into action. "The
odds against me are much greater than those you ex-
press," he wired on June 15, and added flatly: "I consider saving Vicksburg hopeless."

Shocked by his fellow Virginian's statement that he
considered his assignment an impossible one, Seddon
took this to mean that Johnston did not comprehend
the gravity of the situation or the consequences of the
fall of the Gibraltar of the West, which in Seddon's
eyes meant the probable fall of the Confederacy itself.
It seemed to him, moreover, that the general—in line
with his behavior a year ago, down the York-James peninsula—was moving toward a decision not to fight at
all, and to the Secretary this was altogether unthinkable. "Your telegram grieves and alarms me," he replied next day. "Vicksburg must not be lost without a
desperate struggle. The interest and honor of the
Confederacy forbid it. I rely on you still to avert the
loss. If better resources do not offer, you must hazard
attack. It may be made in concert with the garrison, if
practicable, but otherwise without; by day or night, as
you think best."

Still Johnston would not budge. "I think you do not
appreciate the difficulties in the course you direct," he
wired back, "nor the probabilities or consequences of
failure. Grant's position, naturally very strong, is intrenched and protected by powerful artillery, and the

roads obstructed. . . . The defeat of this little army would at once open Mississippi and Alabama to Grant. I will do all I can, without hope of doing more than aid to extricate the garrison."

Fairly frantic and near despair over this prediction that the Father of Waters was about to pass out of Confederate hands, severing all practical connection with the Transmississippi and its supplies of men and food and horses, Seddon urged the general "to follow the most desperate course the occasion may demand. Rely upon it," he told him, "the eyes and hopes of the whole Confederacy are upon you, with the full confidence that you will act, and with the sentiment that it were better to fail nobly daring than, through prudence even, to be inactive. . . . I rely on you for all possible to save Vicksburg."

But no matter what ringing tones the Secretary employed, Johnston would not be provoked into what he considered rashness. "There has been no voluntary inaction," he protested; he simply had "not had the means of moving."

By then it was June 22. Two days later he received a message from Pemberton, suggesting that he get in touch with Grant and make "propositions to pass this army out, with all its arms and equipages," in return for abandoning Vicksburg to him. Johnston declined, not only because he did not believe the proposal would be accepted, but also because "negotiations with Grant for the relief of the garrison, should they become necessary, must be made by you," he replied on June 27. "It would be a confession of weakness on my part, which I ought not to make, to propose them. When it becomes necessary to make terms, they may be considered as made under my authority." In other words, any time Pemberton wanted to throw in the sponge, it would be all right with Johnston.

However, he prefaced this by saying that the Pennsylvanian's "determined spirit" encouraged him "to hope that something may yet be done to save Vicksburg," and two days later, June 29, "field transportation and other supplies having been obtained," he put his four divisions on the march for the Big Black, preceded by a screen of cavalry.

Never one to tilt at windmills, he was unwilling to do so now. The march—or "expedition," as he preferred to call it—"was not undertaken in the wild spirit that dictated the dispatches from the War Department," he later explained, and added scornfully: "I did not indulge in the sentiment that it was better for me to waste the lives and blood of brave soldiers 'than, through prudence even,' to spare them."

He never moved until he was ready, and then his movements were nearly always rearward. The one exception up to now had been Seven Pines, which turned out to be the exception that proved the rule, for it had cost him five months on the sidelines, command of the South's first army, and two wounds that were still unhealed a year later. Moreover, it had resulted in his present assignment, which was by no means to his liking, though his resultant brusqueness was reserved for those above him on the ladder of command, never for those below. To subordinates he was invariably genial and considerate, and they repaid him with loyalty, affection, and admiration. "His mind was clear as a bell," a staff officer had written from Jackson to a friend, two weeks ago, while the build-up for the present movement was still in progress. "I never saw a brain act with a quicker or more sustained movement, or one which exhibited a finer sweep or more striking power. . . . I cannot conceive surroundings more intensely depressing. Yet amidst them all, he preserved the elastic step and glowing brow of the genuine hero."

Desperation never rattled him; indeed, it had rather the opposite effect of increasing his native caution. And such was the case now as he approached the Big Black, beyond which Grant had intrenched a rearward-facing line. On the evening of July 1, Johnston called a halt between Brownsville and the river, and spent the next two days reconnoitering. Convinced by this "that attack north of the railroad was impracticable," he "determined, therefore, to make the examinations necessary for the attempt south of the railroad." On July 3, near Birdsong's Ferry, he wrote Pemberton that he intended "to create a diversion, and thus enable you to cut your way out if the time has arrived for you to do this. Of that time I cannot judge; you must, as it depends upon your condition. I hope to attack the enemy in your front [on] the 7th. . . . Our firing will show you where we are engaged. If Vicksburg cannot be saved, the garrison must."

Next morning, however, before he took up the march southward he noticed a strange thing. Today was the Fourth—Independence Day—but the Yankees over toward Vicksburg did not seem to be celebrating it in the usual fashion. On this of all days, the forty-eighth of the siege, the guns were silent for the first time since May 18, when the bluecoats filed into positions from which to launch their first and second assaults before settling down to the digging and bombarding that had gone on ever since; at least till now. Johnston and his men listened attentively, cocking their heads toward the

beleaguered city. But there was no rumble of guns at all.
Everything was quiet in that direction.

★ <big>8</big> ★

Having failed in his effort to "conquer a peace" by
defeating the principal Union army at Gettysburg,
north of its capital, R. E. Lee had failed as well in his
adjunctive purpose, which had been to frighten the
Washington authorities into withdrawing Grant and
Banks from their strangle-hold positions around Vicksburg and Port Hudson, thereby delivering from danger
not only those two critical locations but also the great
river that ran between them, the loss of which would cut
the South in two.

But Lee's was not the only attempt to forestall that
disaster. In addition to Joe Johnston, whose primary assignment it was, Kirby Smith too, in over-all command
of the Transmississippi, had plans for the relief of Pemberton and Gardner, on whose survival depended his
hope of remaining an integral part of the Confederacy.
Though these included nothing so ambitious as an intention to end the war with a single long-odds stab at
the enemy's vitals, they were at least still in the course of
execution when George Pickett's and Johnston Petti-
grew's men came stumbling back from Cemetery
Ridge, leaving the bodies of their comrades to indicate

the high-water mark of Lee's campaign, which now was on the ebb. Nor were these Transmississippi plans without the element of boldness. Encouraged by John Magruder's success in clearing Texas of all trace of the invader, Smith hoped his other two major generals, Theophilus Holmes in Arkansas and Richard Taylor in West Louisiana, might accomplish as much in their departments. If so, he might attain the aforementioned secondary purpose of causing the Federal high command to detach troops from Grant and Banks, in an attempt to recover what had been lost across the river from their respective positions, and thus lighten the pressure on Vicksburg and Port Hudson. At any rate Smith thought it worth a try, and in mid-June, being frantically urged by Richmond to adopt some such course of action—Davis and Seddon by then had begun losing confidence that anything was going to come of their increasingly strident appeals to Johnston along those lines—he instructed Taylor and Holmes to make the effort.

Taylor, who had just returned disgruntled to Alexandria after his strike at Milliken's Bend—a tactical success, at least until Porter's gunboats hove onto the scene, but a strategic failure, since the objective turned out to be little more than a training camp for the Negro recruits Grant had enlisted off the plantations roundabout—was pleased to be ordered back onto what he considered the right track, which led down to New Orleans. His plan, as he had outlined it before the fruitless excursion opposite Vicksburg, was to descend the Teche and the Atchafalaya, recapture Berwick Bay and overrun the Bayou Lafourche region, which lay between Grand Lake and the Mississippi, deep in Banks's rear, interrupting that general's communications with

New Orleans and threatening the city itself; whereupon
Banks would be obliged to raise his siege of Port Hudson in order to save New Orleans, whose 200,000 citizens he knew to be hostile to his occupation, and
Gardner then could march out to join Johnston for an
attack on Grant's rear and the quick delivery of beleaguered Vicksburg.

Such at least were Taylor's calculations—or more
properly speaking, his hopes; for his resources were admittedly slim for so ambitious a project. He had at Alexandria three small cavalry regiments just arrived from
Texas under J. P. Major, a twenty-seven-year-old Mis-
souri-born West Pointer whose peacetime army career
had included service in Albert Sidney Johnston's 2d
Cavalry, which already had provided the South with
eight and the North with two of their leading generals.
Awaiting instructions on the upper Teche, to which
they had returned in the wake of Banks's withdrawal in
mid-May, were five more such mounted regiments
under Texan Tom Green, the Valverde hero who had
been promoted to brigadier for his share in the New
Year's triumph at Galveston, along with three regiments of Louisiana infantry under Alfred Mouton,
thirty-four years old and a West Pointer, a Shiloh veteran and native of nearby Vermilionville, son of the former governor and brother-in-law to Frank Gardner,
whose rescue was the object of the campaign. The combined strength of the three commands was about 4000
effectives, barely one tenth of the force available to
Banks, but Taylor intended to make up in boldness for
what he lacked in numbers.

The advance was made in two widely divided columns. While Mouton and Green swung down the
west bank of the Teche, marching unopposed through

Opelousas and New Iberia, Taylor rode with Major across the Atchafalaya, then down Bayou Fordoche to within earshot of the guns of Port Hudson. At that point he left him, on June 18, with orders to move rapidly to the rear of Brashear City, the objective upon which the two forces were to converge for a simultaneous attack five days later. The distance was one hundred miles, entirely through occupied territory, but Major made it on schedule.

Skirmishing briefly that afternoon with the bluecoats on guard at Plaquemine, a west-bank landing below Baton Rouge, he bypassed fortified Donaldsonville after nightfall and set off next morning down Bayou Lafourche, which left the Mississippi just above the town. Some thirty miles below on the 20th, he rode into Thibodaux, whose garrison had fled at the news of his approach, and next day he struck the railroad at Terrebonne, thirty miles east of Brashear, then turned due west to complete his share of the convergence Taylor had designed.

Moving crosscountry with relays of quick-stepping mules hitched to his ambulance, that general had joined Mouton and Green on their unopposed march through Franklin to Fort Bisland. By nightfall of June 22 they were at Berwick and were poised for an amphibious attack, having brought with them a weird collection of "small boats, skiffs, flats, even sugar-coolers," which they had gathered for this purpose during their descent of the Teche. Batteries were laid under cover of darkness for a surprise bombardment in support of the scheduled dawn assault on the Brashear fortifications, just eastward across the narrow bay. Taylor's old commander in the Shenandoah Valley doubtless would have been proud to see how well his pupil, whose preparatory work had been done not at West Point but at Yale, had learned the value of well-laid plans when the object was the capture or destruction of an enemy force in occupation of a fixed position.

Old Jack's pride would have swelled even more next morning, when the Louisianian gathered the fruits of his boldness and careful planning. While some 300 dismounted Texans manned the 53 boats of his improvised flotilla—it was fortunate that there was no wind, Taylor said later, for the slightest disturbance would have swamped them—Green's cannoneers stood to their pieces. At first light they opened fire, and as they did so the sea-going troopers swarmed ashore, encouraged by the echoing boom of Major's guns from the east. Flustered by the sudden bombardment, which seemed to erupt out of nowhere, and by the unexpected assault from both directions, front and rear, the blue defenders milled about briefly, then surrendered.

The take was great, for here at the western terminus of the railroad Banks had cached the ordnance and quartermaster supplies he intended to use in his planned return up the Teche and the Red. In addition to 1700 prisoners, a dozen heavy-caliber guns and 5000 new-style Burnside repeaters and Enfield rifles were captured, together with two locomotives and their cars, which were unable to get away eastward because Major had wrecked the bridge at Lafourche Crossing, and commissary and medical stores in such abundance that they brought to more than $2,000,000 the estimated profit from Taylor's well-engineered strike. The general's pleasure was as great as that of his men, who wasted no time before sitting down to gorge themselves on the spoils. Their main concern was food, but his was the acquisition of the implements with which to continue his resistance to the invasion of his homeland. "For the first time since I reached western Louisiana," he exulted afterwards, "I had supplies."

All in all, it was the largest haul any body of Confederates had made since Stonewall followed up his raid on Manassas Junction with the capture of Harpers Ferry, back in September. Like his mentor, however, Taylor did not allow his exultation to delay his plans for the further discomfiture of his adversary. Next morning, leaving one regiment to sort the booty and remove it to Alexandria for safekeeping, he pressed on north and east, once more in two columns. While Green and Major marched for Donaldsonville, near which they were to establish batteries for the purpose of disrupting traffic on the Mississippi and thus sever the main line of supply and communications available to the besiegers of Port Hudson, Mouton's infantry went by rail to Thibodaux, from which point he sent pickets down the line to Bayou des Allemands, within twenty-five miles of New Orleans.

It was during the early morning hours of June 28 that Taylor encountered his first setback, though not in person. Approaching Donaldsonville the night before, Green had meant to bypass it, as Major had done on his way south, but the existence of an earthwork at the junction of the Lafourche and the Mississippi proved irresistible, perhaps in part because the Yankees had given it a hated name: Fort Butler. He disposed 800 dismounted troopers for attack and sent them forward two hours before dawn. The result was a bloody repulse, administered by the 225 defenders and three gunboats that arrived in time to support them. Green, who had suffered 261 casualties and inflicted only 24, pulled back, chagrined, and went about his proper business of establishing his three batteries on the west bank of the river, some ten miles below the town. He opened fire on July 7 and for three days not only kept the Mississippi closed to transport and unarmored supply boats, but also sent out mounted patrols as far downstream as Kenner, barely a dozen miles from the heart of New Orleans, which was already in a turmoil of expectancy as a result of Mouton's continued presence at Thibodaux and nearby Bayou des Allemands.

Secessionists were joyously predicting the imminent entry of the graybacks who were knocking at the gates, and William Emory, with fewer than 1000 men to oppose a rebel host he reckoned at 13,000, was altogether in agreement that the place was the Confederacy's for the taking. What was more, as we have seen already, he had said as much to Banks. "It is a choice between Port Hudson and New Orleans," he informed him on July 4, adding: "You can only save this city by sending me reinforcements immediately and at any cost."

Dick Taylor thus had accomplished the preliminary objective of his campaign; that is, he had brought the pressure he intended upon Banks, who now would be obliged to withdraw from Port Hudson, permitting Gardner to join Johnston for the delivery of Pemberton by means of an attack on Grant's intrenchments from the rear. So much Taylor had planned or anyhow hoped for. But Banks, as we have also seen, refused to cooperate in the completion of the grand design. If New Orleans fell, he told Halleck, he would retake it once the business at hand was completed and his army was free to be used for that purpose; but meantime he would hang on at Port Hudson till it surrendered, no matter what disasters threatened his rear.

Observing this perverse reaction, Taylor was obliged

to admit that once again, as at Milliken's Bend a month ago, though his tactics had been successful his strategy had failed. He had gained much in his brief campaign— particularly at Brashear City, whose spoils would greatly strengthen his future ability to resist the blue invaders —but he had not accomplished the recapture of New Orleans, which he saw as a cul-de-sac to be avoided, or the raising of the siege at Port Hudson.

Theophilus Holmes, though neither as energetic nor as inventive as Zachary Taylor's son and Stonewall Jackson's pupil, was also under compunction to do something toward relieving their hemmed-in friends across the way. Since the turn of the year, when John S. Marmaduke made a successful raid into Missouri, burning the Springfield supply base and bringing a hornet-like swarm of guerillas out of the brush and canebrakes, all the elderly North Carolinian had attempted in this regard was a repeat performance by that same general in late April, this time with twice as many men and instructions to put the torch to the well-stocked military depots along the west bank of the Mississippi north of Cairo, particularly Cape Girardeau, from which Grant was drawing much of his subsistence for the campaign far downriver.

Little came of this, however. Marmaduke and his 5000 troopers—the largest body of horsemen ever assembled in the Transmississippi up to now—struck and routed an inferior blue force at Fayetteville on April 18, then crossed the line into his native state and rode eastward across it in two columns, one through Fredericktown and the other through Bloomfield, driving Yankee outpost garrisons before him as he advanced. Secessionists, many of whom had kinsmen riding with him, greeted their favorite with cheers. His father had been governor before the war and he himself would be governor after it, a bachelor just past thirty now, tall and slender, quick-tempered and aristocratic in manner, with a full beard, delicate hands and feet, and fine hair brushed smooth on top and worn long in back so that it flared in a splendid ruff behind his head. His eyes were kindly and intelligent, though they had a disconcerting squint that came from his being at once near-sighted and unwilling to disfigure himself with glasses. He had studied both at Harvard and Yale before his graduation from West Point six years ago, but neither this formal preparation nor his success on the similar mission back in January stood him in much stead on April 25, when he completed his investment of Cape Girardeau with a demand for an immediate surrender; to which John McNeil, a fifty-year-old former Boston hatter and St Louis insurance agent, who had increased the strength of the garrison to 1700 by bringing in his brigade the day before, replied with an immediate refusal. Marmaduke attacked and found the resistance stiff, all the approaches being covered by well-served artillery. Not only was he repulsed, but scouts reported steamers unloading reinforcements from St Louis at the Cape Girardeau dock. So he withdrew next morning, after launching one more attack designed to discourage pursuit.

It failed in its purpose, however, and the retreat southward across the St Francis bottomlands of the Missouri boot heel required all his skill to avoid being intercepted by the now superior forces of the enemy. By May Day he was back in Arkansas, having suffered 161 casualties, and though he claimed that Federal losses "must have been five times as great as mine in killed and wounded"—McNeil and the others who had opposed him admitted a scant 120, combined—all he had to show for his pains, aside from some 150 recruits picked up in the course of the 400-mile-long ride, was "a great improvement in the number and quality of horses" in his command.

Grant was over the river by then, hard on the march for Jackson, but Holmes attempted nothing more in the way of interference until he received in mid-June an excerpt from a letter the Secretary of War had written Johnston in late May, after Pemberton was besieged, suggesting that he urge the Transmississippi commanders to "make diversions for you, or, in case of the fall of Vicksburg, secure a great future advantage to the Confederacy by the attack on, and seizure of, Helena, while all the available forces of the enemy are being pushed to Grant's aid." Seddon added that, though he was cut off from those commanders and therefore had no means of ordering the adoption of his suggestion, its tactical soundness was "so apparent that it is hoped it will be voluntarily embraced and executed."

He was right, so far at least as concerned its being "embraced," for Holmes had already conferred with Sterling Price on the same notion, and Price, who had taken command in early June of two brigades of infantry, not only declared that his men were "fully rested and in excellent spirits," but also expressed confidence that if Holmes would bring up two more brigades, together they could "crush the foe" at Helena. He had, moreover, an up-to-the-minute report from "an intelligent lady" just arrived from the west-bank Arkansas town, in which she described the enemy garrison as "ex-

ceedingly alarmed," much reduced by downriver calls
for reinforcements, "and apprehensive that you will attack them daily."

Seddon's suggestion reached Holmes at Little Rock
on June 14, together with a covering letter from Kirby
Smith, who left its adoption or rejection up to him.
Holmes was eager, for once, being greatly encouraged
by Price's coincidental approval of the project. "I believe we can take Helena. Please let me attack it," he
replied next day, and Smith consented promptly. "Most
certainly do it," he told him. That was on June 16. Two
days later Holmes issued orders for a concentration of
his forces, preparatory to launching the attack.

He had available for the effort just under 5000 infantry in Price's two brigades and a third under James
Fagan, a thirty-five-year-old Kentucky-born Arkansan
who was a veteran of the Mexican War as well as of Shiloh and Prairie Grove, and just over 2500 cavalry in the
two brigades remaining with Marmaduke—two others
had been detached since his repulse at Cape Girardeau
—and a third under Lucius Walker, who was thirty-
three, a nephew of Tennessee's James K. Polk and a
West Point graduate, though he had abandoned army
life to enter the mercantile business in Memphis until
Sumter put him back in uniform.

Holmes's instructions called for a cavalry screen to be
thrown around Helena as soon as possible, in order to
conceal from its blue defenders the infantry concentration scheduled for June 26 across the St Francis River at
Cotton Plant and Clarendon, within fifty miles of the
objective. Walker and Marmaduke moved out promptly, followed by Price and Fagan. Anxious to get back
onto the victory trail that had led to Wilson's Creek and
Lexington, up in his home state, before he was side-

tracked into defeat at Pea Ridge and more recently at
Iuka and Corinth, Price had announced to his troops
that they would "not only drive the enemy from our
borders, but pursue him into his own accursed land."
The men, who idolized him and affectionately called
him Pap, cheered at the news that these words were
about to be translated into action, and Fagan likewise
reported that his brigade was "ready and in high condition and spirit" as the march got under way.

Those spirits were soon dampened, however, by tor-
rents of rain that turned the roads to quagmires and
flooded the unbridged streams past fording. As a result,
it was June 30 before the infantry reached the areas designated. Holmes remained calm, despite the strain of a
four-day wait, and engaged in no useless criminations.
"My dear general," he wrote Price while the former
Missouri governor was still on the march through calf-
deep mud, "I deeply regret your misfortune."

Revising his schedule accordingly, he moved out
from Clarendon and Cotton Plant on July 1, arrived
within five miles of Helena on the evening of July 3, and
issued detailed instructions for an attack at dawn next
morning. Much depended on concert of action, for the
Union position featured mutually supporting earthworks and intrenchments, but Holmes counted also on
his assumed superiority in numbers. His strength was
7646 effectives, and he reckoned that of the enemy at
"4000 or 5000" at the most.

It was in fact much closer to the lower than to the
higher figure; 4129 bluecoats were awaiting him in the
Helena defenses. But what he did not know was that
they had been warned of his coming and had made special preparations to receive him, including arrangements for the support of the gunboat *Tyler*, whose

8-inch guns had helped to save the day at Shiloh under similar circumstances. The post commander, Benjamin M. Prentiss, had done even stouter service on that bloody field by holding the Hornets Nest until he and his division were overrun and captured. Exchanged in October, the Virginia-born Illinois lawyer had won promotion to major general and assignment to command of the District of East Arkansas—meaning Helena, since this was the only Union-occupied point in the region below Memphis.

For the past four days, disturbed by the rebel cavalry thrashing about in the brush outside his works, Prentiss had had the garrison up and under arms by 2.30 each morning, and just yesterday he had issued an order forbidding a Fourth of July celebration his officers had planned for tomorrow. However, the most effective preparation of all had begun in late December, when Fred Steele went downriver with Sherman and three fourths of his corps, leaving the remnant exposed to a sudden thrust such as Holmes was launching now.

At that time, six months ago, the total defense consisted of a single bastioned earthwork, called Fort Curtis for the then commander of the department, whose guns could sweep the gently rising ground of the hills that cradled the low-lying town beside the river; but since then Prentiss had constructed breastworks and dug rifle pits along the brow of the ridge, an average half mile beyond the fort, overlooking the timber-choked terrain of its more precipitous eastern slopes, and on the three dominant heights, Rightor Hill on the right, Graveyard Hill in the center, and Hindman Hill on the left, he had installed batteries which he designated, north to south, as A, B, C, D. Stoutly emplaced and mutually supporting, so that if one fell those adjoining could turn their fire on it, those four batteries and their protective intrenchments, which linked them into an iron chain of defense, covered the six roads that passed over the semicircular ridge and converged on Fort Curtis like so many spokes on the hub of half a wheel, and the cannoneers who manned them could feel secure—especially after a look back over their shoulders at the *Tyler* riding at anchor beyond the town—in the knowledge that Prentiss and his engineers had made the most of what nature had placed at their disposal.

Frederick Salomon commanded the division Steele had left behind. One of four immigrant brothers who served the Union through this crisis—three of them as colonels and brigadiers and the fourth as wartime governor of Wisconsin, to which they had fled from their native Prussia to avoid the consequences of having fought on the losing side in the Revolution of 1848—he had three small brigades, each led by a colonel: two of infantry, under William McLean and Samuel Rice, and one of cavalry under Powell Clayton. Like Salomon, these three officers were all in their middle or early thirties, nonprofessionals who had risen strictly on merit if not in action, and their troops were Westerners to a man, mostly farm boys out of Missouri, Iowa, and Wisconsin. Except for a single regiment of Hoosiers who had served with Pope in the taking of New Madrid and Island Ten, some fifteen months ago, the total field experience of the garrison had been the recent Yazoo Pass fiasco, in which they had been matched primarily against gnats and mosquitoes while the navy tried in vain to reduce Fort Pemberton. Still irked by the memory of that unhappy experience, and in accordance with Prentiss's standing instructions, they turned out of their bunks and took their posts at 2.30, an hour before dawn

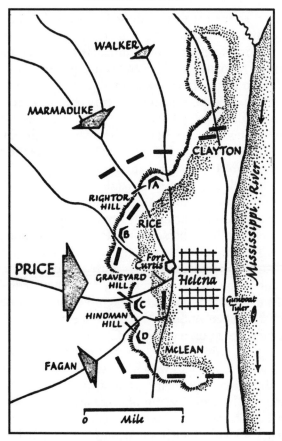

and a good two hours before sunrise of this Independence Day. Clayton's troopers were on the far right, guarding the river road north of town; McLean's and Rice's cannoneers and riflemen were disposed along the hilltop chain of batteries and intrenchments.

Half an hour after they were in position, Holmes's attack opened against the left center. At first it was rather tentative, driving the Federal outpost pickets back up the rugged western slopes of Hindman and Graveyard hills, but presently it exploded in full fury as the butternut pursuers came yelling after them, massed shoulder to shoulder in a solid drive for possession of the two high-sited batteries Prentiss had labeled C and D.

Their repulse was not as sudden as their eruption, but it was equally emphatic. In part this was because they had found the last five miles of road, which they covered after dark, in even worse shape than the hundred-odd they had traversed so painfully during the past week: with the result that they had been unable to bring their guns along and therefore had to attack without artillery support, of which the Federals had plenty. Fagan's brigade struck first, storming Hindman Hill—so called because it was here that the former Confederate commander, Thomas Hindman, had built the fine brick house Samuel Curtis had taken for his headquarters soon after occupying the town the year before. Three successive lines of half-bastions were rapidly penetrated and seized, but not the hilltop battery itself, which met the attackers with volleys of grape that shattered their formation, sent them scrambling for cover, and pinned them down so effectively that they could not even retreat.

Price's two brigades did better, at least at first. Battery C was taken in a rush, the graybacks swarming over Graveyard Hill and whooping among the captured guns. The weaponless rebel artillerymen came up, prepared to turn the pieces on their late owners, only to find that the retreating cannoneers had carried off all the friction primers, which left the guns about as useless to their captors as so much scrap iron. Moreover, they

came under enfilade fire from the two adjoining batteries and took a pounding as well from Fort Curtis, dead
ahead at the foot of the gradual eastern slope. Nor was
that all. Receiving word that Hindman Hill was under
assault, Prentiss had signaled J. M. Prichett of the *Tyler:*
"Open fire in that direction." Now Prichett did, and
with a vengeance, the fuzes of his 8-inch shells cut at ten
and fifteen seconds. So demoralized were the attackers
by the sudden deluge of heavy-caliber projectiles that,
according to one blue officer, two groups of about 250
men each responded "by hoisting a white flag, their own
sharpshooters upon the ridge in their rear firing from
cover upon and cursing them as they marched out prisoners of war."

Holmes did what he could to expand the lodgment,
sending one of Price's brigades to cooperate with Fagan in the stalled drive on Battery D. But to no avail;
McLean and Rice held steady, backed up stoutly by Fort
Curtis and the *Tyler*, whose bow and stern guns were
firing northwest and southwest, respectively, while her
ponderous broadside armament tore gaps in the rebel
center.

The early morning coolness soon gave way to parch-
ing heat; men risked their lives for sips of water from the
canteens of the dead. Around to the north, Marmaduke
had even less success against the defenders of Rightor
Hill, and though he later complained vociferously that
Walker had not supported him on his vulnerable left
flank, the fact was he had already found Batteries A and
B too hot to handle. He and Walker together lost a total
of 66 men, only a dozen of whom were killed. As usual,
it was the infantry that suffered, and in this case most of
the sufferers wore gray. Including prisoners, the three
brigades under Price and Fagan lost better than 1500

men between them. Holmes was not only distressed by the disproportionate losses, which demonstrated the unwisdom of his unsupported assault on a fortified opponent; he also saw that the attack would have been a mistake even if it had been successful, since the force in occupation would have been at the mercy of the *Tyler* and other units of the Federal fleet, which would make the low-lying river town untenable in short order.

By 10.30, after six hours of fighting, all this was unmistakably clear; Holmes called for a withdrawal. By noon it had been accomplished, except for some minor rear-guard skirmishing, although better than one out of every five men who had attacked was a casualty. His losses totaled 1590, nearly half of them captives pinned down by the murderous fire and unable to retreat.

Prentiss lost 239: less than six percent of his force, as compared to better than twenty percent of the attackers. However, even with the odds reduced by this considerable extent, he still had too few men to risk pursuit. Reinforcements arrived next day from Memphis, together with another welcome gunboat, but he was content to break up a rebel cavalry demonstration which he correctly judged to be nothing more than a feint designed to cover a general retirement. By dawn of July 6 the only live Confederates around Helena were captives, many of them too gravely wounded to be moved.

In praising his troops for their stand against nearly twice their number, Prentiss did not neglect his obligation to the *Tyler*, whose skipper in time received as well a letter of commendation from the Secretary of the Navy. "Accept the Department's congratulations for yourself and the officers and men under your command," the Secretary wrote, "for your glorious achievement, which adds another to the list of brilliant

successes of our Navy and Army on the anniversary of
our nation's independence."

★   ★   ★

It was indeed a Glorious Fourth, from the northern
point of view; Gideon Welles did not exaggerate in
speaking wholesale of a "list of brilliant successes"
scored by the Union, afloat and ashore, on this eighty-
seventh anniversary of the nation's birth. For the South,
however, the day was one not of glory, but rather of disappointment, of bitter irony, of gloom made deeper by
contrast with the hopes of yesterday, when Lee was
massing for his all-or-nothing attack on Cemetery
Ridge and Johnston was preparing at last to cross the
Big Black River, when Taylor was threatening to retake
New Orleans and Holmes was moving into position for
his assault on Helena. All four had failed, which was reason enough for disappointment; the irony lay in the fact
that not one of the four, Lee or Johnston, Taylor or
Holmes, was aware that on this Independence Eve, so
far at least as his aspirations for the relief of Vicksburg
or Port Hudson were concerned, he was too late.

At 10 o'clock that morning, July 3, white flags had
broken out along a portion of Pemberton's works and
two high-ranking officers, one a colonel, the other a
major general, had come riding out of their lines and
into those of the besiegers, who obligingly held their
fire. The senior bore a letter from his commander, addressed to Grant. "General," it began: "I have the
honor to propose to you an armistice for several hours,
with a view to arranging terms for the capitulation of
Vicksburg."

Pemberton's decision to ask for terms had been

reached the day before, when he received from his four division commanders, Stevenson, Forney, Smith, and Bowen, replies to a confidential note requesting their opinions as to the ability of their soldiers "to make the marches and undergo the fatigues necessary to accomplish a successful evacuation." After forty-six days and forty-five nights in the trenches, most of the time on half- and quarter-rations, not one of the four believed his troops were in any shape for the exertion required to break the ring of steel that bound them and then to outmarch or outfight the well-fed host of bluecoats who outnumbered them better than four to one in effectives. Forney, for example, though he expressed himself as "satisfied they will cheerfully continue to bear the fatigue and privation of the siege," answered that it was "the unanimous opinion of the brigade and regimental commanders that the physical condition and health of our men are not sufficiently good to enable them to accomplish successfully the evacuation." There Pemberton had it, and the other three agreed. "With the knowledge I then possessed that no adequate relief was to be expected," the Pennsylvania Confederate later wrote, "I felt that I ought not longer to place in jeopardy the brave men whose lives had been intrusted to my care." He would ask for terms.

The apparent futility of submitting such a request to a man whose popular fame was based on his having replied to a similar query with the words, "No terms except an unconditional and immediate surrender can be accepted," was offset—at least to some extent, as Pemberton saw it—by two factors. One was that the Confederates had broken the Federal wigwag code, which permitted them to eavesdrop on Grant's and Porter's ship-to-shore and shore-to-ship exchanges, and from these they had learned that the navy wanted to avoid the troublesome, time-consuming task of transporting thousands of grayback captives far northward up the river. This encouraged the southern commander to hope that his opponent, despite his Unconditional Surrender reputation, might be willing to parole instead of imprison the Vicksburg garrison if that was made a condition of avoiding at least one more costly assault on intrenchments that had proved themselves so stout two times before. The other mitigating factor, at any rate to Pemberton's way of thinking, was that the calendar showed the proposed surrender would occur on Independence Day.

Some among the defenders considered a capitulation on that date unthinkable, since it would give the Yankees all the more reason for crowing, but while Pemberton was aware of this, and even agreed that it would involve a measure of humiliation, he also counted it an advantage. "I am a northern man," he told the objectors on his staff. "I know my people. I know their peculiar weaknesses and their national vanity; I know we can get better terms from them on the Fourth of July than on any other day of the year. We must sacrifice our pride to these considerations."

One other possible advantage he had, though admittedly it had not been of much use to Simon Buckner at Donelson the year before. John Bowen had known and befriended Grant during his fellow West Pointer's hard-scrabble farming days in Missouri, and it was hoped that this might have some effect when the two got down to negotiations. Although Bowen was sick, his health undermined by dysentery contracted during the siege—he would in fact be dead within ten days, three months short of his thirty-third birthday—he accepted the assignment, and that was how it came about that he was the major general who rode into the Union lines this morning, accompanied by a colonel from Pemberton's staff.

However, it soon developed that the past seventeen months had done little to mellow Grant in his attitude toward old friends who had chosen to do their fighting under the Stars and Bars. He not only declined to see or talk with Bowen, but his reply to the southern commander's note, which was delivered to him by one of his own officers, also showed that he was, if anything, even harsher in tone than he had been in the days when Buckner charged him with being "ungenerous and unchivalrous." Pemberton had written: "I make this proposition to save the further effusion of blood, which must otherwise be shed to a frightful extent." Now Grant replied: "The useless effusion of blood you propose stopping by this course can be ended at any time you may choose, by an unconditional surrender of the city and garrison. . . . I do not favor the proposition of appointing commissioners to arrange terms of capitulation, because I have no terms other than those indicated above."

There were those words again: Unconditional Surrender. But their force was diminished here at Vicksburg, as they had not been at Donelson, by an accompanying verbal message in which Grant said that he would be willing to meet and talk with Pemberton between the lines that afternoon.

Worn by strain and illness, Bowen delivered the note and repeated the off-the-record message, both of which were discussed at an impromptu council of war, and presently—by then it was close to 3 o'clock, the hour Grant had set for the meeting—he and the colonel retraced in part the route they had followed that morning, accompanied now by Pemberton, who spoke half to himself and half to his two companions as he rode past the white flags on the ramparts. "I feel a confidence that I shall stand justified to my government, if not to the southern people," they heard him say, as if he saw already the scapegoat role in which he as an outlander would be cast by strangers and former friends for whose sake he had alienated his own people, including two brothers who fought on the other side.

First, however, there came a ruder shock. Despite the flat refusal expressed in writing, he had interpreted Grant's spoken words, relayed to him through Bowen, as an invitation to parley about terms. But he soon was disabused of this impression. The three Confederates came upon a group of about a dozen Union officers awaiting them on a hillside only a couple of hundred yards beyond the outer walls of the beleaguered city. Ord, McPherson, Logan, and A. J. Smith were there, together with several members of Grant's staff and Grant himself, whom Pemberton had no trouble recognizing, not only because his picture had been distributed widely throughout the past year and a half, but also because he had known him in Mexico, where they had served as staff lieutenants in the same division.

Once the introductions were over, there was an awkward pause as each waited for the other to open the conversation and thereby place himself in somewhat the attitude of a suppliant. When Pemberton broke the silence at last by remarking that he understood Grant had "expressed a wish to have a personal interview with me," Grant replied that he had done no such thing; he had merely agreed to such a suggestion made at second hand by Bowen.

Finding that this had indeed been the case, though he had not known it before, Pemberton took a different approach. "In your letter this morning," he observed, "you state that you have no other terms than an unconditional surrender." Grant's answer was as prompt as before. "I have no other," he said. Whereupon the Pennsylvanian—"rather snappishly," Grant would recall—replied: "Then, sir, it is unnecessary that you and I should hold any further conversation. We will go to fighting again at once." He turned, as if to withdraw, but fired a parting salvo as he did so. "I can assure you, sir, you will bury many more of your men before you will enter Vicksburg." Grant said nothing to this, nor did he change his position or expression. The contest was like poker, and he played it straight-faced while his opponent continued to sputter, remarking, as he later paraphrased his words, that if Grant "supposed that I was suffering for provisions he was mistaken, that I had enough to last me for an indefinite period, and that Port Hudson was even better supplied than Vicksburg."

Grant did not believe there was much truth in this, but he saw clearly enough from Pemberton's manner that his unconditional-surrender formula was not going to obtain without a good deal more time or bloodshed. So he unbent, at least to the extent of suggesting that he and Pemberton step aside while their subordinates talked things over. The Confederate was altogether willing—after all, it was what he had proposed at the outset, only to be rebuffed—and the two retired to the shelter of a stunted oak nearby. In full view of the soldiers on both sides along this portion of the front, while Bowen and the colonel talked with the other four Union generals, the blue and gray commanders stood together in the meager shade of the oak tree, which, as Grant wrote afterwards, "was made historical by the event. It was but a short time before the last vestige of its body, root and limb had disappeared, the fragments taken as trophies. Since then the same tree has furnished as many cords of wood, in the shape of trophies, as 'The True Cross.'"

But that was later, after the souvenir hunters had the run of the field. For the present, the oak remained as intact as almost seven weeks of bullets and shells from both sides had allowed, and Grant and Pemberton continued their pokerlike contest of wills beneath its twisted branches. If the Confederate played a different style of game, that did not necessarily mean that he was any less skillful. In point of fact—at any rate in the limited sense of getting what he came for—he won; for in the end it was the quiet man who gave way and the sputterer who stood firm.

In the adjoining group, Bowen proposed that the garrison "be permitted to march out with the honors of war, carrying with them their arms, colors, and field batteries," which was promptly denied, as he no doubt had expected; whereupon Pemberton, after pointing out that his suggestion for the designation of commissioners had been rejected, observed that it was now Grant's turn to make a counteroffer as to terms. Grant agreed; Pemberton would hear from him by 10 o'clock that evening, he said; and with that the meeting broke up, though it was made clear that neither opponent was to consider himself "pledged."

Both returned to their own lines and assembled councils of war to discuss what had developed. Pemberton found that all his division commanders and all but two of his brigade commanders favored capitulation, provided it could be done on a basis of parole without imprisonment. Grant found his officers of a mind to offer what was acceptable, although he himself did not concur; "My own feelings are against this," he declared. But presently, being shielded in part from the possible wrath of his Washington superiors by the overwhelming vote of his advisers, he "reluctantly gave way," and put his terms on paper for delivery to Pemberton at the designated hour. Vicksburg was to be surrendered, together with all public stores, and its garrison paroled; a single Union division would move in and take possession of the place next morning.

"As soon as rolls can be made out, and paroles signed by officers and men," he stipulated, "you will be allowed to march out of our lines, the officers taking with them their side-arms and clothing, and the field, staff, and cavalry officers one horse each. The rank and file will be allowed all their clothing, but no other property." Remembering Pemberton's claim that he had plenty of provisions on hand, Grant added a touch that combined generosity and sarcasm: "If these conditions are accepted, any amount of rations you may deem necessary can be taken from the stores you now have, and also the necessary cooking utensils for them. . . . I am, general, very respectfully, your obedient servant, U. S. GRANT, Major General."

Now that he had committed his terms to paper, he found them much more satisfactory than he had done before. "I was very glad to give the garrison of Vicksburg the terms I did," he afterwards wrote. To have shipped the graybacks north to Illinois and Ohio, he explained, "would have used all the transportation we had for a month." Moreover, "the men had behaved so well that I did not want to humiliate them. I believed that consideration for their feelings would make them less dangerous foes during the continuance of hostilities, and better citizens after the war was over."

So he said, years later, making a virtue of necessity and leaving out of account the fact that he had begun with a demand for unconditional surrender. For the present, indeed, he was so admiring of the arrangement, from the Union point of view, that he did what he could to make certain Pemberton could not reject it—as both had reserved the right to do—without risking a mutiny by the beleaguered garrison. He had Rawlins send the following note to his corps commanders: "Permit some discreet men on picket tonight to communicate to the enemy's pickets the fact that General Grant has offered, in case Pemberton surrenders, to parole all the officers and men and to permit them to go home from here."

He could have spared himself the precaution and his courier the ride. "By this time," a Confederate declared, "the atmosphere was electric with expectancy, and the wildest rumors raced through camp and city. Everyone had the air of knowing something vital." What was more, a good deal of back-and-forth visiting had begun on both sides of the line. "Several brothers met," a Federal remarked, "and any quantity of cousins. It was a strange scene." Whatever the blue pickets might say, on whatever valid authority, was only going to add to the seethe of speculation within and without the hilltop fortress which was now about to fall, just under fourteen months after its mayor replied to the first demand for surrender, back in May of the year before: "Mississippians don't know, and refuse to learn, how to surrender to an enemy. If Commodore Farragut and Brigadier General Butler can teach them, let them come and try."

The upshot was that Grant had come and tried, being so invited, and now Pemberton had been taught, although it galled him. Assembling his generals for a reading of the 10 o'clock offer, he remarked—much as his opponent had done, an hour or two ago, across the way—that his "inclination was to reject these terms." However, he did not really mean it, any more than Grant had meant it, and after he had taken the all but unanimous vote for capitulation, he said gravely: "Gentlemen, I have done what I could," then turned to dictate his reply. "In the main, your terms are accepted," he told Grant, "but in justice both to the honor and spirit of my troops, manifested in the defense of Vicksburg, I have to submit the following amendments, which, if acceded to by you, will perfect the agreement between us. . . ."

The added conditions, of which there were two, were modest enough in appearance. He proposed to march his soldiers out of the works, stack arms, and then move off before the Federals took possession, thus avoiding a confrontation of the two armies. That was the first. The second was that officers be allowed "to retain their . . . personal property, and [that] the rights and property of citizens . . . be respected." But Grant declined to allow him either, and for good cause. As for the first, he replied, it would be necessary for the troops to remain under proper guard until due process of parole had been formally completed, and as for the second, while he was willing to give all citizens assurance that they would be spared "undue annoyance or loss," he would make no specific guarantees regarding "personal property," which he privately suspected was intended to include a large number of slaves, freed six months ago by Lincoln's Proclamation. "I cannot consent to leave myself under any restraint by stipulations," he said flatly. Denial of the proposed amendments was contained in a dispatch sent before sunrise, July 4. Pemberton had until 9 A.M. to accept the original terms set forth in last night's message; otherwise, Grant added, "I shall regard them as having been rejected, and shall act accordingly."

Now it was Pemberton's turn to bend in the face of stiffness, and this he did the more willingly since the morning report—such had been the ravages of malnutrition and unrelieved exposure—showed fewer than half his troops available for duty as effectives. "General," he answered curtly about sunrise: "I have the honor to acknowledge the receipt of your communication of this day, and in reply to say that the terms proposed are accepted."

The rest was up to Grant, and it went smoothly. At 10 o'clock, in response to the white flags that now fluttered along the full length of the Confederate line, John Logan marched his division into the works. Soon afterwards the Stars and Stripes were flying over the Vicksburg courthouse for the first time in two and a half years. If the victors were somewhat disappointed professionally that seven weeks of intensive shelling by 220 army cannon, backed up by about as many heavier pieces aboard the gunboats and the mortar rafts, had done surprisingly little substantial damage to the town, it was at least observed that the superficial damage was extensive. Not a single pane of glass remained unbroken in any of the houses, a journalist noted. It was also observed that, despite the southern commander's claim that he had ample provisions, the gauntness of the disarmed graybacks showed only too clearly, not only that such was not the case, but also that it apparently had not been so for some time.

One Federal quartermaster, bringing in a train of supplies for the troops in occupation, was so affected by

the hungry looks on the faces of the men of a rebel brigade that he called a halt and began distributing hardtack, coffee, and sugar all around. Rewarded by "the
heartfelt thanks" of the butternut scarecrows, he said afterwards that when his own men complained that night
about the slimness of their rations, "I swore by all the
saints in the calendar that the wagons had broken down
and the Johnny Rebs had stolen all the grub."

Not only was there little "crowing," which some
Confederates had feared would be encouraged and enlarged by a Fourth of July surrender, but according to
Grant "the men of the two armies fraternized as if they
had been fighting for the same cause." Though that was
perhaps an overstatement of the case, there was in fact a
great deal of mingling by victors and vanquished alike —
"swapping yarns over the incidents of the long siege," as
one gray participant put it — and even some good-
natured ribbing back and forth. "See here, Mister; you
man on the little white horse!" a bluecoat called out to
Major Lockett, whose engineering duties had kept him
on the move during lulls in the fighting. "Danged if you
aint the hardest feller to hit I ever saw. I've shot at you
more'n a hundred times." Lockett took it in good part,
and afterwards praised his late adversaries for their generosity toward the defeated garrison. "General Grant
says there was no cheering by the Federal troops," he
wrote. "My recollection is that on our right a hearty
cheer was given by one Federal division 'for the gallant
defenders of Vicksburg!'"

Pemberton did not share in the fraternization, not
only because of his present sadness, his sense of failure,
and his intimation of what the reaction of his adoptive
countrymen would be when they got the news of what
had happened here today, but also because of his nature,

which was invariably distant and often forbidding. For him, congeniality had been limited mainly to the family circle he had broken and been barred from when he threw in with the South. Even toward his own officers he had always been stiffly formal, and now toward Grant, who came through the lines that morning on his way to confer with Porter at the wharf, he was downright icy; indeed, rude. Perhaps it was the northern commander's show of magnanimity, when he knew that such concessions as had been granted—parole of the garrison, for example, instead of a long boat ride to prison camps in Ohio and Illinois—had been the result of hard bargaining and a refusal to yield to his original demand for unconditional surrender. In any event, one of his staff found Pemberton's manner "unhandsome and disagreeable in the extreme." No one offered Grant a seat when he called on Pemberton in a house on the Jackson road, this officer protested, and when he remarked that he would like a drink of water, he was told that he could go where it was and help himself. He did not seem perturbed by this lack of graciousness, however; he went his way, taking no apparent umbrage, content with the spoils of this Independence Day, which were by far the greatest of the war, at any rate in men and materiel.

Confederate casualties during the siege had been 2872 killed, wounded, and missing, while those of the Federals totaled 4910; but now the final tally of captives was being made. It included 2166 officers, 27,230 enlisted men, and 115 civilian employees, all paroled except one officer and 708 men, who preferred to go north as prisoners rather than risk being exchanged and required to fight again. In ordnance, too, the harvest was a rich one, yielding 172 cannon, surprisingly large amounts of ammunition of all kinds, and nearly 60,000 rifles, many of such superior quality that some Union regiments exchanged their own weapons for the ones they found stacked when they marched in.

One additional prize there was, richer by far than all the rest combined and to which they had served as no more than prologue. The Mississippi would return to its old allegiance as soon as one remaining obstruction had been removed, and that allegiance would be secure as soon as one continuing threat had been abolished. The obstruction—Port Hudson—was not really Grant's concern except for the dispatching of reinforcements, which he could now quite easily afford, to help Banks get on with the job. He kept his attention fixed on Joe Johnston—the threat—who continued to hover, off to the east, beyond the Big Black River. Conferring with Porter, Grant requested his cooperation in flushing out the rebels up the Yazoo, reestablished there by Johnston while the Federals were concentrating on the reduction of Vicksburg. As usual, the admiral was altogether willing; he assigned an ironclad and two tinclads the task of escorting 5000 infantry upstream to retake Yazoo City, which the Confederates had refortified since their flight from the approaching gunboats back in May. But the northern army commander's main concern was Johnston himself and the force he was assembling west of Jackson.

Yesterday, while surrender negotiations were under way, Grant had notified Sherman, whose troops were already faced in that direction, that he was to strike eastward as soon as Vicksburg fell. "I want Johnston broken up as effectually as possible, and roads destroyed," he wired. This message was followed shortly by another, in which he was more specific as to just what breakage was

expected. "When we go in," he told his red-haired lieutenant, "I want you to drive Johnston from the Mississippi Central Railroad, destroy bridges as far as Grenada with your cavalry, and do the enemy all the harm
possible. You can make your own arrangements and
have all the troops of my command, except one corps—
McPherson's, say. I must have some troops to send to
Banks, to use against Port Hudson."

As it turned out, there was no need for more troops at
Port Hudson. All that was required was valid evidence
that its companion bluff 240 miles upriver was in Union
hands, and this arrived before the reinforcements: specifically, during the early hours of July 7.

That evening Gardner received from one of his three
brigade commanders—Miles, whose position on the far
right afforded him a view of the river, as well as of the
extreme left of the Federal intrenchments—a report of
strange doings by the enemy, ashore and afloat: "This
morning all his land batteries fired a salute, and followed it immediately [by another] with shotted guns,
accompanied by vociferous yelling. Later in the day the
fleet fired a salute also. What is meant we do not know.
Some of them hallooed over, saying that Vicksburg had
fallen on the 4th instant. My own impression is that
some fictitious good news has been given to his troops
in order to raise their spirits; perhaps with a view of
stimulating them to a charge in the morning. We will be
prepared for them should they do so."

The colonel's men shared his skepticism as well as his
resolution, even when confronted with documentary
evidence in the form of a "flimsy" tossed into their
lines, bearing the signature of the Federal adjutant-gen-
eral and announcing Pemberton's surrender three days

ago. "That's another damned Yankee lie!" a butternut defender shouted back. But Gardner himself was not so sure. He had fought well, inflicting 4363 casualties at a cost of only 623 of his own, and though by now the trenches were less than twenty feet apart in places and the enemy was obviously about to launch another massive assault, which was likely to succeed at such close range, he was prepared to fight still longer if need be. On the other hand, it was no part of his duty to sacrifice the garrison for no purpose—and obviously Port Hudson's purpose, or anyhow its hope of survival, was tied to that of Vicksburg. If the Mississippi bastion had fallen, so must the Louisiana one, exposed as it would be to the possible combination of both Union armies.

So Gardner adopted the logical if somewhat irregular course of inquiring of his opponent, by means of a flag of truce next morning, as to whether the report of Vicksburg's fall was true. And when Banks supplied confirming evidence, in the form of a dispatch Grant had sent on the surrender date, Gardner decided that the time for his own capitulation was at hand. Final details were not worked out until the following day, July 9, when the besiegers marched in and took possession, but a train of wagons had already entered Port Hudson the previous afternoon, loaded with U.S. Army rations for the half-starved garrison.

Banks combined firmness and generosity. Though his terms had been unconditional, he paroled his 5935 enlisted captives and sent only their 405 officers to New Orleans to await exchange or shipment north. Moreover, having acquired some 7500 excellent rifles and 51 light and heavy guns, he closed the formal surrender ceremony with "a worthy act, well merited." Thus his adjutant characterized the gesture in describing it years later. "By General Banks's order, General Gardner's sword was returned to him in the presence of his men, in recognition of the heroic defense."

If there was haste in the northern commander's method, including parole of all his enlisted prisoners, there was also method in his haste. Albeit they were the sweeter, being his first, Banks was no more inclined than Grant to sit down and enjoy the fruits of his victory; for just as the latter took out after Joe Johnston as soon as Vicksburg fell, so did the former concern himself with Dick Taylor as soon as Port Hudson followed suit.

Faced as he was with the departure of the nine-month volunteers who made up a considerable portion of his army, Banks had to choose between using the remainder as guards for the captured garrison or as a mobile force for driving out the reported 13,000 Confederates who had moved into his rear and were threatening New Orleans from Bayou Lafourche and Berwick Bay. Quite aside from the pleasure he derived from being generous to a defeated foe, that was why he paroled nearly 6000 of his 6340 prisoners: to get them off his hands and thus be free to deal with Taylor.

Having decided, he wasted no time. While the surrender ceremony was in progress he put Weitzel's and Grover's divisions aboard transports and sent them at once to Donaldsonville, where they would begin their descent of the Lafourche, disposing of infiltrated rebels as they went. The debarkation was completed on July 11; next afternoon the two blue divisions began their advance down opposite banks of the bayou. Early the following morning, however—July 13 at Koch's Plantation, six miles from Donaldsonville—Weitzel's two west-bank brigades, and indirectly Banks himself, were

given a cruel demonstration of the fact that haste sometimes made waste, even in pursuit.

Tom Green, with his own and Major's brigade of
mounted Texans, had been having a fine time disrupting traffic on the Mississippi with the guns he had established on its right bank, ten miles below the town.
Though they could do no real damage to the *Essex*,
which came down to challenge them, they did succeed
in driving the ironclad off and puncturing the steam-
drums of several less heavily armored vessels. A battery
commander referred to the 12-foot levee as "the best of
earthworks," and Green was prepared to stay there in-
definitely, finding balm in his present success for the
sting of the recent setback at Fort Butler. After three
days of such fun, however, he learned of the arrival of
ten transports at Donaldsonville and the debarkation of
two blue divisions with better than five times his number of men. Determined not to leave without a fight,
whatever the odds, he pulled back from the river,
crossed the Lafourche, and lay in wait for what was
coming.

What was coming was Weitzel, supported by Grover
across the way. Green struck hard, soon after sunrise of
July 13, caught the bluecoats off guard, and threw them
into such hasty retreat that they abandoned three of
their guns to their pursuers. They lost 50 killed, 223
wounded, and 186 captured or missing, while Green
lost 9 killed and 24 wounded. He withdrew westward,
unmolested, and rejoined Taylor at Vermilionville, that
general having retired with all his spoils from Brashear
City when he learned of Gardner's surrender and the
intended return downriver of the besieging army. By no
means strong enough for a full-scale battle with the
greatly superior forces of the Federals near their base,

he was content to wait for them to attempt a second ascent of the Teche. They would find him better equipped for resistance than he had been before his recent brief but profitable drive to the outskirts of New Orleans.

Banks accepted the Koch's Plantation check with his usual grace, even setting aside a court-martial's findings that one of Weitzel's brigade commanders had been guilty of drunkenness on duty and misconduct in the presence of the enemy. The former Speaker was looking for no scapegoat; he would take whatever blame there was, along with the praise, as designer and director of the campaign from start to finish. And of praise there was much. It was Banks, after all, who had removed the final obstruction to Union control of the Mississippi, following Grant's extraction of "the nail that held the South's two halves together."

On July 16, one week after the fall of Port Hudson, the unarmed packet *Imperial* tied up at New Orleans and began unloading cargo she had brought unescorted from St Louis. For the first time in thirty months, the Father of Waters was open to commerce from Minnesota to the Gulf.

Meanwhile Porter and Sherman had gone about their assignments, though for both there had been irksome delays followed by mishaps for which irksome was all too mild a word; Porter's, in fact, had occurred on the same day as Weitzel's, and while it had been considerably less bloody it was also a good deal more expensive.

Originally intended as reinforcements for Banks, since they had spent less than a month in the Vicksburg trenches, 5000 men of Herron's division were shifted to lighter-draft transports on July 11, when news of the fall

of Port Hudson arrived, and set out up the Yazoo next
morning, escorted by two 6-gun tinclads and the 14-
gun ironclad *Baron de Kalb*, formerly the *St Louis* but
rechristened when it developed that the navy already
had a warship by that name. One of the original seven
built by James Eads in the fall of '61 and a veteran of all
the major engagements on the Tennessee, the Cumber-
land, and the Mississippi north of Vicksburg, she had
carried the flag eight weeks ago on a similar expedition
to Yazoo City and beyond, which had resulted in much
damage to the enemy at no cost to the fleet.

This last was not to be the case this time, however.
Isaac Brown, who had sunk the *De Kalb*'s sister ship
Cairo with a demijohn of powder up this same winding
river in December, was back again with forty survivors
of the crew from his lost ram *Arkansas*, and he had plans
for a repeat performance. His navy artillerists managed
to drive the ironclad back around the bend when she
appeared below the town at noon of July 13, but a Tar-
heel regiment assigned to the place by Johnston withdrew on learning that Herron had landed three of his
own regiments with instructions to bag the defenders.
Obliged to pull back for lack of support, Brown and his
sailors left something behind them in addition to their
guns: as Porter and Herron presently discovered.

The two were on the bridge of the flagship, steaming
slowly upstream toward the undefended town, when—
just after sunset, abreast of the yards where, about this
time a year ago, the *Arkansas* had acquired her rusty
armor—one of Brown's improvised torpedoes exploded
directly under her bow. As she began to settle, another
went off under her stern, which hastened her destruction. Within fifteen minutes, though all aboard managed to escape with nothing worse than bruises, she was

on the muddy bottom, providing a multichambered home for gars and catfish.

Herron, having survived this violent introduction to one of the dangers involved in combined operations, went ashore to complete his share of the mission, afterwards reporting the destruction of the Yazoo City fortifications and five of the nine rebel steamboats found lurking in the vicinity, together with the capture of some 300 prisoners, six guns, and about 250 small arms, as well as 2000 bales of cotton and 800 horses and mules which he commandeered from the planters roundabout. He was enthusiastic; no less than 50,000 more bales were awaiting discovery and seizure in the region, he declared. Porter, on the other hand, summed up the operation somewhat ruefully. "But for the blowing up of the *Baron de Kalb*, it would have been a good move," he informed his superiors, and he added, by way of extenuating this loss of his fourth ironclad since December: "While a rebel flag floats anywhere the gunboats must follow up. The officers and men risk their lives fearlessly on these occasions, and I hope the Department will not take too seriously the accidents which happen to the vessels when it is impossible to avoid them."

Sherman made no such apology, though his particular mishap had occurred the day before and had been preceded by a week of hot and profitless activity. Grant's instructions for him to "do the enemy all the harm possible," accompanied as they were by the prospect of having close to 50,000 troops with which to carry them out, had put the red-haired Ohioan in what he liked to call "high feather," and when they were followed next day—July 4—by the news that Vicksburg had fallen, his excitement reached fever pitch. "I can hardly restrain myself," he replied. Nor did he: adding,

"This is a day of jubilee, a day of rejoicing to the faith-
ful. . . . Already are my orders out to give one big huzza
and sling the knapsack for new fields."

Those new fields lay on the far side of the Big Black,
however, which was now past fording because of a sudden four-foot rise resulting from heavy rains upstate.
Sherman spent two days throwing bridges at Birdsong's
Ferry and Messinger's Ford and due east of Bovina, thus
providing a crossing for each of his three corps, and on
July 6 the "Army of Observation," so called from the
days of the siege, passed over the river in pursuit of
Johnston, who had retired toward Jackson the day
before, on learning of Pemberton's surrender. As the
rebels withdrew eastward along roads that were ankle-
deep in dust—no matter how many inches of rain had
fallen upstate, not a drop had fallen here in weeks—
they made things difficult for their pursuers by leading
animals into such few ponds as had not dried in the heat,
then killing them and leaving their carcasses to pollute
the water. It was Johnston's intention not only to delay
his opponent by such devices, but also to goad him into
attempting a reckless, thirst-crazed assault on the Jackson intrenchments, which the Confederates had repaired and improved since Grant's departure and in
which they had taken refuge by the time the superior
Federal force completed its crossing of the Big Black,
twenty-five miles away.

The crafty Virginian's attempt to discourage and torment his pursuers with thirst was unsuccessful, however, for several reasons. For one, the siege-toughened
bluecoats simply dragged the festering carcasses from
the ponds, gave the water a few minutes to settle, then
brushed the scum aside and drank their fill, apparently
with no ill effects at all. For another, the rain soon

moved down from the north, sudden thunderous showers under which the marchers unrolled their rubber ponchos and held them so that the water trickled into their mouths as they slogged along. Lifted so recently by the greatest victory of the war, their spirits were irrepressible, whether the problem was too little moisture or too much. "The dirt road would soon be worked into a loblolly of sticky yellow mud," one veteran was to recall. "Thereupon we would take off our shoes and socks, tie them to the barrel of our muskets, poise the piece on the hammer on either shoulder, stock uppermost, and roll up our breeches. Splashing, the men would swing along, singing 'John Brown's Body,' or whatever else came handy."

They gloried in their toughness and took pride in the fact that they never cheered their generals, not even "Uncle Billy" Sherman. A surgeon wrote home that they were "the noisiest crowd of profane-swearing, dram-drinking, card-playing, song-singing, reckless, impudent daredevils in the world." They would have accepted all this as a compliment, second only to one Joe Johnston had paid them in warning his Richmond superiors not to underrate Grant's westerners, who in his opinion were "worth double the number of northeastern troops." They thought so, too, and were ready to prove it on July 10 when their three columns converged on the rebel intrenchments outside Jackson and took up positions before them, Ord's four divisions to the south, Steele's three in the center, and Parke's two on the north.

Within the semicircular works—which, as usual, he considered "miserably located"—Johnston had four divisions of infantry confronting the Union nine, plus a small division of cavalry which he used to patrol the flanks along Pearl River, above and below the town. He made several brief sorties in an attempt to provoke the bluecoats into attacking, but Sherman, though he enjoyed a better than two-to-one numerical advantage, had had too much experience with earthworks these past eight weeks to be tempted into rashness. Instead, he spent two days completing his investment, meantime sending raiders north and south to break the Mississippi Central and thus cut Jackson off from any possible rail connection with the outside world, the bridge in its rear not having been rebuilt since its destruction back in May. Then on July 12, despite his admonitions as to caution, the mishap came.

On Ord's front, Lauman was advancing his division through an area obscured by trees and brush, when the lead brigade of 880 veterans suddenly found itself exposed to a withering crossfire from guns and rifles, losing 465 men and three stands of colors, as well as most of the cannoneers and horses of a section of artillery, before the remnant could recover from the shock and backpedal. "I am cut all to pieces," Lauman lamented; Ord relieved him of command.

Sherman approved the brigadier's removal, but refused to be disconcerted by the affair, which had at least confirmed his assumption that Joe Johnston was a dangerous man when cornered: so much so, in fact, that the Ohioan began to wish the Virginian gone. "I think we are doing well out here," he informed Grant two days later, "but won't brag till Johnston clears out and stops shooting his big rifle guns at us. If he moves across Pearl River and makes good speed, I will let him go."

That was just what Johnston had in mind, now that Sherman had the capital invested on three sides. "It would be madness to attack him," he wired Richmond that same day. "In the beginning it might have been done, but I thought then that want of water would compel him to attack us." By next morning, July 16, he was convinced that his only hope for survival lay in retreat. "The enemy being strongly reinforced, and able when he pleases to cut us off," he notified Davis, "I shall abandon this place, which it is impossible for us to hold."

Accordingly, after nightfall, he proceeded to carry out the most skillful of his withdrawals so far in the war. Previously—at Manassas and Yorktown, as well as here at Jackson two months ago yesterday, on the day after his arrival from Tennessee—it had been his practice to leave guns and heavy equipment in position lest their removal, which was likely to be noisy, warn the enemy of his intention; but not now. Silently the guns were withdrawn by hand from their forward emplacements while the sick and wounded were being sent eastward across the river, followed by brigade after brigade of soldiers who had been kept busy with picks and shovels till after midnight, drowning out the sounds of the evacuation. Breckinridge's Kentuckians, who had accomplished Lauman's discomfiture four days ago, went last.

The lines of the aborted siege, which had cost the Federals 1122 casualties and the Confederates 604, yawned empty in the darkness and remained so until daylight brought a blue advance and the discovery that Johnston had escaped across the Pearl, much as Lee had done across the Potomac three nights earlier with somewhat less success.

He took with him everything movable but he could not take the railroad or the town. Undefended, Jackson was reoccupied—and reburned. That task was assigned to Sherman's old corps, primarily to Blair's division, which was fast becoming proficient in such work, while Ord moved south with instructions to break up the Mississippi Central "absolutely and effectually" for a distance of ten miles, and Parke did the same in the opposite direction. Steele's men did a thorough job on the capital, sparing little except the State House and the Governor's Mansion. Pettus had departed, but the victorious generals held a banquet in his mansion on the second night of the occupation, and when one brigadier was missing next morning he was found asleep beneath the table, so freely had the wine flowed.

"You can return slowly to Black River," Grant replied to news that the town had fallen, but Sherman stayed on for a week, supervising the extensive demolition his chief had prescribed at the outset. Added to what had been done in May, this new damage converted the Mississippi capital into what he referred to as "one mass of charred ruins." (Blair's exuberant veterans had a briefer, more colorful description of the place; "Chimneyville," they called it.) Though he found the stripping of the countryside by his foragers for fifteen miles around "terrible to contemplate," Sherman thought it proper to add that such was "the scourge of war, to which ambitious men have appealed rather than [to] the judgment of the learned and pure tribunals which our forefathers have provided for supposed wrongs and injuries."

Characteristically, however, before his departure he distributed supplies to civilian hospitals and turned over to a responsible committee enough hard bread, flour, and bacon to sustain five hundred people for thirty days, his only condition being that none of this food was to be converted "to the use of the troops of the so-called Confederate states." Despite the damage to their pride,

the committeemen were glad to accept the offer, whatever the condition. "The inhabitants are subjugated.
They cry aloud for mercy," Sherman informed his commander back at Vicksburg.

How lasting the damage would be, either to their
pride or to their property, was open to some question.
Up to now, particularly in regions where the occupation
had been less than constant, the rebels had shown remarkable powers of recovery from blows about as
heavy. On the march eastward from the Big Black, for
example, one of the Federal columns had crossed a portion of the field that took its name from Champion Hill,
which the shock of battle had left all torn and trampled,
scorched and scored by shells and strewn with wreckage. That was how the marchers remembered the scene
from their passage this way a little less than two months
back; but now, to their considerable surprise, they
found that much of the field had been plowed and
planted and corn stood four feet tall in neat, lush rows,
not only as if the battle had never been fought, but also
as if, except for the reappearance of the soldiers, there
had never been a war at all, either here or anywhere else.
It was in a way discouraging.

This time, though, as Johnston faded back before
them without fighting, they were less distracted and
could give their full attention to the destruction which
had been more or less incidental on the western march.
They blazed a trail of devastation; gins, barns, farm-
houses, almost everything burnable went up in flames
and smoke; rearward the horizon was one long smudge.
Looting took on new dimensions, sometimes of absurd-
ity. One officer, watching a cavalryman stagger along
with a grandfather's clock in his arms, asked what on
earth he planned to do with it, and the trooper ex-

plained that he was going to take it apart "and get a pair of the little wheels out of it for spur rowels."

There was time, too, for bitterness. A colonel viewing a porticoed mansion set back from the road in a grove of trees, neatly fenced and with a well-kept lawn and out-buildings, including slave quarters, burst out hotly: "People who have been as conspicuous as these in bringing this thing about *ought* to have things burned! I would like to see those chimneys standing there without any house." That his troops had taken his words to heart was evident on the return from Jackson, when the regiment passed that way again. His wish had been ful-filled. All that remained of the plantation house was its blackened chimneys. "Sherman monuments," they were called; or, perhaps more aptly, "Sherman tomb-stones."

Some among the Confederates in and out of uniform, but most particularly Richmond friends of Davis and Seddon, put the blame for much of this on Johnston, whose policy it had ever been to sacrifice mere territory, the land and all it nourished, rather than risk avoidable bleeding by any soldier in his charge. Always, every-where in this war except at Seven Pines—which battle, poorly fought as it was, had done more to sustain than refute his theory: especially from the personal point of view—he had backed up after a minimum of fighting, leaving the civilians of the evacuated region to absorb the shocks he evaded. So some said, angered by his ap-parent lack of concern for the fate of Vicksburg, which he had been sent to save. Others not only disagreed; they even pointed to the recent campaign as an example of his superior generalship. Unlike Pemberton, who had lost his army by accepting risks Johnston had advised him to avoid, the Virginian had saved his men to fight another day, and in the process had inflicted nearly twice as many casualties as he suffered.

Mainly such defenders were members of his army, who not only had good cause to feel thankful for his caution, but also had come under the sway of his attractive personality. A genial companion, as invariably considerate of subordinates as he was critical of superiors, he won the affection of associates by his charm. There were, however, a few who were immune, and one among them was Pemberton, though this was only recently the case. At the outbreak of the war they had been friends; Johnston in fact had chosen the Pennsylvanian as his adjutant before the northern-born officer's transfer to South Carolina and afterwards to Mississippi. But that was far in the past, in the days before the siege one friend had waited in vain for the other to raise.

Soon afterwards, in mid-July and in accordance with Grant's instructions for the paroled lieutenant general to report to his immediate superior, Pemberton found the Virginian "sitting on a cleared knoll on a moonlight night surrounded by members of his staff." Thus a witness described the scene, adding that when Johnston recognized the "tall, handsome, dignified figure" coming toward him up the slope, he sprang from his seat and advanced to meet him, hand outstretched.

"Well, Jack old boy," he cried. "I'm certainly glad to see you!"

Pemberton halted, stood at attention, and saluted.

"General Johnston, according to the terms of parole prescribed by General Grant, I was directed to report to you."

The two men stood for a moment in silence as Johnston lowered his unclasped hand. Then Pemberton saluted once more, punctiliously formal, and turned away.

They never met again.

★   ★   ★

News that Meade had stopped Lee at Gettysburg sent Lincoln's expectations soaring; he foresaw the end of the war, here and now, if only the victory could be pressed to its logical conclusion with "the literal or substantial destruction" of the rebel host before it recrossed the Potomac. Then came the let-down, first in the form of the northern commander's Fourth of July congratulatory order to his troops, calling for still "greater efforts to drive from our soil every vestige of the presence of the invader."

Lincoln's spirits took a sudden drop. "My God, is that all?" he exclaimed, and presently he added: "This is a dreadful reminiscence of McClellan. . . . Will our generals never get that idea out of their heads? The whole country is our soil." His fears were enlarged the following day by word that Lee had stolen away in the night, and no dispatch from Meade, that day or the next, gave any assurance of a vigorous pursuit. Lincoln fretted as much *after* as he had done before or during the three-day battle, so high were his hopes and so great was his apprehension that they would be unfulfilled. At a cabinet meeting on July 7 his expression was one of "sadness and despondency," according to Welles, "that Meade still lingered at Gettysburg, when he should have been at Hagerstown or near the Potomac, in an effort to cut off the retreating army of Lee."

That afternoon he was conferring with Chase and a

few others in his office, pointing out Grant's progress to
date on a map of Mississippi, when Welles came running into the room with a broad smile on his face and a
telegram from Porter in his hand. The admiral had sent
a fast boat up to Cairo, the Memphis wirehead having
broken down, and beat the army in getting the news to
Washington: "I have the honor to inform you that
Vicksburg has surrendered to the U.S. forces on this 4th
day of July."

Lincoln rose at once. "I myself will telegraph this
news to General Meade," he said, then took his hat as if
to go, but paused and turned to Welles, throwing one
arm across the shoulders of the bearer of good tidings.
"What can we do for the Secretary of the Navy for this
glorious intelligence? He is always giving us good news.
I cannot in words tell you my joy over this result. It is
great, Mr Welles; it is great!" The Secretary beamed as
he walked to the telegraph office with his chief, who
could not contain his pleasure at the outcome of Grant's
campaign. "This will relieve Banks. It will inspire me,"
he said as he strode along. He thought it might also inspire Meade, and he had Halleck pass the word to him
that Vicksburg had surrendered; "Now if General
Meade can complete his work so gloriously prosecuted
thus far . . . the rebellion will be over."

A wire also went to Grant: "It gives me great pleasure
to inform you that you have been appointed a major
general in the Regular Army, to rank from July 4, the
date of your capture of Vicksburg." Moreover, on
Grant's recommendation, Sherman and McPherson
soon were made permanent brigadiers, the reward that
had gone to Meade at Frederick that same day.

The following day, however, when Grant's own announcement of Pemberton's capitulation came limping in behind Porter's—which had said nothing about terms—there was cause to think that his victory was by no means as complete as had been supposed before details of the surrender were disclosed. Surprise and doubt were the reaction to the news that practically all of the nearly 30,000-man garrison had been paroled. Halleck, for instance, protested by return wire that such terms might "be construed into an absolute release, and that the men will immediately be placed in the ranks of the enemy." Grant had already noted that the arrangement left his and Porter's "troops and transports ready for immediate service" against Johnston and Gardner, which otherwise would not have been the case, and when he explained that the parolees had been turned over to an authorized Confederate commissioner for the exchange of prisoners, which made the contract strictly legal, Old Brains was mollified.

So was Lincoln, who was a lawyer himself and knew the dangers that lurked in informalities, though what appealed to him most was Grant's further contention that the surrendered troops were "tired of the war and would get home just as soon as they could." There, he believed, they would be likely to create more problems for the Confederacy than if they had been lodged in northern prison camps, a headache for the Union, which would be obliged to feed and guard them while awaiting their exchange.

Others not only disagreed, but some among them formed a delegation to call on Lincoln with a protest against Grant's dereliction and a demand for his dismissal from command. What rebel could be trusted? they asked, and predicted that within the month Pemberton's men would violate their parole and be back in the field, once again doing their worst to tear the fabric of the Union.

Referring to his callers as "crossroads wiseacres," though they must have included some influential dignitaries, Lincoln afterwards described to a friend his handling of the situation. "I thought the best way to get rid of them was to tell the story of Sykes's dog. Have you ever heard about Sykes's yellow dog? Well, I must tell you about him. Sykes had a yellow dog he set great store by—" And he went on to explain that this affection was not shared by a group of boys who disliked the beast intensely and spent much of their time "meditating how they could get the best of him." At last they hit upon the notion of wrapping an explosive cartridge in a piece of meat, attaching a long fuze to it, and whistling for the dog. When he came out and bolted the meat, cartridge and all, they touched off the fuze, with spectacular results. Sykes came running out of the house to investigate the explosion. "What's up? Anything busted?" he cried. And then he saw the dog, or what was left of him. He picked up the biggest piece he could find, "a portion of the back with part of the tail still hanging to it," and said mournfully: "Well, I guess he'll never be much account again—as a dog."

Lincoln paused, then made his point. "I guess Pemberton's forces will never be much account again as an army." He smiled, recalling the reaction of his callers. "The delegation began looking around for their hats before I had got quite to the end of the story," he told his friend, "and I was never bothered any more after that about superseding the commander of the Army of the Tennessee."

Now as always he shielded Grant from the critics

who were so quick to come crying of butchery, whiskey, or incompetence. "I can't spare this man. He fights," he had said after Shiloh, and more than a month before the surrender of Vicksburg he had called the campaign leading up to the siege "one of the most brilliant in the world."

In a sense, this latest and greatest achievement was a vindication not only of Grant but also of the Commander in Chief who had sustained him. Perhaps Lincoln saw it so. At any rate, though previously he had corresponded with him only through Halleck, even in the conferring of praise and promotions, this curious hands-off formality, which had no counterpart in his relations with any of the rest of his army commanders, past or present, ended on July 13, when he wrote him the following letter:

My dear General

I do not remember that you and I ever met personally. I write this now as a grateful acknowledgment for
the almost inestimable service you have done the country. I wish to say a word further. When you first reached
the vicinity of Vicksburg, I thought you should do what
you finally did—march the troops across the neck, run
the batteries with the transports, and thus go below; and
I never had any faith, except a general hope that you
knew better than I, that the Yazoo Pass expedition and
the like could succeed. When you got below and took
Port Gibson, Grand Gulf, and vicinity, I thought you
should go down the river and join General Banks; and
when you turned northward, east of the Big Black, I
feared it was a mistake. I now wish to make the personal
acknowledgment that you were right and I was wrong.

Yours very truly
A. Lincoln.

List of Maps

(Maps drawn by George Annand, from originals
by the author. All are oriented north.)

A Note on the Type

The principal text of this Modern Library edition ·
was set in a digitized version of Janson, a typeface that dates
from about 1690 and was cut by Nicholas Kis,
a Hungarian working in Amsterdam. The original matrices
have survived and are held by the Stempel foundry in
Germany. Hermann Zapf redesigned some of the weights and
sizes for Stempel, basing his revisions on the original design.